Representations of Technoculture in Don DeLillo's Novels

This book is the first to explore technoculture in all of Don DeLillo's novels. From *Americana* (1971) to *The Silence* (2020), the American author anatomizes the constantly changing relationship between culture and technology in overt and layered aspects of the characters' experiences. Through a tendency to discover and rediscover technocultural modes of appearance, DeLillo emphasizes settings wherein technological progress is implicated in cultural imperatives. This study brings forth representations of such implication/interaction through various themes, particularly perception, history, reality, space/architecture, information, and the posthuman. The chapters are based on a thematic structure that weaves DeLillo's novels with the rich literary criticism produced on the author, and with the various theoretical frameworks of technoculture. This leads to the formulation and elaboration on numerous objects of research extracted from DeLillo's novels, namely: the theorization of DeLillo's "radiance in dailiness," the investigation of various uses of technology as an extension, the role of image technologies in redefining history, the reconceptualization of the ethical and behavioral aspects of reality, the development of tele-visual and embodied perceptions in various technocultural spaces, and the involvement of information technologies in reconstructing the beliefs, behaviors, and activities of the posthuman. One of the main aims of the study is to show how DeLillo's novels bring to light the constant transformation of technocultural everydayness. It is argued that though such transformation is confusing or resisted at times, it points to a transitional mode of being. This transitional state does not dehumanize DeLillo's characters; it reveals their humanity in a continually changing world.

Laila Sougri, PhD is a Moroccan translator, writer, and researcher. She has published numerous translations, short stories, and papers. Some of her current interests include methodologies of interdisciplinarity, American literature, memory studies, and speculative realism in literature and psychology.

Routledge Research in American Literature and Culture

Lynd Ward's Wordless Novels, 1929–1937
Visual Narrative, Cultural Politics, Homoeroticism
Grant F. Scott

Authoritarianism and Class in American Political Fiction
Elite Pluralism and Political Bosses in Three Post-War Novels
David Smit

Death, Time and Mortality in the Later Novels of Don DeLillo
Philipp Wolf

Asian American War Stories
Trauma and Healing in Contemporary Asian American Literature
Jeffrey Tyler Gibbons

The Mercurial Mark Twain(s)
Reception History, Audience Engagement, and Iconic Authorship
James L. Machor

From Subjection to Survival
The Artistry of American Women Writers
Molly J. Freitas

Representations of Technoculture in Don DeLillo's Novels
Laila Sougri

For more information about this series, please visit: www.routledge.com/Routledge-Research-in-American-Literature-and-Culture/book-series/RRAL

Representations of Technoculture in Don DeLillo's Novels

Laila Sougri

NEW YORK AND LONDON

First published 2024
by Routledge
605 Third Avenue, New York, NY 10158

and by Routledge
4 Park Square, Milton Park, Abingdon, Oxon, OX14 4RN

Routledge is an imprint of the Taylor & Francis Group, an informa business

© 2024 Laila Sougri

The right of Laila Sougri to be identified as author of this work has been
asserted in accordance with sections 77 and 78 of the Copyright, Designs
and Patents Act 1988.

All rights reserved. No part of this book may be reprinted or reproduced or utilised
in any form or by any electronic, mechanical, or other means, now known or
hereafter invented, including photocopying and recording, or in any information
storage or retrieval system, without permission in writing from the publishers.

Trademark notice: Product or corporate names may be trademarks or registered trademarks,
and are used only for identification and explanation without intent to infringe.

Library of Congress Cataloging-in-Publication Data
Names: Sougri, Laila, 1990– author.
Title: Representations of technoculture in Don DeLillo's novels / Laila Sougri.
Description: New York, NY : Routledge, 2024. | Series: Routledge research in
American literature and culture | Includes bibliographical references and index. |
Identifiers: LCCN 2023012632 (print) | LCCN 2023012633 (ebook) |
ISBN 9781032526652 (hardback) | ISBN 9781032526669 (paperback) |
ISBN 9781003407768 (ebook)
Subjects: LCSH: DeLillo, Don–Criticism and interpretation. |
Technology in literature. | Culture in literature. | LCGFT: Literary criticism.
Classification: LCC PS3554.E4425 Z877 2024 (print) |
LCC PS3554.E4425 (ebook) | DDC 813/.54–dc23/eng/20230516
LC record available at https://lccn.loc.gov/2023012632
LC ebook record available at https://lccn.loc.gov/2023012633

ISBN: 9781032526652 (hbk)
ISBN: 9781032526669 (pbk)
ISBN: 9781003407768 (ebk)

DOI: 10.4324/9781003407768

Typeset in Sabon
by Newgen Publishing UK

To my parents, with love.

Contents

Acknowledgments   *x*

Introduction   1

1   Don DeLillo's Technoculture   11
    The Interrelatedness of Culture and Technology 11
      "Radiance in Dailiness" 11
      Prototypical Extensions in Ratner's Star *and* Zero K *13*
      Clearing Technological Determinism: "They Shoot Horses,
        Don't They?" 25
    Breaching the Beyond: *Attaining the Extraordinary*
    through the Ordinary 30
      "The Electric Stuff of the Culture" 30
      Promethean Shiny Shield in White Noise
      and The Names *31*
      Television as "Waves and Radiations" in Americana
      and White Noise *37*
        The Other-Worldly Dimension of the Screen in
         White Noise *37*
        Pixeled Synesthesia in Americana *43*

2   Latent History and Techno-Progress   53
    The Implication of Image Technologies in the
    Rise of Latent History 55
      "Latent History" in Great Jones Street *and* Running Dog *55*
      From Truth to Technocultural Possibilities within History 61
    Historical Uncertainty and the Televisual Event in Libra *66*
      Kennedy's Filmed Assassination: a Pioneer of Historical
        Uncertainty 66

viii *Contents*

*Oswald's Third Line of History: the Fall of Historical
Causality 70
Oswald's Dailiness: the TV Child as Underprivileged
Cripple 71
The Third Line of History 75
Oswald as a Technocultural Construct of Latent
History 78*

3 Reconceptualizing the Real   89
The Simultaneity of Recording and Receiving Events:
Underworld *and* Falling Man *90*
Visual Insertion of the Unusual in Dailiness 90
*The Superreal and Underreal Aspects of the
Televisual Event 94*
*The Proximity of Latent History and the
Hyperreality of the Event 94*
The 9/11 Live Broadcast: Reality in the Age of Terror 99
The Reprogrammed Mind in Mao II, The Body Artist,
and The Silence *105*
The Emergence of a Third Reality 105
Mediated Gaze: "the Virus of the Future" 111

4 The Phenomenology of Technocultural Space   125
"Technocultural Space" in End Zone *126*
Perception at the Margins of Civilization 126
The Ontological Internalization of Outer Space 130
Tele-Visuality in the Desert 135
Encounters with Technocultural Parallax in Players *141*
The Complexity of Postmodern Architecture 141
Pammy's Phenomenological Mode of Being 144
"Boxing in" the Self 144
The Suburban Unboxing of the Self 148

5 Perception in the Informational Era   159
*The "Dominant Metaphor" of Postmodern
Technoculture 159*
Information in DeLillo's Novels 159
The Vitality of Information: a Reading of Cosmopolis *164*
The Micro-Liveliness of Dailiness 164
The Limo-Stage of Data 169
The Grin without a Body: Uncertainty in Fleeting Data 170
The Zero-Oneness of Being 173

Contents ix

DeLillo's Posthumans 174
   Seeking the Beyond: *the Other Side of the Screen 176*
   Transhumanism: the Emancipation of Consciousness in
     Point Omega *and* Zero K *180*
   Toward a Virtual Reality 185

Conclusion   199

Works Cited   *203*
Index   *213*

Acknowledgments

I would like to thank my mother Rajae Naciri and my father Hamid Sougri, my brothers, Reda and Azeddine, my sister-in-law, and my nephew. This journey would have never been possible without your undying support.

I owe my deepest gratitude to my supervisor and mentor, Prof. Cherki Karkaba, whose guidance, feedback, patience, and kindness were crucial to the completion of this work.

I would like to warmly thank Prof. Brahim Houban, Prof. Driss Bakka, Prof. Mohamed Sghir Syad, Prof. Mohamed Behnassi, and Prof. Mohamed Rakii for their immense kindness and encouragements. I would also like to thank the wonderful Routledge/Taylor & Francis editorial team, particularly Jennifer Abbott, Anita Bhatt, and Anna Callander, for their professionalism and patience.

And finally, I am very grateful to all my dear friends, especially Anton Jurčević, M'bark Bouzzit, Miloud Rahmoun, Leila Bouziane, and François Gastineau for believing in me and for their support.

Introduction

In Max Frisch's *Homo Faber* (1957),[1] some travelers engage in a discussion about the relevance of technology to their lives. The protagonist, Walter Faber, remarks that even the ship on which they are voyaging is "the product of technology" (78). This remark seems to take the other characters aback. Up to this point, they have not been paying attention to the "technological" nature of their stay on the vessel. They are absorbed by close-to-hand activities such as reading and playing table tennis. Meanwhile, Faber is captivated by the meticulousness of the components of the ship. He gazes at the engine-room as if it were a sculpture in the Louvre. He goes as far as to think that "sculptures and things like that are nothing more (to my way of thinking) than forbears of the robot" (78). Faber disregards a whole cultural heritage, as culture, for him, has mutated into a set of algorithmic data, devoid of the "primitive symbols" of spirituality. Conversely, the other travelers are oblivious to the cultural importance of the ship itself. They derive their vitality chiefly from familiar proximate activities.

These antithetical views raise a number of crucial questions as regards the nature of the cultural impetus in the technological era. Is it necessary to render spirituality and emotions obsolete in order to keep up with the growing insertion of technology in everyday life? Does "living technologically" necessitate terminating all sorts of cultural imperatives that have existed alongside technology for millennia? Can technology ever be separated from culture?

This study approaches such questions through the novels of Don DeLillo. As one of the prominent authors of postmodern fiction, DeLillo demonstrates that the world does not stand on neutral ground. With this aim, he dredges up the interrelatedness of cultural imperatives with various technologies. Similarly to other authors such as Philip K. Dick, Joseph McElroy, Thomas Pynchon, William Gibson, and Douglas Coupland, DeLillo explores the implications of technology in contemporary culture as if the former were a ship of which one is not always aware. For DeLillo, the advance of technology does not imply the marginalization of

DOI: 10.4324/9781003407768-1

2 Introduction

culture. On the contrary, the postmodern world for him is rich with "a spirit of cooperation"[2] that should not be considered as impure. DeLillo describes himself as a translator of the things he sees and hears,[3] and what he sees seems to be the impossibility of separating culture and technology. He translates the various manifestations of culture through the mediating nature of technology.

The manner in which DeLillo approaches the technology–culture interrelatedness is best abridged through what has been neologized "technoculture." The term "technoculture" was coined by Henry Burger in the 1960s. In a letter to a journal, Burger suggested the term to designate a new discipline that focuses on "the interplay between technology and culture" (260).[4] The concept of technoculture brings forth the simultaneous workings of culture and technology. It presupposes that the two "spheres" have always been complementary constituents. As such, the interconnectedness implied in "technoculture" requires redefining culture to include its technological aspect and redefining "technology" in a way that acknowledges an important cultural involvement.

Generally speaking, culture refers to "a society's shared and socially transmitted ideas, values, emotions, and perceptions that are used to make sense of experience, generate behavior, and are reflected in that behavior" (Haviland et al., 28).[5] Even if this definition concentrates on the social aspect of culture, it reveals an important point. The task of culture is to transmit the beliefs, behaviors, and activities that shape one's life. Technology has become one of the major mediums for transmitting these imperatives. The advance of technology casts cultural imperatives in a new light. Image technologies, information technologies, nanotechnology, digitalization inform the individual's need to live better and even to live fully. They reveal the possibility of transcending the human being, which problematizes the distinction between the human and the technological.

The function of technological implication is not limited to being "the direct material manifestation of rational thought."[6] From late twentieth century onward, technology has usually been related to efficiency. It implies for some of DeLillo's characters that the newly formed cultural imperatives can provide superhuman capacities. However, when seen from a more objective viewpoint, it means mostly that culture is being rebuilt on previously unfamiliar associations. Seeing technology in terms of culture has brought about new expressions of designation that do not connote technological determinism. One speaks of technoculture as "collaboration," "implication," "intermingling," rather than a negative "effect," or a numbing "imposition." Sadie Plant[7] favors the term "weaving":

[sic] the digital machines of the late twentieth century weave new networks from what were once isolated words, numbers, music, shapes,

smells, tactile textures, architectures, and countless channels as yet unnamed. Media become interactive and hyperactive, the multiplicitous components of an immersive zone.... The yarn is neither metaphorical nor literal, but quite simply material, a gathering of threads which twist and turn through the history of computing, technology, the sciences and arts.

(11–12)

Plant's concept of weaving is important in the investigation of DeLillo's novels because it seeks to break free both from cultural determinism and from technological determinism. Its quality of forming a construct that avoids considering culture and technology as two distinct spheres facilitates the process of "interlacing" the two terms into a layered whole.

Plant's "weaving" enables the possibility of understanding technoculture in a way that undermines determinism. For this reason, the concept returns throughout the study to offer a technocultural relationship that is based on interrelatedness rather than on a favored aspect of culture or technology. This weaving is represented in various ways in DeLillo's novels. Familiar extensions are woven with unfamiliar ones (*Ratner's Star, Zero K*). Ordinary spaces radiate with the brightness of the transcendental (*White Noise, The Names*), and the pixels of the house of myths, television, open doors to warm colors of synesthesia (*White Noise, Americana*). History is woven with anonymous spaces, and recorded historical events are woven with famous and nameless men (*Great Jones Street, Running Dog, Libra*). Reality is woven with breaking news, and screens are woven with psychological distress (*Mao II, Underworld, The Body Artist, Falling Man, The Silence*). Deserts are woven with a tele-visual stream of consciousness, and skyscrapers are woven with fleeting identities (*End Zone, Players*). Faith is woven with posthuman aspirations and the Internet is woven with spiritual connections (*Underworld, Cosmopolis, Point Omega, Zero K*).

The unusual patterns that DeLillo weaves create a degree of ambiguity. Albert Bergmann suggests that dealing with this ambiguity starts with laying bare the approximate function of technology through that which seems to be the mundane activities of everydayness.[8] In his novels, DeLillo pays particular attention to the interaction between technology and culture in what he calls "dailiness." Dailiness refers to the overlooked ordinary beliefs, behaviors, and activities adopted by the characters in their constant interaction with technology. It could be claimed that DeLillo belongs to a category of writers who "tear through [the everyday] to reveal the living spirit enshrouded within, not above, or beyond, but within—and in doing so to liberate something strange, mysterious and bizarre."[9] DeLillo's purpose in disclosing such a setting is to anatomize a crucial involvement of technology in culture and vice versa. He declares that he seeks to unravel

4 Introduction

a sort of "radiance in dailiness"[10] that seems to underlie his fiction. This radiance involves the characters' spiritual and intrinsic technological functioning in a context of everyday activities.

While there has been research on DeLillo's concern with technology, none has extensively investigated the technocultural aspect of his novels. In *Postmodern American Fiction: a Norton Anthology* (1994),[11] DeLillo is added under the section "technoculture." He is quoted for his depiction of his characters' interactions with image technologies in the postmodern world. Generally speaking, DeLillo's critics provide extensive readings on culture (Mark Osteen), subjectivity and technology (Randy Laist, Joseph Tabbi), history and memory (Bob Batchelor and Philipp Wolf), time/space and atoms (Lilla Farmasi and Samuel Coale), ethics and faith (Jesse Kavadlo and Paul Giaimo), the environment (Elise Martucci), and language (David Cowart). These critics usually form complete, partial, or marginal connections between their inquiry and technology. However, it is noticed that more often than not technology and the self are established either against each other or next to each other but rarely, if ever, *within* each other. This tendency creates a dualistic view between technology and the individual. At times, the division leads to seeing technology as an extension that absorbs one's humanity, falling in this way into technological determinism.

Human beings, as Donna Haraway insists, are "cyborgs."[12] They are not dualistic constructs of mind/body, subject/object. Multiplicity and contingency are intrinsic to the cyborg's mentality and identity. In this context, multiplicity and contingency mean simply the possibilities that technology opens through its interaction with the "dailiness" of characters. The possibilities that characterize technology reflect the layers of culture. The experience of the "cyborg" does not depend on his/her interaction with just humans. It also depends on the behaviors caught from humanizing or being exposed to various technologies. This is best shown in novels such as *Underworld*, *Cosmopolis*, and *Zero K* where characters weave together spiritual practices with advanced technology.

The connections that DeLillo's characters draw between unfamiliar forms of technologies and their background extend their experiences. As an extension, technology reflects the physical as much as the mental apparatuses. While structures such as supermarkets and cars provide the external extensions of the characters' dailiness, television and computers constitute their visual/virtual extensions. The paraphernalia of extensions points out the diversity and growing uses of technology. In order to avoid a narrow view, instances of both dated and advanced technologies are given to demonstrate their implication in the characters' beliefs, behaviors, and activities. If advanced technology is believed to overcome spiritual practices, it is shown that this is not the case. To this aim, particular attention is given

Introduction 5

to the hermeneutical processes of the characters' interaction with various sorts of technologies in the late twentieth century and early twenty-first century. This timespan corresponds to the postmodern age.

The diverse nature of the world that DeLillo investigates is intrinsically connected to postmodern technology. From *Americana* (1971) to *The Silence* (2020), DeLillo zooms in on the particularities of contemporary life in relation to corresponding technologies. Despite denying his title as a postmodern author,[13] DeLillo deals with "predominantly post-modern sensibilities."[14] It could be claimed that these postmodern sensibilities concern the implication of image technologies and information technologies, among others, in the characters' dailiness.[15] This implication comes with a degree of uncertainty and confusion, as the possibilities of technological advance usually convey complex messages to the viewer. However, technological advance is not the essence of such disposition. To avoid an apologetic technological stance, technology *reveals* rather than *creates* uncertainty. Instead of being a parasitic injection, uncertainty is intrinsic to DeLillo's characters, which is apparent in novels such as *Libra* (1988) and *Falling Man* (2007).

DeLillo's approach to technoculture in his novels reveals the growth of unusual connections. Such connections bring together spheres that have been distant to an extent, as has been mentioned. DeLillo could be said to highlight the interrelatedness of technology and culture in different periods and through different modes of appearance. Technology becomes a surface to be discovered and rediscovered in new ways, as it keeps advancing. In order to remain aware of the hidden workings of technology, DeLillo constantly reformulates a binary ontology. This ontology is symbolized by the characters' constant shift of perspective caused by the growing intertwinement between the physical environment and virtuality. The resulting traffic pushes DeLillo to keep returning to themes such as visuality, history, time, reality, space, architecture, information, and the posthuman. DeLillo returns to these themes not because he is unable to find new horizons, but because they constantly redefine the perception of the postmodern individual.

DeLillo's characters perceive a partial view of technology since they perpetually relate the unfamiliar to the familiar. Consequently, their beliefs, behaviors, and activities reflect internal struggles. This does not imply that technology is the nucleus of their struggles. Rather, their interaction with technology brings out new perceptions of their uncertainties. As technocultural beings, DeLillo's characters embody a transitional rather than an inauthentic mode of being.

By investigating the subtle but vital interconnectedness of technology and culture, DeLillo is an early advocate of postmodern technoculture. The term itself was neologized by Burger one decade before DeLillo's first novel,

6 Introduction

Americana (1971). In essence, technoculture is a compound that cannot be separated from an interdisciplinary field of study. It is a bricolage in the sense that it does not focus on one independent discipline.[16] A number of works have focused on theorizing technoculture or reading available theories concerned with technocultural connections.[17] Miscellaneous philosophies clarify the interrelatedness of culture and technology, and such diversity is beneficial to this thesis.[18]

Being a bricolage implies that "technoculture" is compatible with the diversity inherent in DeLillo's novels. It also means that "technoculture" can circulate with ease between various fields such as ontology, phenomenology, and information theory. Even if the neologism "technoculture" in itself is not central to several references used in this project, these references still give vitality to the theoretical framework of "technoculture." A number of philosophers have investigated the relationship between culture and technology in their respective fields. Particularly crucial are the writings of Sadie Plant, Marshall McLuhan, Katherine Hayles, Jean Baudrillard, Gilles Deleuze, Donna Haraway, Martin Heidegger, Maurice Merleau-Ponty, and Slavoj Žižek. The correlation between technoculture and the theories of these thinkers may seem vague or confusing. Consequently, defining their relevant concepts is not sufficient. The method adopted creates synergy between "technoculture" and concepts such as technological extension, hyperreality, information overabundance, and posthuman. This approach not only pinpoints DeLillo's investigation of the technology–culture interaction, but it also expands the involvement of technoculture in literary readings.

To maintain an interdisciplinary approach, the chapters are based on various thematic representations of technoculture. These themes are built in such a way as to stress the collaboration between technology and culture in space and within the mind. In his 17 novels and novellas, DeLillo discloses the history of how technologies have progressed and migrated from a limited external space to the very "space" of the psyche. However, DeLillo is distinguished by his sincere interest in the physical involvements of technology in his characters' dailiness despite the ascendency of virtual extensions. Therefore, the chapters simultaneously investigate space as an external technocultural environment and as a virtual and/or visual technoculture.

Chapter 1 argues that DeLillo's conception of dailiness is compatible with technoculture. A definition is given of technoculture as an extension that concerns not only the daily use of objects, but also the transcendental implication of technologies. The emergency of dealing with technological determinism has led to adding a section that shows DeLillo's awareness of this propensity. Such a detour facilitates the introduction of the transcendental dimension of technoculture. The second part of the chapter

Introduction 7

describes more thoroughly the nature of dailiness as a woven set of cultural imperatives and technologies. DeLillo delineates the various implications of technology in space and in the psyche of the characters. It is argued that ordinary objects and spaces are rich with transcendental connotations. To that end, televisual experiences are investigated from the lens of myth and synesthesia. The televisual experience comes in the form of a protective coat and pixelated trance.

Chapter 2 discloses the role of image technologies in redefining the meaning of past and lived historical events. The first part of the chapter argues that the televisual event has contributed to changing the structure of historical accounts. Because history is transmitted directly through image technologies, it has undergone a temporal and orientational transition. This transition is dubbed "latent history" by DeLillo to explain the state and manifestation of history in the technocultural era. Latent history no longer deals with past events only but also with actual events. Not only does it transcend official accounts of history, but it also validates imaginative possibilities. The second part of the chapter locates, through the Kennedy assassination, a turning point of the American consciousness. The assassination is a precursor to a line of uncertainty that defines the individual's immersion in a culture of images. Lee H. Oswald is chosen as a case study connected both to the rise of latent history and to the insertion of image technologies in the individual's dailiness.

Chapter 3 reveals the manner in which reality itself is reconceptualized through the characters' interaction with live events. The first part argues that the recorded event has become a simulacrum among a large heritage of simulacra. The Kennedy assassination is no longer exclusive. Events such as taped murders and the 9/11 attacks revive the sense of uncertainty born with the Kennedy assassination. However, they do not necessarily resuscitate a sense of ethical values, even when the tragic event is lived. Tragic events contribute to the mutation of one's lived or televisual experience. They become familiar in spaces from which they were remotely distant, such as supermarkets and motels. As a consequence, this forced familiarity creates a shift in the manner in which the characters gaze at the televisual medium. The second part of the chapter argues that reality is not eradicated but transformed into a mediated construct. The physical presence of the individual is compared to the televisual one to assess the nature of a mediated experience of reality.

Because of the importance DeLillo gives to direct and mediated sense of space, Chapter 4 explores the characters' experiences of technocultural space in dailiness. It is argued that technocultural space is heightened in metropolises as much as in natural environments. The first part of the chapter argues that spaces such as the desert incite tele-visuality despite the lack of image technologies. Tele-visuality is understood as an

8 Introduction

intrinsic component that adapts to different environments. This poses a phenomenological question of perception. In *End Zone*, the individual seems to adopt a tele-visual method of perception even when image technologies are scarce because space itself is informational in nature. The phenomenological question of perception is also tested in an advanced technocultural space. If scarceness allows the mind to construct its own tele-visual process of understanding, how does the mind react to a technologically enhanced space? The second part of the chapter demonstrates that technocultural space is implicated in the individual's behavior. The individual can respond to her/his environment either by adapting to it or by giving in to its grandeur. Investigating the material environment, in *Players*, clarifies the role of the phenomenology of space in the structure of ontological perception. Technocultural space, be it as barren as the desert or as complex as a metropolis, invites the characters to adapt. Hermeneutical processes seem to correspond to the space in which characters are found. This shows that characters are not indifferent to different technocultural environments.

Chapter 5 draws on the previous chapters to reveal the proliferation of information in the postmodern age. The first part introduces the role of information in re-structuralizing the characters' understanding of technocultural space. It is suggested that encounters with various sources of information lead to ontological and spiritual revelations. In the second part of the chapter, it is argued that these revelations are concretized or fantasized through advanced technology. The characters gathered have recourse to advanced technology to breach the limits of what it means to be human. They become thus posthuman. They make use of the possibilities of information, which are encouraged by advanced technology, to transcend their limitations. The question posed is whether the characters' attempt to transcend their limits is equal to an attempt to transcend their humanity. Do they remain human even when they try to merge fully with technology? To answer this question, abstract realms such as cyberspace are set, in comparison to the material world, as primary environments of existence.

The main aim of the study is to demonstrate that technoculture is inevitably involved in the dailiness of Don DeLillo's characters. More specifically, technoculture is intrinsic to understanding the characters' beliefs, behaviors, and activities. The chapters bring forth representations of the interaction between technology and culture to show that they are continuously woven together in different forms. Instead of being increasingly driven apart, culture and technology have reached a point of indiscernibility. It is argued that the gradual insertion of technology in the characters' dailiness does not necessarily imply that reality is swallowed by technological rigidity. Rather, DeLillo's novels bring to light the transformation of technocultural dailiness decade after decade. Though this transformation is confusing or

Introduction   9

resisted at times, it points out a transitional mode of being. This transitional state does not dehumanize DeLillo's characters as much as it reveals their humanity in relation to the changing technoculture.

Notes

1 Frisch, Max. *Homo Faber*. Translated by Michael Bullock, San Diego, A Harvest Book, 1987.
2 DeLillo, Don. "Unmistakably DeLillo." Interview by Mark Feeney. *Conversations with Don DeLillo*, edited by Thomas DePietro, Jackson, University Press of Mississippi, 2005, p. 169.
3 Robert McCrum reports in an article the words of DeLillo who declares that "I'm just translating the world around me in what seems to be straightforward terms.... But I'm not trying to manipulate reality. This is just what I see and hear." www.theguardian.com/books/2010/aug/08/don-delillo-mccrum-interview
McCrum, Robert. "Don DeLillo: 'I'm Not Trying to Manipulate Reality–This Is What I See and Hear'." *The Observer*. Guardian News and Media, August 7, 2010. Accessed May 16, 2017.
4 Burger, Henry G. "'Technoculture'." *Technology and Culture*, vol. 2, no. 3, 1961, pp. 260–261. *JSTOR*, www.jstor.org/stable/3101029
5 Haviland, William A., et al. *Cultural Anthropology: The Human Challenge*. 14th ed., Belmont, Wadsworth/Cengage Learning, 2013.
6 Roderick, Ian. *Critical Discourse Studies and Technology: A Multimodal Approach to Analysing Technoculture*. London, Bloomsbury Academic, 2016, p. 9.
7 Plant, Sadie. *Zeros + Ones: Digital Women + the New Technoculture*. London, Fourth Estate, 1997.
8 Borgmann, Albert. *Technology and the Character of Contemporary Life: A Philosophical Inquiry*. London, University of Chicago, 1984.
9 Lefebvre, Henri. *Critique of Everyday Life*. Translated by John Moore, vol. 1, London, Verso, 1991, p. 107.
10 DeLillo, Don. "'An Outside in this Society': An Interview with Don DeLillo." Interview by Anthony DeCurtis. *Conversations with Don DeLillo*, edited by Thomas DePietro, Jackson, University Press of Mississippi, 2005, p. 70.
11 Geyh, Paula, et al., editors. *Postmodern American Fiction: A Norton Anthology*. New York, W. W. Norton, 2006.
12 Haraway, Donna Jeanne. *Simians, Cyborgs, and Women: The Reinvention of Nature*. London, Free Association, 1991.
13 When asked how he reacts to his novels being called postmodern, DeLillo answers that he remains indifferent. "I don't react. But I'd prefer not to be labeled. I'm a novelist, period. An American novelist" (Nadotti 115).
DeLillo, Don. "An Interview with Don DeLillo." Interview by Maria Nadotti. *Conversations with Don DeLillo*, edited by Thomas DePietro, Jackson, University Press of Mississippi, 2005, pp. 109–119.
14 DeLillo, Don. "Dangerous Don DeLillo." Interview by Vince Passaro. *Conversations with Don DeLillo*, edited by Thomas DePietro, Jackson, University Press of Mississippi, 2005, p. 77.

10 *Introduction*

15 Postmodernism is read at times as the age of visual extensions such as television. In "Toward a Concept of Postmodernism," Ihab Hassan reflects on the conceptual constitution of postmodernism. The first conceptual problem that he discusses concerns the word "postmodernism" itself. He suggests that, though the word sounds "awkward," it is still a better substitute for calling contemporary age "the atomic, or space, or television, Age" (588). What is relevant to this context is that, for instance, image technologies or information technologies are intrinsically connected to postmodernism as the house of multiplicity.
Hassan, Ihab. "Toward a Concept of Postmodernism." *Postmodern American Fiction: A Norton Anthology*, edited by Paula Geyh, et al., New York, W. W. Norton, 2006, pp. 586–595.

16 The first major work on technoculture is a set of papers amassed by Constance Penley and Andrew Ross. The premises of "technoculture" are set in the introduction to stress a rational of inclusion.

> Technologies are not repressively foisted upon passive populations, any more than the power to realize their repressive potential is in the hands of a conspiring few. They are developed at any one time and place in accord with a complex set of existing rules or rational procedures, institutional histories, technical possibilities, and, last, but not least, popular desires.
>
> (xiv)

Penley and Ross add that "cultural negotiations" are necessary to unearth and analyze the hidden workings of technology.
Penley, Constance, and Andrew Ross, editors. *Technoculture*. London, University of Minnesota Press, 1991.

17 See Borgmann, *Technology and the Character of Contemporary Life*; Davis, Eric. *TechGnosis: Myth, Magic & Mysticism in the Age of Information*. Berkeley, CA, North Atlantic Books, 2015; Cooper, Simon. *Technoculture and Critical Theory: In the Service of the Machine?* London, Routledge, 2014; Davis, Gregory H. *Means without End: A Critical Survey of the Ideological Genealogy of Technology without Limits, from Apollonian Techne to Postmodern Technoculture*. Lanham, University Press of America, 2006; Genosko, Gary. *When Technocultures Collide: Innovation from below and the Struggle for Autonomy*. Waterloo, Canada, Wilfrid Laurier University Press, 2014; Roderick, *Critical Discourse Studies and Technology*.

18 In 2008, for instance, Debra Benita Shaw has published a study that gathers different philosophies to highlight their technocultural implications.
Shaw, Debra B. *Technoculture: The Key Concepts*. Oxford, Berg, 2008.

1 Don DeLillo's Technoculture

The Interrelatedness of Culture and Technology

"Radiance in Dailiness"

In *Zeros + Ones: Digital Women + the New Technoculture* (1997),[1] Sadie Plant suggests that "man and his tools exist 'only in relation to the interminglings they make possible or that make them possible'" (77). Plant edits the quote she borrows from Deleuze and Guattari's *Mille Plateaux* in a way that breaks the dichotomies between man and tool. Tools, for her, are not only technological objects to be *used*. Man is not the *superior* user whose tools endow him with extended power. She rather conceives them as the two "perceptible elements" working simultaneously in a particular process (77). In his novels, Don DeLillo adopts a similar perception. He views everyday tools in particular and technology in general as a complementary necessity to his characters' daily life. He calls the daily processes of this necessity "radiance in dailiness."

DeLillo uses the description "radiance in dailiness" during an interview with Anthony DeCurtis, an editor and writer from Rolling Stone. DeCurtis propounds that DeLillo's particular attention to the details of everyday life reflects his fondness of "the trappings of suburban middle-class existence."[2] DeLillo answers that he rather attempts to find a "kind of radiance in dailiness" through writing.[3] The author does not aim to "bind his characters to suburbs and bedrooms" (Dewey 5).[4] Instead, he observes and peels off the layers of a radiance present in dailiness. "Radiance," as conceived by DeLillo, could be understood as the everyday technological brightness and "waves and radiations." Dailiness could be interpreted as the highlighted beliefs, behaviors, and activities adopted on a daily basis, and how undertaking or understanding them is mediated by technology. The manner in which technology mediates daily life is not an optional addition. It is, as Plant suggests, a complementary necessity. In this way,

DOI: 10.4324/9781003407768-2

12 Don DeLillo's Technoculture

investigating any aspect of culture would inevitably comprise a technological implication.

Viewing radiance in dailiness as a relationship of implication is compatible with the definition of technoculture. For centuries, technology has been defined as the application of scientific knowledge only. It implies that technology is capable of being neutral as regards the world it modifies. However, a number of philosophers and critics have refuted this demarcation.[5] They believe that technology is neither "simply a tool"[6] nor "subservient to other value spheres."[7] Technology becomes rather an active component in various cultural aspects of life. Technology and culture have never been separate spheres. They form what has been recently introduced as technoculture.[8] Ian Roderick[9] defines technoculture as an interactional relationship presupposing that technology and culture "are not distinct spheres of activity and knowledge but rather that the one is always implicated in the other" (1). Technoculture as a relationship of implication invalidates the dualism that has characterized technology and culture since the nineteenth century (9). Technology is, therefore, not only the production of new machines in factories or the mere assemblage of cars, smartphones, television. Culture is not only the social domain upon which humans organize beliefs, behaviors, and activities.

It is with this spirit that DeLillo defines radiance in dailiness. Rather than observing technology and culture from without, DeLillo adopts a technocultural "reflexive analysis from within, as it were, the belly of a beast that has grown to monstrous proportions" (Shaw 4). This analysis avoids compartmentalizing the two terms, so radiance in dailiness functions in terms of technocultural inclusion rather than addition. Thus, radiance *in* dailiness suggests that technology is implicated in culture and vice versa.

DeLillo's conception of radiance in dailiness as implication is not always recognized. Many critics acknowledge DeLillo's capacity as a "cultural anatomist," in Joseph Dewey's words (6), but they view the deep involvement of technology in daily life negatively. Dewey himself, when he describes DeLillo as a cultural anatomist, adds that the author's analysis of fin de millennium America is "not a particularly comforting one" (6). The critic accuses the "invasive technologies" present in DeLillo's novels of creating a culture where "the real becomes distant, the familiar estranged, the everyday irrelevant" (8). Even if Dewey constructs a valid narrative analysis of DeLillo's novels, he still laments a gradual loss of authenticity provoked by technology. Randy Laist develops a similar perception.[10] His view is however relatively less extreme than Dewey's. "More than any other major American author, DeLillo has examined the manner in which contemporary American consciousness has been shaped by the historically unique *incursion* into daily life of information, military, and consumer technologies" (3; emphasis added). Laist offers an important synthesis of the manner in which technology affects the "soul and the world," and he acknowledges the involvement of technology in daily life. However, he views technology as an intrusion rather than as implication. Both critics agree that DeLillo explores the relationship between technology and culture, but neither view it in terms of technoculture. They rather adhere to an extreme or relative technological determinist view, which reduces DeLillo's credibility as a "cultural anatomist."

Technoculture could restore this credibility, as it offers a less radical view of "radiance in dailiness." DeLillo describes himself as a translator of the things he sees and hears.[11] "Radiance in dailiness" encompasses his perception, for it translates the various manifestations of technoculture. These manifestations include how DeLillo's characters understand themes such as technology, history, the self, time, space, death, and information. The manifestations also include the manner in which characters make use of technological devices, spaces, and knowledge to extend their capacities. "Radiance in dailiness" is built on the expression of beliefs, behaviors, and activities, and it is equipped with a paraphernalia of extensions for everyday usage. Therefore, technoculture as "radiance in dailiness" presupposes that culture and technology have never been separate spheres of functioning. They are rather united for the better or for the worse in DeLillo's novels to "reveal what it means to be American, and perhaps, what it means to be human" (Kavadlo 9).[12]

Prototypical Extensions in Ratner's Star and Zero K

"Culture is technoculture," Erik Davis insists (2015).[13] Culture has never stood alone; technology has always assisted it. Indeed, technology and culture have always collaborated with each other to set ways of living and to improve these ways. DeLillo seems to be aware of this perpetual intermingling. This view is corroborated by Alexandra Glavanakova who suggests that DeLillo bases his writings on the philosophy that humans have always been "technological and prosthetic" (101).[14] "Radiance in dailiness," as DeLillo's expression of contemporary technoculture, discloses more than a means-to-end relationship between technology and culture. For DeLillo, to be human does not mean to be solely culturally predetermined, as "[h]uman beings have been cyborgs from year zero" (E. Davis 1). To be part cyborg does not mean that humans are losing their humanity either. Being part cyborg is compatible with Marshall McLuhan's representation of extension. McLuhan[15] suggests that human beings undergo autoamputation to extend their capacities (47). They give up their natural capacities to rely on tools that serve as extensions for the body. From the most primitive flint knife to the most advanced smartphone, technological extensions have always been a complementary part of the human body.

14   *Don DeLillo's Technoculture*

McLuhan repeats this statement with fervent highlight. However, his representations of media extensions remain broad. They do not touch upon the intrinsic processes of humans' responses to a world they understand through media.[16] In his review of *Understanding Media*, Patrick D. Hazard derides McLuhan's use of inadequate literary figures in his analysis.[17] For the critic, figures such as Charles Baudelaire and James Joyce have "probably taught us all they can about media they never saw.... Which artists in the new media are the Baudelaires and Joyces of film, radio, and television?" Hazard asks. The answer could be novelists such as Don DeLillo, as he employs intuitive vigor to delineate the anatomy of postmodern technoculture.

Before investigating the manner in which DeLillo anatomizes postmodern technoculture, it is worthwhile to look into the modernist/postmodernist debate revolving around DeLillo's oeuvre. James Joyce remains one of the strongest references that both DeLillo and his critics acknowledge. "For the richness of his language and the scope of his literary ambition, James Joyce looms largest in DeLillo's imagination."[18] It could be said that DeLillo is considered the Joyce of the postmodern movement, but the appellation itself sets forth additional layers of undecidedness. Indeed, the question regarding DeLillo's literary affiliation remains unexhausted. Henry Veggian asks: "is DeLillo a late modernist, or a postmodernist who recycles literary modernism in the way that a sculptor might recycle everyday objects into 'found art'"?[19] Some critics believe that DeLillo is a postmodern writer (Cowart, Laist, Johnston), while others insist that he remains modernist (Nel, Lentricchia). Even if there are also critics who abstain from labeling DeLillo (Kavadlo, Yehnert, Martucci), they do not clarify DeLillo's stance. In order to avoid a restricted view of DeLillo's position in the literary heritage, it is safer to suggest that he works his novels at the crossroad of modernism and postmodernism. He makes use of the modernist aesthetic structure in an attempt to understand the postmodern world.

DeLillo mutates the modernist structure to anatomize the postmodern society. He does not stop at describing technology as a physical extension of man. He goes a step further by interrogating the psyche's response to technology while it growingly becomes an abstract extension. DeLillo's notion of "radiance in dailiness" could be said to focus on applied technoculture. It describes technoculture as a constant interdependence between culture and technology in the context of everyday experience.[20] "Radiance in dailiness" also points to the flow created between the ontological understanding of life and the set of technological media enacted to shape that life.[21] The everyday technological brightness and "waves and radiations" enclosed in dailiness function as extensions to the characters' beliefs, behaviors, and activities.

Since DeLillo's characters adopt different ways of life, technology translates their beliefs, behaviors, and activities in different ways. The technologies that DeLillo's characters use in daily life vary in terms of sophistication and usage. Therefore, it is not sufficient to disclose the relationship between technology and culture as a linear construct. It is important to keep in mind that technology upholds multiplicity as much as culture does. Two characters are chosen in order to explore simultaneously DeLillo's method to build technological extensions and the various technologies used for that purpose. Henrik Endor from *Ratner's Star* and Ross Lockhart from *Zero K* epitomize how technoculture adapts to their needs in a context of dailiness. At the beginning of their quest, the two characters have similar beliefs, technologies, and goals. However, as their changing beliefs diverge, they choose different sets of technologies to express them. Juxtaposing these two characters shows DeLillo's different representations of technological implication in daily life.

Ratner's Star (1976) is DeLillo's exploration of a reality too mysterious to be contained and too intriguing to be ignored. It is structured as Alice's journey in wonderland.[22] Billy Twillig, a 14-year-old prodigy, flies to central Asia to work in a subterranean scientific center. Billy is summoned in order to decode a message supposedly coming from space, specifically from Ratner's Star. During his stay, Billy discovers a completely new context that supposedly focuses on explaining the world scientifically. He compares such scientific milieu with recollections from life back home. The novel resists any linear plot. With an "extravagant architecture," DeLillo opens his novel to genres such as sci-fi, Menippean satire, bildungsroman.[23] The novel is itself built as an extension that goes in all directions. The whole structure of the novel is based on multiplicity. Its very purpose seems to be indicating how the characters mediate their lives through various kinds or levels of technology.

The novel is divided into two parts. The first part is undertaken outward. Billy discovers the various compounds of the center, with futurist and most of the time uncanny findings. The second part is a journey inward. Billy is selected among a few scientists to decode the message and create a universal language. In addition to pursuing his goal, that is, doing mathematics, Billy meets different individuals and discovers a whole new world in the center. One of these individuals is his predecessor Henrik Endor.

Endor is a renowned mathematician and astrophysicist, who abandons a life of fame and science in order to dedicate his time to digging. Early in the novel, Billy finds a picture of Endor taken a few years before. In the picture, Endor is "bearded, in his sixties, and wore a star pentagram on a chain around his neck" (*Ratner's Star* 21). Endor's bodily expression translates his lifestyle before becoming a digger. In order to highlight the transition, the reader is given an account of Endor's previous lifestyle:

16   *Don DeLillo's Technoculture*

Endor had married three times, suffered injuries in two wars, flown jet aircraft to nearly record-breaking altitudes to do photographic research in astronomy. He had written several books of a speculative nature, best-sellers every one. He was an accomplished cellist and founder of an all-mathematician chamber group. Heads of state had honored him in marble halls.

(Ratner's Star 83)

Endor is a man who dives into the extreme multiplicity of postmodern technoculture, as he flies to the highest altitudes and succeeds in many fields. Endor's motility, which is assisted by advanced technology, extends his capacities.[24] In this description, Endor's embodiment transcends the immediate spatiotemporal context within which he is found. The body, which is extended by advanced technology, is used as a medium[25] for celestial accomplishments. When he flies a jet aircraft to a high altitude, his aim is not related to a physical experience. His body and the advanced technology at his disposal are the mediums through which he undergoes research in astronomy.

The use of the body as a medium for "capacity extension" is equally represented in *Zero K* (2016). Similarly to Billy Twillig, Jeffrey Lockhart, the narrator of the novel, witnesses a radical and uncanny transformation in the human psyche and body. Jeffrey is invited to a subterranean scientific center called the Convergence. True to his faithfulness to isolated underground locations, DeLillo transports the reader to the "carious teeth" of the Uzbekistani desert. Ross Lockhart, a self-made billionaire, sends for Jeffrey, his son, to observe the miracles of science. Ross invests his wealth in cryogenic research to "pause" his wife's life. Artis Martineau suffers from several incurable diseases. Her only option for survival is life after death. Seeing no other available option, Ross tries to push the limits of science to find the best cryonic formula. Similarly to many of DeLillo's characters, Ross does not shy away from having recourse to unorthodox methods. He founds the Convergence with the aim of freezing Artis's consciousness until technology is advanced enough to build her anew.

Similarly to Endor, Ross is described as a bearded man in his mid-to-late sixties. He too uses his body as an extension for his aims. His space of comfort consists of his office mostly. Ross seeks to save his wife through the possibilities made available by the vast network he has established. Seen from the first-person point of view of his son, Ross seems to be connected to physical and virtual extensions. They allow him to maintain control over the progress of the Convergence.

This [office] was improvised, several screens, keyboards and other devices set about the room. I was aware that he'd put major sums of money into this entire operation, this endeavor, called the Convergence, and the office was a gesture of courtesy, allowing him to maintain convenient contact with his network of companies, agencies, funds, trusts, foundations, syndicates, communes and clans.

(*Zero K* 7)

Ross adheres to that which Albert Borgmann calls "the persistent glamour of the promise of technology" (105).[26] The pattern of technology is implicitly implicated in his choices. Technology promises to extend his power far enough to defy death itself.

Ross sees in the collaboration between science and technology the promise of achieving what has been so far impossible for Man, that is, immortality. DeLillo chooses cryopreservation as an example of that collaboration.[27] The author seeks to expose the extreme measures that individuals are ready to take to ensure survival. Combined with his expertise in finance, technology offers Ross the means to advance fast in cryonic actions. The purpose behind this urgent need is not profit as much as having the burden of loss lifted off his shoulders.

Endor and Ross share their Faustian need to push the limits of technological possibility and to mobilize the necessary means to achieve their goals. However, the expression of their technological extension is not exclusive to their work hours. Their dailiness is itself adjusted to their beliefs. They both make sure that the architecture of technology mirrors their erudite aspirations. They try not only to achieve a goal but also to translate possibilities to reflect it. Technological possibilities could be read in terms of metaphors. Drawing from George Lakoff and Mark Johnson, Ian Roderick explains that metaphors are not merely figurative forms of language.[28] They are deeply integrated in the processes of thoughts and actions.[29] Roderick then suggests that the individual's daily use of technology is not experienced as a neutral set of tools that interact with other tools. Rather, the individual experiences technology in accordance with his or her own background or lived experiences. As it is the case for Endor and Ross, the continuous dialogue between technologies and their personal experiences opens possibilities previously unimaginable. In this way, their reality does not draw its strength solely through weaving connections with other human beings. It depends also on the behaviors caught from humanizing or being exposed to various technologies.

Endor and Ross construct their environment to be a constant reminder of the conclusions they reach, as will be shown. Their radiance in dailiness is an internal as well as an external affair. It encompasses not only the education and control of the self but its very production (Barglow 143). For Raymond Barglow,[30] procedural activity transitioned from ritual practices[31] to formal structures.[32] Ritual practices "connect

18 Don DeLillo's Technoculture

individuals within a lifeworld of meanings and values," and formal structures "articular a social reality where personal identity and personal relationships are irrelevant" (144). While Ross maintains the formal structure of contemporary life through anonymous transactions, Endor returns to ritualistic practices.

Put together, the two characters represent the process through which two similar individuals would drastically diverge in worldview. The most apparent divergence noticed between the two characters is the technology they use. It will be argued that the bodily and technological extensions of both characters mirror their changing beliefs.

When Endor leaves the center and starts his daily activity of clawing the earth, the extensions he takes with him consist of the clothes he is wearing and a clothes hanger. Even if Endor does not share his worldview with a community, his digging and humming is a return to worldly practices. The refined man Billy sees in the aforementioned picture has disappeared. Endor's shirt and trousers are worn out, the chain is gone, his sagacious face is tanned and unwashed (*Ratner's Star* 84). Endor stands near a "fifteen feet long, eight wide and twelve deep" hole, which resumes his life's work (*Ratner's Star* 83). Upon close inspection of Endor's figure, Billy notices that "small crawling things moved about in his white beard" (*Ratner's Star* 84). As wondered in *Zero K*, "[w]as this the beard a man grows who is eager to enter a new dimension of belief?" (7). Billy finds it unusual that such erudite icon would abandon the center to indulge in larvae diet. The teenager's first guess is that Endor could not decode the message; but, as it is revealed near the end of the novel, Endor does succeed in decoding it before departing. Therefore, Billy's questions remain so far unanswered: "what does he [Endor] want? Why is he behaving this way?" (*Ratner's Star* 83).

Once he has decoded the message, Endor realizes that all routes lead to the same destination. He comes to understand that the message "tell us something of importance about ourselves" (*Ratner's Star* 91). The message received had been sent from earth. It has boomeranged back to announce the date of an eclipse. The radio signals that have sent it have been elaborated by an extinct civilization. This incites Endor to believe that the technology of those considered primitives is not as inferior as the modern man thinks. Maybe it has been even more advanced than the technology used in late twentieth century. This theory is shared by an anthropologist, Maurice Wu, whose research includes discovering the nature of the beings who have sent the message:

> In the very distant past on this planet, there was a species of life that resembled modern man both outwardly and otherwise. Intellectually I've managed to accept this without reservation. Now, thanks to Walter,

Don DeLillo's Technoculture 19

we know precisely what these people were capable of doing, technologically. They were capable of beaming radio signals into space.

(*Ratner's Star* 403)

Another theory suggests that the original evolutionary thread of man has been interrupted because of an unidentified degeneration. It is assumed that man had to rebuild everything anew. "The answer we've arrived at here is probably the answer we've known, at some dim level of awareness, since the beginning" (*Ratner's Star* 404). These theories reiterate the tendency of the human being to return to anterior conclusions, reached spontaneously if not methodically. As such, any message sent by man is bound to repeat earlier happenings despite technological variances.

Since the message does not have an expeditor other than man himself, Endor decides to deny the senses no more. "We don't extend the senses to probe microbe and universe.... We deny the evidence of our senses. A lifetime of such denial is what sends people into larva-eating rages" (*Ratner's Star* 87). Nevertheless, Endor does not relinquish his identity as a scientist; he rather changes his mode of daily existence. In Mark Osteen's words,[33] "[Endor] embraces the notion that science is a matter of faith...." (70). This leads to more confusion about his motive for abandoning the center. If Endor does not lose faith in science, why does he adopt a "primitive" dailiness?

For Joseph Dewey, Endor retreats to the hole because of the traumatic realization that the world is not as orderly and containable as science seeks to prove. The world is not only made of calculations but of contradictions and spontaneity (44). Endor is believed to commiserate with those that remain unaware of the treachery and retreats to primitivism as an act of protest. However, science itself is not the system that he walks against. It is suggested that Endor loses faith in advanced technology rather than in science. He denounces the legacy of the mind/body separation that stretches up to the twentieth century through advanced technology. Endor realizes that such separation does not lead to a transcendence of the mind. It is a conviction that has been accreting before his departure from the center.

I've had a strong conviction for quite some time. Both before and since the hole. Better light out for a hole, Endor. Find yourself a hole and light out fast. That was my conviction. I still have it. Things here aren't what they seem, Big B. I don't think I'm any closer to dying than I was before the hole. Excluding pure chronology, of course. In other words I didn't come here to meet a quick end. Another thing. The sorrow of simply being is no greater here than it was in pre-hole environments. When you talk about simply being, you're talking about things like holes and rusty mud. My mind is the same, my eyesight, the way I dream, the way

20   *Don DeLillo's Technoculture*

I smell to myself. It's surprisingly easy to adjust to living in a hole. Out there, in other words, there's just as much holeness and mudness.

(*Ratner's Star* 90–91)

Endor believes that advanced technology is imposed to fulfill certain political aims. This view is shared by Borgmann, who suggests that "technology is seldom offered as a choice, i.e., as a way of life that we are asked to prefer over others, but is promoted as a basis for choices" (103). By retreating to the hole, Endor unburdens himself from the glamor of advanced technology.

Endor's choice does not find its roots in repressed nostalgia for nature. His radiance in dailiness adjusts to a simpler lifestyle. The purpose of digging with a cloth hanger, for instance, is not to project a message of desperation but to strengthen his choice. It could be said that Endor adapts his cloth hanger to his main goal. Shilling shares this view when he suggests that "[b]y developing expertise in the use of objects, we effectively embody new means of projecting ourselves onto the world" (55). Endor trades the artificiality of "Translucent polyethylene"[34] for the sun's light. Even the center's rooms do not seem optically dissimilar from the hole. Billy describes Endor's room early in the novel. The bareness of the room recalls the bareness of Endor's hole:

There were no windows. The lighting was indirect, coming from a small carbon-arc spotlight focused on a reflecting plate above it. The walls were slightly concave and paneled in a shimmering material decorated with squares and similar figures, all in shades of the same muted blue and all distorted by the concave topography. The optical effect was such that the room seemed at first to be largely devoid of vertical and horizontal reference points.

(*Ratner's Star* 17)

For Endor, the major difference between the advanced technology of the center and his new environment is the degree of "self-amputation." As an extension, Endor considers advanced technology a long and misguiding detour to the truth. A shorter path to truth could be found through trusting natural senses.

Endor discovers that digging protects him from danger, that a clothes hanger is all the extension he needs, and that eating larvae can sustain him. Nevertheless, it would be erroneous to assume that Endor proceeds to a total removal of technological identity. In *Technology in Western Civilization* (1967),[35] Melvin Kranzberg explains that "Homo sapiens cannot be distinguished from Homo Faber, Man the Maker." Since the dawn of time, Man the Maker has existed alongside Man the Thinker, as tools were necessary for the survival of man (Vol. I 8). Tools cannot be constructed without Man but Man needs these tools to survive. Endor mentally revives characteristics belonging to an anterior time. Nevertheless, he takes with him a clothes hanger for digging, and he returns to the center, "[h]oping it would all come together.... but it stayed apart" (*Ratner's Star* 84). These responses translate Endor's decision, not to stand against technology itself, but to stand against a particular sort of technological use.

When Billy meets Endor, the "bearded man" invites the teenager to take a look at the particularity of his room. "It's not one of those shimmery canisters. I designed it myself. Had things shipped in special.... It's a room in and of time" (*Ratner's Star* 92). Contrarily to Billy's expectation, the room is plain and uninspiring, or so it seems to him:

> The room had hardwood floorboards that needed waxing. From the ceiling hung a single light bulb, unshaded. There was a rocking chair, plain in appearance, located in the far corner. A rectangular segment on one wall was cleaner than the rest of the wall.... The only other thing in the room was a Coca-Cola wall clock.
>
> (*Ratner's Star* 380)

If both Billy and the reader fail to detect what makes this room "special," Endor views it as a "[n]ice place to sit and think" (*Ratner's Star* 92). As already explained, Endor has never fully adhered to a contemporary view of life. He is liberated from this view by rejecting the advanced technology method of enlightenment. Endor views "primitivism" as a collaboration between tool and reason to uncover the secrets of life through digging and chanting.

While Endor travels back in time to uncover the secrets of life as perceived by the senses, Ross chooses to take a leap of faith toward the future. Unable to live without his wife, Ross decides to end a life of ambition to be cryopreserved next to his beloved. Two years after the "temporary" death of Artis, Ross prepares his sabbatical retreat. The process of the transition starts by removing any physical excess (body hair) and material identity (his profession). Ross becomes "a lost shorn figure without a suit or tie or personal database" (*Zero K* 236). While observing this transition, Jeffrey confesses that all he is seeing is "a man with nothing left to him but the clothing he wore" (*Zero K* 233). Covered only with a "loose white garment,"[36] the only extension he is offered, Ross undergoes a ritual of preparation.

Before looking into Ross's transformation, it is useful to explain how *Zero K* probes the possibilities born from the intermingling of revolutionary technology and spiritual distress. One of DeLillo's enquiries in the novel revolves around the capacity of technology to create posthumans and the

22   Don DeLillo's Technoculture

relevancy of religious belief in such context. As supported by Glavanakova, "Although not directly formulated by DeLillo, the question whether the posthuman entities of the twenty-first century are contemporary pilgrims in need of protection and prayer is inevitably posed by the text" (98). In simple terms, the "posthuman" could be defined as the aim to step over the threshold of what is possible and as the belief in the attainability of that which lies *beyond*. In Ross's case, the process of the ritual seems to be defined as a pilgrimage made possible through a whole technological body. As DeLillo posits in an interview, this posthuman endeavor "is about pushing the limits of what it means to be human. Death is no longer read in terms of religion, as a spiritual afterlife, but in terms of technology" [my translation] (38).[37] As is the case in most of his work, DeLillo seeks to highlight the importance of technology in the expression of faith and spirituality. In *Zero K*, this expression makes of technology its very space.

Despite the common belief, technology and religion have not been built separately within culture. DeLillo seems to agree with David F. Noble when the historian argues that "modern technology and religion have evolved together and that, as a result, the technological enterprise has been and remains suffused with religious belief" (Noble 5).[38] Technology becomes in this context the basis of a new faith. Ross defines cryonic transition as a sort of technological Gnosticism. "Faith-based technology. That's what it is. Another god. Not so different, it turns out, from some of the earlier ones. Except that it's real, it's true, it delivers" (*Zero K* 9). Similarly to Endor, Ross considers his decision faith-based. However, Ross does not aim to return to the "earlier gods." He rather aims to *weave* his consciousness completely with technology.

As a metaphor, technocultural weaving explains the interrelatedness of the human body and advanced technology. Sadie Plant introduces this concept best. For her, Man has been made mutant thanks to the "softwares linings of all technology."[39] From the dawn of time, weaving has involved layers of meanings. It has not only been used for the fabrication of clothes against the cold. It has also been a way to create and send a message of identity, a message that highlights a need to innovate and "invoke magic."[40] Weaving webs of patterns has opened a matrix of significance and multiplicity. This multiplicity exists, but it is not always felt in one's embodied "radiance in dailiness." Plant's inference is fortified by Donna Haraway's structure of technological embodiment. Haraway points to Man's kinship with the machine:[41] "By the late twentieth century, our time, a mythic time, we are all chimeras, theorized and fabricated hybrids of machine and organism; in short, we are cyborgs" (150). It could be said that the postmodern man is woven together with technological extensions, be they external or internal. The deep implication of technology in the human body redefines not only its appearance but its very structure.

Don DeLillo's Technoculture   23

In *Zero K*, the human body becomes a fabric upon which novel and unrecognized patterns are woven. This is the basis of Ross's faith. He explores a new dimension of technology. This dimension not only renders the body a medium for technological advance, it also contributes in reshaping consciousness. Such is the price of risking never being restored to life, a choice that requires both faith and trust. In a way, Ross's technological extension is not only an attempt to master the future. It is also a rejection of contemporary technology.[42] This recalls Borgmann's statement about technology as imposition. Ross seeks to restore or rebuild technology in his image, rather than allow the existing technology to dictate his lifestyle:

> Technology has become a force of nature. We can't control it. It comes blowing over the planet and there's nowhere for us to hide. Except right here, of course, in this dynamic enclave, where we breathe safe air and live outside the range of the combative instincts, the blood desperation so recently detailed for us, on so many levels.
>
> *(Zero K* 245)

Ross decides when and how he would die, or rather how he would "temporarily" die. However, is Ross really in control of the technological extension he himself builds?

In terms of McLuhan's philosophy, Ross would be said to give in to the technology he himself designs in order to become numb to the pain of loss (48). Ross, it would be said, is proceeding to a "desperate and suicidal autoamputation"[43] to denounce the weakness of the body, Artis's as much as his. Such weakness is best described during Ross's "biomedical redaction:"

> He was naked on a slab, not a hair on his body. It was hard to connect the life and times of my father to this remote semblance. Had I ever thought of the human body and what a spectacle it is, the elemental force of it, my father's body, stripped of everything that might mark it as an individual life. It was a thing fallen into anonymity, all the normal responses dimming now. I did not turn away. I felt obliged to look. I wanted to be contemplative. And at some far point in my wired mind, I may have known a kind of weak redress, the satisfaction of the wronged boy.
>
> *(Zero K* 251)

Jeffrey cannot help but see a pitiful nearly extension-less entity despite his father's pleading to "respect the idea" (*Zero K* 10). Jeffrey is biased not entirely because he resists envisaging the possibility of immortality. Rather, seeing his father in a state of vulnerability is Jeffrey's way to legitimate a

24 *Don DeLillo's Technoculture*

grudge he has always held against his father for abandoning him. Beyond Jeffrey's somewhat unreliable account, the reader still recalls the philosophy behind Ross's decision, as DeLillo offers the revolutionary aspect of the project prior to its implementation. Ross considers the episode of his transition as an unavoidable step, for it announces the arrival of a new era. He is to be postmarked Zero K: Man's bold attempt to claim victory against nature.

"Zero K" is an appellation destined to those who choose "to enter the portal prematurely."[44] A representative, known only as Zara, believes that the five heralds, Ross and four other anonymous volunteers, are going to move toward "a complex of ideas and aspirations and hard-earned realities" (*Zero K* 238). Since this state is an absolute transition into abstractness, it could be said that it has its own form of radiance in dailiness. Prior to enacting the Zero K project, Zara gives a "sermon" on rebirth. She explains, with conviction, the state in which the heralds will find themselves after the biomedical redaction.

> It will not be total darkness and utter silence.... In time you will re-encounter yourself. Memory, identity, self, on another level. This is the main thrust of our nanotechnology. Are you legally dead, or illegally so, or neither of these? Do you care? You will have a phantom life within the braincase. Floating thought. A passive sort of mental grasp. Ping ping ping. Like a newborn machine.
>
> (*Zero K* 238)

Zara promises a new form of existence in the capsule that will contain Ross's frozen body. In this scenario, there would be a new form of light, not too dim and not too bright. There would be also a new sort of noise, a constant humming, either that of the capsule or that of consciousness. Whether this is a superior or inferior form of life is contestable and even irrelevant to an extent. It could be read either as a primitive form of digitally abstract dailiness or as a transcendence from the physical body. Either way, there is a degree of familiarity, as "memory, identity, self" are to be restored. Beliefs, behaviors, and activities are supposedly reconstructed on the basis of the former (embodied) life. This poses the question concerning the ontology of the new (upgraded) form of the human being as a cyborg.[45]

Endor and Ross demonstrate that technology is not only an external extension but a spiritual and behavioral extension as well. It has been suggested that technology is not a neutral tool; it is the looking glass of identity and reason. "Radiance in dailiness" as conceived by DeLillo represents the interrelated of technoculture and the individual. However, if technology is implicated in the internal as much as the external aspects

Don DeLillo's Technoculture   25

of life, to what extent does it influence the decisions of the characters? The urgency to deal with this question emanates from its relatedness to technological determinism. In the face of the slippery relationship between technoculture and the individual, DeLillo poses the question of the role of technology in the consequences of human actions and decisions.

Clearing Technological Determinism: "They Shoot Horses, Don't They?"

If Ross ends up in a restricted space by choice, the protagonist of *They Shoot Horses, Don't They?* (1935) is not as lucky. Robert Syverten, an optimistic but jobless young man, is convinced by a debutant actor Gloria Beatty to participate in a marathon dance contest. The dancers are entrapped for weeks in a suffocating building whose only luxury is a rare glimpse at the setting sun. Horace McCoy portrays the commodification of human beings for the sake of entertainment. No more than a means of profit, the participants' struggle becomes the object of the audience's voyeuristic greed. The endless fight against elimination abruptly ends after a tragic incident. Robert not only loses a chance at winning the contest; he also loses a chance at building a future. He walks to the pier to remember how it feels like to breathe fresh air, not knowing it is a farewell to his freedom. While standing on the pier, Gloria pleads Robert to shoot her. He contemplates ending her life, as he knows that she has been and always will be no more than a wounded animal. While he is holding the gun against her head, Robert remembers how his grandfather had to put to death a cherished horse because of a broken leg. By associating the wounded animal to Gloria's inadequacy to live, Robert thinks of the murder as an act of mercy.

The title of the novel, which is the answer Robert gives when asked about the reason for the murder, poses a question concerning intention[46] and extension. When it comes to extensions such as a gun, is technology always a neutral tool that "makes" people do wrong or does one's intention matter? If McCoy builds the premises for this question in the thirties, DeLillo attempts to answer it in the nineties through *Underworld* (1997). In this context, DeLillo's representation of intention and extension consists of exploring the "radiance" of technology as an active component in "dailiness."

Part Six of the novel focuses on the psychology of an "innocent" murderer living in the early fifties, a couple of decades after the Great Depression. Near the end of the reversed chronology of *Underworld*,[47] the omniscient narrator relates a traumatic experience that marks the end of Nick Shay's childhood. A troubled teenager at the time, Nick visits his friend and mentor George Manza, also referred to as George the Waiter. George is described as a "face on a pole.... who carried something stale

26 Don DeLillo's Technoculture

and unspontaneous, an inward tension that kept him apart" (*Underworld* 663). George lives literally and symbolically in the underworld (*Underworld* 770). Nick usually finds him in the basement of the restaurant in which he works. He is referred to as George the Waiter not only because it is his job, but also because "his life seemed suspended in some dire expectation" (*Underworld* 663). Nick soon learns that, similarly to Gloria, George awaits death.

Being a junkie and a "bachelor for life," George does not respond to Nick's silent plea to fill the void left by his father's abandonment. During Nick's last visit to George, they play cards for an hour, hoping it would help George fall into a deep slumber. When they finish playing, George shows Nick a gun he has found in a car he was supposed to park. George's reason for stealing the gun is that he "didn't want to leave it in the car where somebody who's not responsible" (*Underworld* 779). George's inability to articulate his thoughts correctly reflects an insurmountable apathy. Nick excitedly takes the shotgun and poses with it. He aims it at George's head and asks whether the gun is loaded or not. George answers that it is not loaded, with "the slyest kind of shit-eating grin."[48] While "an interested look moved across his mouth,"[49] George waits for Nick's next move with curiosity. Nick notices that "he had a look on his face that was more alive and bright than George had ever looked" (*Underworld* 780). Thinking that they were having a good time, Nick pulls the trigger and shoots George in the head.

Nick is unable to understand how a supposedly unloaded gun results in a "sucking sound com[ing] out of the man's face" (*Underworld* 781). For an undetermined time, Nick stands two yards away from the corpse, rewinding the scene over and over again "in the videotape of his mind."[50]

> The way the man said no when he asked if it was loaded.
>
> He asked if the gun was loaded and the man said no and the smile was all about the risk, of course, the spirit of the dare of what they were doing....
>
> He asked if the thing was loaded and the man said no and now he has a weapon in his hands that has just apparently been fired.
>
> He force-squeezed the trigger and looked into the smile on the other man's face.
>
> But first he posed with the gun and pointed it at the man and asked if it was loaded.
>
> Then the noise busted through the room and he stood there thinking weakly he didn't do it....
>
> Why would the man say no if it was loaded?
>
> But first why would he point the gun at the man's head?
>
> (*Underworld* 781)

The shock and uncertainty that Nick witnesses destabilize him. He fails to develop any recognizability with "the man" who is supposed to be his mentor. George becomes "the man" who has opened the gate to the underworld, and "the man" who has symbolically dragged Nick to a path of unredeemable sin. This view is shared by Osteen when he argues that the murder marks a point of no return: Nick Shay becomes a "fallen angel, a once-bright star who begins in glory but ends in the darkness of self-imposed damnation" (223).

For several critics, Nick pulls the trigger in order to overcome the oedipal conflict he has been struggling with since the disappearance of his father.[51] During one of his sessions with his psychiatrist, Nick looks back to the day of his falling. Dr. Lindblad insists that he must probe the history of the murder because she believes that his "father was the third person in the room that day" (*Underworld* 509). For her, Nick has a responsibility to explore the connection between the disappearance of his father and the murder he commits six years later. According to Leonard Wilcox,[52] "Nick's killing of Manza resonates with oedipal impulses and hostilities left unresolved by Nick's father's disappearance" (125). In this context, the moment of the murder represents the point where Nick's past hostilities converge with George's inability to take his father's vacant place. As Osteen remarks, "the Oedipal motivations behind the crime seem almost too obvious. Nick must kill the surrogate father out of rage at the real one" (225).

Focusing on the oedipal interpretation of the murder shadows a technocultural reading of Nick's and the gun's role in the crime. Nick's affirmation that the crime "had no history" has been viewed as a weak response to an unstable psychological state. The words of his psychiatrist "there was a third man in the room that day" are not to be dismissed. Nevertheless, Nick's unconscious disappointment for not finding a paternal surrogate is not the sole reason for pulling the trigger. Nick believes that by handling and bouncing the "harmless" object in his hands he is "doing something simple and maybe halfway clever" (*Underworld* 156). The one thing that Nick is aware of is that the gun is illegal as it appears to be sawed-off. Other than this, Nick does not know for sure what he is holding, "a pirate's pistol or an old Kentucky flintlock" (*Underworld* 780).

Nick seems to pose with the pistol both to show George his bravery and to test the realness of the cold metal. The gun, as a random extension, is not the only component that has led to the murder. For DeLillo, there is a multitude of usual and unusual technocultural connections implicated in that crucial moment. In a way, the particularity of the murder lies in the randomness that such unusual connections harbor in daily life.

Elaborating on this point requires first a reminder of the nature of technoculture. Culture and technology *intermingle* in various ways to form infinite layers or unusual connections. As has been explained, technology

28   *Don DeLillo's Technoculture*

is not only that which is technological, and culture is not only that which is cultural. This is the case not only because one is part of the other, and distinguishing them proves itself to be difficult in the postmodern world, but also because culture is constituted of layers of chaotic elements inter-mingling, dialoguing, and even contradicting each other. This chaos is felt in daily life. Usual and unusual connections appear either explicitly or implicitly to break an orderly unfolding of dailiness. Nick's intention when visiting George has not been killing him but spending time with him. Similarly, Robert's intention in standing on the pier has not been planned as a setting for murder. Nick and Robert have not foreseen the tragic development of their evening because they were in a *familiar* and ordinary context.

The multitude of connections freeze in the moment Nick shoots George, as it brings infinite questions and suppositions. In the quoted passage, Nick is unable to believe that "now he has a weapon in his hands that has just apparently been fired." In the history of violence that he had accumulated before the murder such randomness has never occurred: "Why would the man say no if it was loaded? But first why would he point the gun at the man's head?" (*Underworld* 781).

Nick wonders why George would claim that the gun is not loaded. If Nick does not have an answer to this question, Robert Syverten does. George "the Waiter" does not feel adequate for living. However, even if it is the case, he has asked Nick neither to aim the gun at him nor to fire it. Perhaps Nick fires in order to murder the father figure, but perhaps he fires the gun just because he has thought that it is an extension like any other. This leads to yet another question: who/what has killed George, Nick or the gun? This question is differently approached by Jennifer Daryl Slack and J. Macgregor Wise.[53] They question the National Rifle Association's slogan that "guns don't kill people, people do." Slack and Wise read it against the critique staged by the British comedian Eddie Izzard. This latter acknowledges the possibility that guns do not necessarily kill people, but "the gun helps, you know...." (qtd. in Slack and Wise 49). Slack and Wise then list a number of questions, testing the finiteness of the slogan (49). They conclude that both the association and the comedian may be right. For each argument defending the slogan there is a counter-argument demurring it.

The complexity of George's murder reflects Slack and Wise's vacilla-tion. Nick could not have shot George in the head if he had no gun, if he had no good aim, and if the gun were not loaded. However, Nick has never had any intention of killing, and since he is still under legal age, should he be held responsible for a murder he has unwillingly caused? Viewing the murder in terms of causality may give a finite answer, by directing the blame either toward Nick or toward the gun, but it remains

Don DeLillo's Technoculture 29

appallingly reductive. It is possible to say that once enacted, technologies "do seem to encourage the alignment of all sorts of possibilities" (technological determinism); however, it is also possible to say that "[t]he effect of the gun—that is, killing and/or violence—follow directly from that cultural need and desire" (cultural determinism) (54). Nick's desire has not been to commit murder but to be reckless without consequences. Since George's death is the consequence, whose fault is it? This question does not seem to have a satisfying answer, as it harbors named and unnamed ambiguities.

DeLillo is purposefully ambiguous about the details of the murder, as ambiguity defines it largely. By not limiting the murder down to the gun, DeLillo dodges technological determinism. Even if the gun is the extension by which Nick commits the murder, it is not the cause. The slogan declaring that "guns don't kill people, people do" in its turn conceals the conundrums of the technocultural context within which Nick, the gun, and George interact. Restricting the murder in terms of "Hobson's choice" does not change the fact that George dies either because of Nick or because of the gun, or because of everything involving them both. It is not the dominance of one element over the others that leads to the slaying of George. Rather, the completion of such an eminent possibility involves random but connected circumstances.

By the late-twenties, technology had become deeply ingrained in daily life. Technology had become associated not only with specific fields, but also with the simplest tasks done at home.[54] This implies that dailiness has become a field where everything and anything can happen in a glimpse of an eye. This is shown by the randomness of the murder because it involves a degree of technological uncertainty. In his novels, DeLillo usually explores, either explicitly or implicitly, the manner in which uncertainty has penetrated the technoculture of postmodern America.[55] Samuel Coale argues that by doing so, DeLillo is "cutting across causality, helping to produce the quantum flux, the postmodern spell of uncertainty and skepticism" (79).[56] DeLillo seeks in his novels to examine phenomena such as "the shattering randomness of the event."[57]

By stressing the randomness of the event, DeLillo not only dodges technological determinism, but he also looks into that which could be considered unusual connections. These connections bring together the technologically advanced objects and "primitive" beliefs, ordinary behaviors, and uncanny outcomes. However, DeLillo does not seek to highlight a sense of hopelessness by uniting technology and belief in unusual connections. Rather, he seeks once more to stress how individuals are woven together with technology. If the first part of the chapter deals mainly with the material aspect of this extension, the second part explores deeper layers of the characters' technocultural implication in dailiness.

30   *Don DeLillo's Technoculture*

Breaching the *Beyond*: Attaining the Extraordinary through the Ordinary

"The Electric Stuff of the Culture"

The weaving metaphor seen in the previous section is not limited to a material level; it works itself down to hidden layers of dailiness. In his novels, DeLillo is particularly interested in the concealed meanings perceived by his characters, for he follows them wherever *they* take him.[58] By walking beside them, DeLillo observes "the electric stuff of the culture"[59] that they see, hear, and sense. His characters' sight, hearing, and feelings allow him to describe and even define radiance in dailiness.[60] These extensions offer " 'a way into' a fundamental phenomenon at the heart of our mental culture" (Laist 3). Peeling off layers of everyday life to reach this "fundamental phenomenon" does not point to a growing irrelevancy. DeLillo attempts to reveal the feelings and mysteries hidden in the radiance of dailiness. Radiance appears in the most ordinary moments, but it also reaches the most remote fears and desires. As Kavadlo insists, "DeLillo does nothing less than locate and expose fear, love, and evil.... [and] explore mystery" (7). Feelings are amplified by the sense of mystery. This amplification is the result of sensing the existence of something transcendental, reached through breaking the boundaries between that which is solely technological and that which is solely cultural.

The layered dailiness breaks the boundaries between opposites in order to understand the self and the world. As Gerhard Hoffmann expresses it, DeLillo "invests the quotidian with revelatory power."[61] This power is the result of the interconnectedness of culture and technology. As already mentioned, technology as brightness, and "waves and radiations" is implied in culture as a set of beliefs, behaviors, and activities. This implication breaks the "bulwark between banality and profundity, between innocuous everydayness and transcendental menace, between triviality and significance" (Laist 66). In DeLillo's novels, "banality" refers to basic activities such as shopping, watching television, or observing objects of interest. These activities have the potential of leading to unusual philosophical and spiritual insights. This gives them the capacity to reveal "profound" meanings. The "trivial" distractions of everyday life are the ways through which the characters attempt to escape the hovering presence of death. Whatever the stance characters take, they are usually seeking (or are exposed to) something that transcends the immediacy of their activities.

Radiance in dailiness ultimately aims at restoring a sort of balance between the transcendental aspects of culture and technology. Neither element cancels the other because they continuously create connections. As Erik Davis suggests, technologies not only "serve as the vehicles for spells, ghosts, and animist intuitions," but they also launch "pads for transcendence, for the disembodied flights of gnosis" (6). DeLillo seeks to unveil this transcendence,[62] not through exclusive cultural activities, but through technologically mediated cultural activities. The transcendental aspect of radiance serves as a background for DeLillo's work:

> this radiance can be almost frightening. Other times it can be almost holy or sacred. Is it really there? Well yes.... that's something that has been in the background of my work: a sense of something extraordinary hovering just beyond our touch and just beyond our vision.[63]

DeLillo does not attempt to celebrate a transcendental atmosphere of culture, be it religious, magical, or strange but he does not condemn its importance either. The rationality that is supposed to accompany technology has so far failed to eradicate the *beyond*. In DeLillo's novels, technology ironically amplifies transcendence. John A. McClure rewords this idea when he affirms that DeLillo combines the transcendental/spiritual and the technological by "loosening the fabric of everyday reality so that something else presence or emptiness shines through" (65).[64]

Promethean Shiny Shield in White Noise and The Names

The novel that most breaks the boundaries between the banal and the transcendental through brightness is DeLillo's satirical novel *White Noise* (1985).[65] The novel follows Jack Gladney's attempts to protect this dailiness from the reminder of a pending death. Jack is the chairman of a department called "Hitler studies," which he had created in the sixties. He lives in the small town of Blacksmith with his fourth wife, Babette, and four children from different marriages, Heinrich, Stephanie, Denise, and Wilder. Jack's routine of shopping, watching television, and working remains undisturbed until a toxic chemical named Nyodene D is dispersed in the atmosphere. The family evacuates, but on the way to safety, Jack is exposed to the chemical. His fear of death rendered not only mental but physical as well, he seeks ways to rid himself from the doom that has "entered" him. He discovers that his wife has been having an affair with a scientist, Willie Mink, in exchange for a drug called Dylar. Dylar is supposed to eliminate the fear of death. Jack then tries to acquire the drug for himself. During his quest, he is usually found discussing life and death with his colleague Murray J. Siskind.

DeLillo dedicates the first part of *White Noise* entitled "waves and radiations" to describing the "radiance" of technology through Jack's eyes. In the 20 chapters that constitute this part, the reader is introduced to Jack's everyday activities. "Waves and radiations" are usually considered

32 Don DeLillo's Technoculture

DeLillo's synthesis on the role of consumerism and information technologies in fragmenting the postmodern family. For Joseph M. Conte,[66] Jack's daily life represents "the randomness of postmodern America in terms of pervasive and indirected 'Energy waves, incident radiation'" (125). In this context, energy waves refer to the "constant bombardment of media message and sound" (Kavadlo 17). Jack is, indeed, usually exposed to the images of television and sounds of radio. They randomly fill his vision and reach his ears in various places. This involvement (not to say "invasion") is also explained by "society's envelopment and displacement of nature through the technologies of the late twentieth century" (Martucci 79). For Elise Martucci,[67] the displacement that nature has suffered gives place to buildings, such as the supermarket, that mimic an amplified sense of symbolism. The supermarket is "filled with myriads of signs and symbols that the characters are bombarded with" (102). All in all, "waves and radiations" is seen as DeLillo's condensation of random (not to say "crushing") set of packages, brightness, and sounds filling Jack Gladney's daily life.

Although "waves and radiations" is undoubtedly concerned with the random glow and sounds of television and the supermarket, their heavy presence in Jack's dailiness is not the cause of his existential discomfort. Part One of the novel is concerned with the role that consumerism and information technologies play in Jack's life. However, the expression "waves and radiations" does not aim at showing "that life in America today is boring, benumbing, dehumanized."[68] It rather invites the reader to locate the transcendental implication that technology discloses daily. "Wherever Jack looks," Randy Laist suggests, "his manmade environment appears to brim with transcendental implications" (67). This transcendental implication is most directly experienced through brightness. Brightness is understood in *White Noise* as the direct visual manifestation of technoculture. As early as the first paragraph, Jack is found in his office watching "a long shining line [of station wagons] that coursed through the west campus" (*White Noise* 3). The arrival of a massive number of students, which he calls the "brilliant event," energizes him each September. He observes the students as they unload the "suitcases full of light" (*White Noise* 3), and he admires their parents that seem to "glow a little" with their expensive clothes (*White Noise* 7).

Upon returning home, Jack reminds his wife, Babette, about the "brilliant event." He is sorry that she has missed the "Blue, green, burgundy, brown [station wagons that] gleamed in the sun" (*White Noise* 6). Babette admits that she has "trouble imagining death at that income level" (*White Noise* 7). "Maybe," Jack answers, "it is no death as we know it. Just documents changing hands" (*White Noise* 7). Without knowing it, Babette has touched upon a fear that Jack is unable to shake away. Jack comforts himself by suggesting that death is merely a process of "documents changing hands."

Don DeLillo's Technoculture   33

This re-immerses him in the routine of daily life. Objects seem to shield Jack from his hopelessness. He tries to avoid being reminded of everything he cannot control.

Mark Osteen advances that Jack describes students' commodities more than the students themselves because he considers them commodities as well (167). Osteen adds that Jack knows that "he is another commodity," so he perceives everything in terms of packaging (167). To understand better the reason why Osteen gives much importance to Jack's materialistic inclination, it is important to quote at length the second half of the first paragraph of *White Noise*:

> As cars slowed to a crawl and stopped, students sprang out and raced to the rear doors to begin removing the objects inside; the stereo sets, radios, personal computers; small refrigerators and table ranges; the cartons of phonograph records and cassettes; the hairdryers and styling irons; the tennis rackets, soccer balls, hockey and lacrosse sticks, bows and arrows; the controlled substances, the birth control pills and devices; the jurik food still in shopping bags—onion-and-garlic chips, nacho thins, peanut creme patties, Waffelos and Kabooms, fruit chews and toffee popcorn; the Dum Dum Pops, the Mystic Mints.
>
> (3)

Packaging is represented in Osteen's work as an aura radiating enough brightness to outshine the students and Jack himself. However, listing objects does not "eliminate the human, and humane, elements of the novel" (Kavadlo 14). Listing objects is understood rather as Jack's ritual. Laist reads the same passage in terms of narrative cataloging. He believes that the first paragraph of the novel functions as a sort of "précis" of Jack's narration technique (66). Throughout the novel, Jack catalogs the objects he notices, not because he feels that he is a commodity himself, but because their brightness offers a protective warmth. This passage could be therefore interpreted as Jack's use of electricity and its host of commodities and services to ward off dread. Osteen does not deny this, but he does fall in a technologically deterministic view of the passage. Jack is not redefined as an object, but he is under the pressure of an incessant dread, and brightness eases this dread.

Going back to brightness, in particular, and electricity, in general, implies a movement that transcends commodities themselves. Electricity, and its host that form the electric stuff of culture, seems to radiate with protecting energy. The college professor is fascinated by that which Raymond Williams calls "the gift of power."[69] This gift represents the evolution of "the steam power, the petrol engine, electricity, these and their host of products in commodities and services" (Williams, "Culture is

34 Don DeLillo's Technoculture

Ordinary" 9). For Jack, this gift comes in the form of visual energy, which gives brightness its transcendental meaning. Throughout the novel, Jack is exposed to all sorts of colors and lights. For instance, while he is driving across an accident, he is dazzled by a "strong and eerie light" (*White Noise* 143). When the nuclear catastrophe hits Blacksmith, it provokes "high-tension discharge of vivid light" (*White Noise* 184). Jack eats from "shiny bags of potato chips" (*White Noise* 8), and the air at times seemed to be "bright, swirling around [his] head" (*White Noise* 341). During the last few years, Jack even starts seeing "colored spots.... so gaily animated" even when there is nothing (*White Noise* 46). In short, brightness is deeply integrated into his sight.

In *White Noise*, electricity could easily be defined as the "very source of life, light, and consciousness" (qtd. in E. Davis 107). Jack is not so much interested in learning about electricity in itself. He does not know how electricity functions, or what it is exactly. He does not know the technical terms and the parts involved. After the toxic event, the family is obliged to make do with the bare minimum in a camp located a few miles out of town. The displacement provokes a sense of alienation in the characters.

The displacement makes Heinrich self-conscious about the limited knowledge of the modern man. Heinrich asks his father "what is electricity? What is light?" (*White Noise* 172). Jack is unable to answer. All that concerns the father is that "[we]'re doing alright," as long as "[w]e have heat, we have light" (*White Noise* 172). Jack is comfortable in the camp because "electricity does not just catapult [his] imagination into the metaphysical empyrean; it also grounds [him] on the earth" (E. Davis 35). As a sort of technocultural galvanism, electricity does not only power devices; it also protects Jack from the evil that hides in the shadows of life. As Laist seems to suggest: "electric technology is so like a human dream made real, some possibility culled from the murky depths of the mythological unconscious and wrested Prometheus-like into diurnal, society activity" (21). Jack believes that the world has gained unprecedented brightness. What is important for Jack is that it is there. He tricks himself into thinking that darkness cannot reach him when he wraps himself with brightness. He feels safer when he turns on the light. When he turns it off to sleep, he reaches out to the light of his digital watch that "glowed green in the dark" (*White Noise* 257).

This brightness is present wherever the protagonist looks, as long as he seeks it. Jack finds reassurance in the results of a whole technological progress. He gives technology, in general, and the brightness of electricity, in particular, the task of making his life better, of giving him the possibility to hide rather than face his fears. In the end, it is the gift of protection.

The gift of protection does not find its origins in postmodern technology. Its origin does not even go back to the first experiments of electricity that

Don DeLillo's Technoculture   35

began in the enlightenment period. Rather, the origins of brightness go back to the "fire marks and artifacts" Katheryn, the protagonist's estranged wife in *The Names* (1982),[70] searches for in the ruins of Greece. After James Axton admits to having committed adultery, Katheryn moves to Kouros with their son Tap. She works as a pseudo-archeologist in an excavation directed by the 60-year-old Owen Brademas, who serves as a protector for Katheryn and as a father figure for Tap. In an attempt to regain his role as husband and father, James accepts a job as an insurance risk analyst in a firm called the Northeast Group. He frequently visits Katheryn to make amends, but she prefers "to dig" (*The Names* 145). James believes that her activity is a way to "carry on the singleminded struggle she'd always thought life was supposed to be" (*The Name* 15).

Katheryn is one of the most descriptive characters of an existential struggle. This struggle is understood here as ontological disquiet or dread of the unknown, which requires "a strenuous personal engagement" (*The Names* 15). According to Greek mythology, this struggle goes back to Epimetheus's failed task to bestow Man with a way to protect himself. Epimetheus, the Titan whose name means "after-thinker," has gifted all animals inborn ways to protect themselves. Fur, claws, wings among many tools have been distributed to all creatures except Man. After finding nothing to gift Man, Epimetheus asks Prometheus for assistance. The latter, whose name means "fore-thinker," steals fire from Hephaestus and craft-knowledge from Athena to give them to humans. Read as the essence of technoculture, the gift of Prometheus is destined to allow humans to protect themselves and to survive.

Prometheus's gift to humans does not come without a price. Upon learning of the "godly" tools given to Man, Zeus punishes Prometheus by chaining him to a rock and condemning him to eternal suffering (until Heracles frees him). In their turn, humans are punished by turning Prometheus's good action against them. With the power of fire and craft comes Pandora's box. Pandora, a woman as beautiful as she is mischievous, is sent as a wife to Epimetheus to access a jar, or rather a pithos. She opens the pithos and releases all the evils of the world. Pandora's action has brought "...humans grievous pain: / And only hope in its unbroken dwelling did remain" (Hesiod 60).[71] Katheryn's digging is symbolically motivated by finding the residue of that hope to struggle her way through life. When James asks Kathryn about her findings in the ruins, she answers "fragments" of "storage jars" (*The Names* 16). Those technocultural fragments help her counter the struggle. James notices that after a day's work, Kathryn is radiant with the energy she has gained from digging. Even if the digging wears her down, "she was also charged by it, bright with it, giving off static" (*The Names* 14). The power of the gods is transferred to her on a daily basis to survive yet another day. She is energized physically and spiritually by her activity.

36   Don DeLillo's Technoculture

Similarly to Kathryn, Jack's attraction toward the brightness of technology could be understood as a way to cope with the evils of the world. As Kavadlo words it, "technology…. attempts to camouflage something concomitant with death: a sense of evil" (23). However, Jack does not find protection in the ruins of Athens, contrarily to Kathryn. For Jack, "[t]he sources of 'radiance' are not in Asia or Africa, but across the street and in the living room" (Osteen 166). Jack does not dig the earth to ease his dread. He searches the shiny shelves of the supermarket where "buckets of power and white beyond white" reside (*Americana* 207).

The light of the supermarket is a strong source of reassuring brightness. When Jack enters the vast space, he is hit by a "blast of colors;" as "[e]verything seemed to be in season, sprayed, burnished, bright" (*White Noise* 42). Jack believes that as long as the supermarket stands strong and shiny, "[e]verything was fine, would continue to be fine, would eventually get even better" (*White Noise* 197). The reassuring feeling Jack gets when he enters the supermarket emanates from its characteristic as that which John Frow calls the "phenomenology of surfaces" (47).[72] On these surfaces, Jack finds "tales of the supernatural and the extraterrestrial. The miracle vitamins, the cures for cancer, the remedies for obesity" (*White Noise* 375). With its vivid atmosphere, the supermarket stimulates feelings of mystical energy, capable of making everything better.

Jack's regular trips to the supermarket are not limited to the activity of getting groceries. He considers the supermarket, with its bright colors, as a spiritual boost. Osteen states that "consuming attaches persons to the things whose reproducibility betokens immortality" (171). The products of the supermarket channel with Jack, which provides him with "therapy for body and soul" (166). Because Jack always finds "sprayed, burnished, bright" goods when he comes back to the supermarket, he develops an illusion of constancy.[73] This constancy not only concerns the figurative immortality of the identical products that Jack finds. It also gives Jack the feeling that nothing would change for him as long as products return to the supermarket's shelves.

Unlike Ross's transhumanist apparatus, Jack is unable to summon tremendous technological possibilities to ward off death. He is surrounded by humbler technocultural constructs, so Jack "channels" back with the brightness of products. In this context, "channeling" with products means deflecting unwanted thoughts (Osteen 166). Thus, the tabloids, for instance, with their "vivid lettering" channel "myriads of pseudo-religious beliefs into a curious species of postmodern faith"[74] to quieten the "dull and unlocatable roar" (*White Noise* 43). This channeling is possible because the brightness of products reassures "some snug home in our souls" (*White Noise* 24). The brightness spotlights unusual technocultural connections that provide Jack with unexpected insight or meaning. "In

Don DeLillo's Technoculture   37

the commonplace I find unexpected themes and intensities" (*White Noise* 211). Being able to see such connections makes Jack believe that he has "achieved a fullness of being" unknown to "people who need less, expect less" (*White Noise* 20).

The brightness and "blast of colors" that surrounds goods are thus important sources of constancy. Constancy takes a larger proportion when the supermarket becomes an "unconscious system of representation" that serves as "a temporary way to step outside death by entering an aestheticized space of consumption" (Duvall 128).[75] All the processes that constitute shopping become part of a ritual to avoid thinking about "the vast and terrible depth.... The inexhaustibility.... The whole huge nameless thing.... The massive darkness," that is, death (*White Noise* 331). These processes begin when Jack enters the "magical" sliding doors and conclude when he reaches the supermarket's checkout line. The supermarket in this sense constitutes a "communal experience of the invisible, a sense of mysteriousness that implies that neither life nor death has been settled, closed" (LeClair 228).[76] In other words, it implies that Jack has entered a suspended realm, where neither the responsibilities of life nor the fear of death can reach him.

The wall remains low between the power of consumerism and the brightness of products as a symbol of constancy and "the massive darkness" as a constant reminder of death. Jack cherishes the "routine universe" he has been able to develop, so he seeks to maintain it. This desire makes him dread an upcoming end. The role of the supermarket and its products seems to be shielding him from hopelessness; the same hopelessness Kathryn seeks to chase away through her digging. Shiny products adopt the role of Pandora's box. Each time Jack opens a plastic wrap, a sense of dread is countered by detritus of lost hope, the hope of immortality in his case. In this way, products could be said to radiate a sense of constancy and strength unfound in the naked human body.

Television as *"Waves and Radiations" in* Americana *and* White Noise

The Other-Worldly Dimension of the Screen in White Noise

If spending time in the supermarket leads to all sorts of enchantment, time in front of television opens metaphors of "myth and dream" (Laist 70). These myths and dreams reach the characters' televisions by the means of invisible energies. For DeLillo, invisible energies are as important as daily brightness. He refers to these energies as "waves and radiations." In *White Noise*, waves and radiations are translated as the energies that Jack is capable of sensing in the supermarket's invisible manifestations of brightness, and they are transmitted through various devices. The gift of

38 *Don DeLillo's Technoculture*

power, electricity in particular, allows the practical use of these invisible energies. The outcome is the technocultural assemblage of images and sounds received by Jack through television.

Waves and radiations are part of a succession of modern technological discoveries, technically speaking. Radiations are energies transported in space through waves. Radio waves transfer these energies through a particular frequency of sound waves from one point to another. However, by powering devices, electric technology does not activate neutral responses in individuals. It extends not only their vision but also their mind's imagination. Raymond Williams defines television as a broadcasting technology "of varied messages to a general public" (*Television* 13).[77] However, television extends down to viewers' nervous system, as McLuhan continuously repeats. Television's role is not only to broadcast information; but, as Osteen puts it, television also "channels" the superficial to the spiritual aspects of DeLillo's characters. Television, for Osteen, creates a link between consumerism, the spiritual, and the transcendental (166). Laist inserts that television is an "atmospheric presence in *White Noise*, rather than a localizable object" (73). Through a technocultural relation, television becomes a "gospel of consumerism" (Osteen), one that is watched as well as felt (Laist). Televisual "waves and radiations" represent a spiritual aura that extends beyond its concealed components. As will be shown, television not only touches the characters' visual system, it also recharges them spiritually.

One rainy evening, Murray invites Babette and Jack to dine with him. The couple listen to Murray's revelations while sipping coffee in a small "off-white room." Jack asks his host what insights he has gained from watching television every morning for two months. "Waves and radiations," Murray answers, "the medium is a primal force in the American home. Sealed-off, timeless, self-contained, self-referring. It's like a myth being born right there in our living room" (*White Noise* 60). For Murray, television creates its own setting, as it is "self-contained" and "self-referring."

This view is elaborated in Jersy Kosinski's *Being There*[78] when the protagonist, Chance, remarks that television establishes its own space:

> Chance went inside and turned on the TV. The set created its own light, its own colour, its own time. It did not follow the law of gravity that forever bent all plants downward. Everything on TV was tangled and mixed and yet smoothed out: night and day, big and small, tough and brittle, soft and rough, hot and cold, far and near.
>
> (5)

Moreover, Murray believes that television unites radiations as a technological discovery to myths as cultural expressions to relate events. Williams

Don DeLillo's Technoculture 39

explains that television is not an invention that came into being as a single event. "It depended on a complex of inventions and developments in electricity, telegraphy, photography and motion pictures, and the radio" (*Television* 144). Murray summarizes all the inventions that allowed the creation of television as "waves and radiations;" for without waves and radiations, the medium would have never become the house of myths.

Murray finds a meaningful connection between radiations and myths because the world in which he lives allows the emergence of such connection through technoculture. As Murray suggests, television as known today resembles a myth because of its cultural mysteries and symbols. Television is a mediator that functions thanks to "waves and radiations" in order to transmit vocal and pictorial meanings, which are more mythical than real. The "sealed-off" and "timeless" energies allow the reception of sound and image. As Jack and Murray agree, this makes television a source of deep codes and messages that "mark our species as unique" (*White Noise* 60). The sealed-off components of television consist of all the hidden parts of the box and the invisible energies of radio waves. Television endlessly detects the messages carried by these waves since it can be cyclically reconstructed anew by putting together new components that detect "waves and radiations." The constancy of radio waves offers endless choices of information reception. This set of information discloses nothing new. It rather rephrases endlessly the mythical messages that already exist, and which are revisited over and over again. In this way, television eradicates absence, for the American home is always filled with the sounds and images of television.

The description of the relationship between television and myths is only the first layer of what television represents for Murray and Jack. Murray gives a deeper meaning to television as a manifestation of spiritual "radiance in dailiness." Murray does not content himself with describing television as the house of myths. His conclusion, after his nearly mystical experience, is that adults have to set aside their "irritation, weariness, and disgust" in order to internally connect with television. The objective is to behold television "like something we know in a dreamlike and preconscious way" (*White Noise* 60). The reason behind Murray's insistence on transcending "our first-person selfhood"[79] is to acknowledge the fact that contemporary life is breaking the boundaries between reality and dream. In this contemporary life, "the goings-on of dreams are no longer wholly the prerogative of sleep" (Cecchetto et al. 3).[80] Instead, the whole contemporary life may be viewed as a mere dream whose "flows of images, sounds, feelings, ambiences, ideas promises, and meanings are proximate and promiscuous as any fantasy" (3). The technocultural amalgam of contemporary life blurs the distinction between reality and myth, the medium and the message. The medium, television in this case, becomes a portal to whatever the viewer desires. Because of its "incredible amounts of psychic

40   Don DeLillo's Technoculture

data," television channels its vast web of images to the viewer's desires. Its images and sounds adapt to whatever the characters need, to the extent of becoming part of them. McLuhan suggests that "With TV, the viewer is the screen.... He is bombarded with light impulses" (341), which Murray calls "little buzzing dots." These dots "make up the picture pattern. There is light, there is sound" (*White Noise* 61).

For McLuhan, "the TV image is visually low in data" (341). Unlike pictures, it is not attractive because of visual consistency or lasting images. Unlike movies and series, television lacks in image data level and it lacks planning, rehearsal, and plot. However, television offers the watcher a high participation level in the series of moving images. Because television is a cool medium, it does not block the viewer's participation in what he is watching. It means that the viewer is able to fill the gaps that television overlooks. This is why television seems to Murray a "primal force." It "welcomes us into the grid" (*White Noise* 61), and holds us there. Its force emanates from its ability to engage Murray, even when television images are a blur of "bright packaging, the jingles, the slice-of-life commercials, the products hurtling out of darkness...." (*White Noise* 61). It does not matter what program Murray finds on television. It is the atmosphere that attracts him, that is, the ability to interpret the flick of images. Television activates an ancient atmosphere for Murray. "The TV image is now a mosaic mesh of light and dark spots," McLuhan offers (342), that "opens ancient memories of world birth" Murray concludes (*White Noise* 61). Television is capable of opening a door to the "world birth" because it allows the participation of Murray in its movement. Murray looks at the medium as a box of magic that "overflows with sacred formulas" (*White Noise* 61). Television adapts itself to Murray's interpretation.

Jack Gladney has a different relationship with television. He rarely watches it; he mostly hears it. Television as voice refers to what Roland Barthes calls a mythical "speech," parole, which invades Gladneys' space and mediates their cultural imperatives.[81] In this context, myths refer not only to the linguistic constructs of past legends, or to the original and unreal stories of bedtime; myths, such as the invasive information Jack hears, also refer to the concealed meanings built on an already completed construct of signifier and signified. Myths unsettle that construct from its original (historical) meaning to endow it with a new implication. Even though meaning loses its originality, it still lives through a fabricated meaning capable of being regenerated endlessly.

This capacity for regeneration intrudes on Jack's space, and fills it with unidentified voices. As Laist suggests, Jack's "chief relation to the physical object of television is as something he overhears rather than something he watches" (73). Jack hears television either willingly or unwillingly. His narration is continuously interrupted by the sound of the medium. He hears the miscellaneous information television transmits even when he does not intend to listen. For instance, while he is having an intimate moment with Babette in their bedroom, he hears "Someone turn[ing] on the TV set at the end of the hall" (*White Noise* 33). He remains tuned to the television coming to life as "a woman's voice said: 'If it breaks easily into pieces, it is called shale. When wet, it smells like clay'" (*White Noise* 33). For Osteen, Jack is usually tuned to television because he is a "human TV set" (173). It is true that Jack is woven with the technocultural radiations of television, but he is not a human TV set as much as a receptor of sound waves that his consciousness absorbs and translates. Television is part of Jack's "aural landscape, a dull murmur, invisible and everywhere" (Laist 73). His consciousness is channeled to the sounds and images of television. In this way, television becomes an extension, not only of his sight but of his hearing as well. Even when television is located in another room and is switched on by another person, Jack cannot help channeling with it.

Each time it is switched on by one of the Gladneys, television brings to life a mesmerizing power that goes beyond the room where the medium is located. Television becomes a strong source of sound, a call heard beyond walls. Contrarily to painting, reading, or any other activity that requires concentration, television does not need full attention. This is where its efficiency lies. Its presence could be interpreted either as background noise or as sought distraction. With neither effort from Jack, nor invitation, television fills Jack's thoughts while he is in the bedroom deciding with Babette which one of them will read erotica to the other. Jack's whole house radiates with the announcements and assertions coming through television about life, nature, fashion, and so on. This, for Osteen, renders television "a prayer book or archive of spells" that "reveals the religious yearnings beneath postmodern culture" (173). Television is such reference because, whether invited or not, it comforts Jack. Read this way, television represents the reconstruction of a longstanding warmth that finds its expression through the "waves and radiations" of technoculture.

Each Friday night, Babette invites her family to watch television together. Everyone has to be present in order to "de-glamorize the medium in their eyes, make it wholesome domestic sport" (*White Noise* 18). Most Friday television sessions are uneventful. Even if the Gladneys are all sitting in the same space, they are still not together in spirit. Steffie leaves the room whenever there is an embarrassing or shameful scene. Denise does not lose a chance to teach Steffie about toughness and the ability to *watch*. Heinrich pays attention neither to television nor to the rest of the family.

Despite their usual apathy, the Gladneys fail to de-glamorize television completely. Misplaced euphoria is stimulated when there is something that interests them. One Friday evening, when they gather for their "Friday assembly," the Gladneys cannot tear their eyes away from television.

42 Don DeLillo's Technoculture

Heinrich is not sullen, Steffie is absorbed, Jack is not bored as they watch images of natural disasters.

> There were floods, earthquakes, mud slides, erupting volcanoes. We'd never before been so attentive to our duty.... Babette tried to switch to a comedy series.... She was startled by the force of our objection. We were otherwise silent, watching houses slide into the ocean, whole villages crackle and ignite in a mass of advancing lava. Every disaster made us wish for more, for something bigger, grander, more sweeping.
>
> (*White Noise* 75–76)

Babette is startled by the objections of the members of her family because, contrarily to her, they channel to catastrophes and violence. Jack, for instance, is not filled with sadness as he sees people dying and forests burning. He is rather relieved that he watches rather than lives misfortune. Televisual catastrophes decrease his own "brain fade," and misery.

Jack's colleague, Alfonse Stompanato, suggests that "brain fade" is provoked by the endless information individuals watch on TV, that is why, "[w]e need an occasional catastrophe to break up the incessant bombardment of information" (*White Noise* 77). As long as catastrophes and violence happen somewhere else, they are welcome to happen in order to break the huge flow of ceaseless information. Dennis A. Foster[82] confirms this view by suggesting that "[o]ur society can live with violence—or rather could not survive without it—so long as it is rationalized, represented within a myth and a technology" (161). Mythologized catastrophes lose their original meanings, their touch on reality, and become reoccurring reminders of distanced calamities.

Television, in this way, becomes a shield that offers inconsequential catastrophes; it also becomes a space of safety that distracts the viewers from their own internal viciousness. As expressed in *The Names*, "I feel I'm safe from myself as long as there's an accidental pattern to observe in the physical world" (205). By confronting the televisual voyeurism, DeLillo seeks to point out the manner in which the desire for safety is remolded. For DeLillo, individuals seem to have displaced and miniaturized desire:

> I imagine people, individuals, watching their TV screens and having their own private apocalypses because right in front of them they have vivid images of real earthquakes and the like. Something is happening which has to do with the displacement of desire.
>
> (114)[83]

The waves and radiations of television seem to have miniaturized the watcher's expectations and desires. The technocultural "waves and

Don DeLillo's Technoculture   43

radiations" is confronted with ethical integrity. If such integrity is forgotten while viewing natural catastrophes, the characters nevertheless demonstrate the perpetual need for protection.

Television provokes this response in Jack, in particular, because he perceives the medium in terms of touch rather than sight. McLuhan explains that "TV is, above all, an extension of the sense of touch, which involves maximal interplay of all senses" (364). When Jack watches natural catastrophes, his whole being is touched. His eyes follow the images; his ears hear the comments, he breathes the "erupting volcanoes" and tastes the ashes of others' dying. He is, most of all, enthralled by the sensations because distant catastrophes attest to both dread and safety. During these nights, television becomes the center "where the outer torment lurks, causing fears and secret desires" (*White Noise* 101). Such paradoxical conception of television is not without foundation, as "touch is [sometimes] the feeling that nothing is safe" (Plant 186). Television, as a technocultural symbol, contains contradictions, as it is a web of data to be interpreted as Jack wishes. What Jack wishes is to gain life credit by watching others die. Such settings provoke dread in him because he knows that, sooner or later, he will die as well. Nevertheless, the setting also reassures him. Jack feels that he is still alive and that death is not coming yet.

Either for Jack or for Murray, television is a source of mild synesthesia. Magical or not, transcendental or not, television still opens a door to something beyond what they are watching. While television opens the time of world birth to Murray, it offers Jack a way to console himself and to forget about his misery. The magical, spiritual, and transcendental atmospheres of television emanate from its synesthesia.

Pixeled Synesthesia in Americana

Provoking synesthesia through television finds its fuller definition in DeLillo's first novel, *Americana* (1971). DeLillo has never acknowledged the use of synesthesia. Nevertheless, it is manifested when his characters are caught trying to interpret "wave and radiations." Generally speaking, synesthesia, from the Greek "joined sensation," denotes the ability "to hear colors, taste shapes, or experience other equally strange sensory fusions" (Cytowic 2).[84] Synesthesia precepts do not conform to the common ways of perceiving the world. They are rather characterized by "spatial extension and dynamism, and are involuntary, automatic, and consistent over time" (2). These spatial extension and dynamism are highlighted in *Americana*[85] through the manner in which the protagonist, David Bell, experiences television. Instead of involving his sight only, David activates various senses in the process of watching television. David represents the forebear of the way DeLillo's characters experience something other than gaining

44   Don DeLillo's Technoculture

information. DeLillo's characters are more often than not barely concerned by the programs broadcast on television. They seek, similarly to Kathryn, a hope they believe is buried in the screen. This is compatible with the weaving that technoculture reiterates through combinations of the technological and the spiritual.

In *Americana*, David counters the monotony of his life by absorbing the spiritual energy of waves and radiations through television. David works for an advertising network, a job for which he has no passion. He attends parties with individuals to whom he feels no attachment. After divorcing his wife, he maintains a meticulously arranged life. His daily life consists of a repeated set of activities that he breaks temporarily away from by watching television. One night, after showering, he tries to remember whom he has wanted to call. Unable to remember, he "looked at the television screen for a moment and then found [himself] in a chair about a foot away from the set, watching intently" (*Americana* 43). David's intention has never been to watch television. He had switched it on when he arrived home from work as usual, but he usually pays no particular attention to the broadcasts. Similarly to Jack, David channels to the sounds television much more than to the meanings it is supposed to convey. However, a force seems to have compelled him toward the medium. He cannot understand it, but he submits to it.

David cannot assimilate the content of the screen, but that is not what makes him watch television for half an hour. He sits so close to the screen that he can see "that meshed effect, those stormy motes" (*Americana* 43). These effects "drew [him] in and held [him] as if [he was] an integral part of the set" (*Americana* 43). Television, as a cool medium allowing high participation, "leaves much more for the listener or user to do" (McLuhan 348). This is true for David, but not as a program viewer. This is why his experience is synesthetic. David is "touched" by television. In this context, "touch" is defined in terms of the McLuhanian philosophy of sense interplay. Watching television, thus, becomes "a matter of fruitful meeting of the senses, of sight translated into sound, and sound into movement, and taste and smell" and even transcendence (McLuhan 66). David participates body and soul in an experience that is not about television. It is rather about a bond being created between visual "meshed effects" and an abstract force emanating from David. In Elias Canetti's words, David "wants to *see* what is reaching toward him, and to be able to recognize or at least classify it" (qtd. in Plant 186; emphasis in original). David glimpses his soul; he senses his "molecules" transcending his body and touching or "mating with those millions of dots" (*Americana* 43). He transcends the voices and integral fast-paced images in order to use television as a medium to bond with his essence.

Perceiving his soul requires avoiding being distracted by the images and sounds of television. To succeed, David develops an atomistic view of television by connecting his "molecules" with television's "millions of dots." This atomistic view of television is not hazardous. DeLillo has a tendency to explore transcendental matter through particles and waves. His aim is to describe "the process of consciousness itself" (Coale 94). Indeed, DeLillo's aim is not to show how television affects David, but which process fills David while staring at the enmeshed effect. This process implicates the medium as a technocultural door that opens his deepest desires and fears. David, thus, channels on a deeper level with the screen to experience a moment "close to mystical," as Murray would word it.

This nearly mystical experience is the result of a synesthetic process triggered by David's channeling with television. The goal of this process amounts to perceiving his soul and developing a better understanding of his own self. As McLuhan confirms, "it would seem to be the *synesthesia*, or tactual depth of TV experience, that dislocates [one] from usual attitudes of passivity and detachment" (367; emphasis in original). David awakens from the trance only after the announcement of a commercial break. The post-synesthetic experience makes him feel "numb and sleazy, the way an awakening man feels when he realizes he passed out drunk on his host's sofa the night before" (*Americana* 44). The experience consumes his capacity to feel, as it demands the unification of all his senses.

Once his soul has bonded with the meshed effect of television, David begins to see himself more clearly. He loses his sense of time and space to reach another level of self-understanding. David realizes that he has been stumbling "through life, waiting for some change, some new dispensation, to complete the displacement of the old order" (Cowart 132). In other words, he understands that "he who is drunk by a passing shadow / Always carries within them the cost / Of wishing a change of place" [my translation] (Baudelaire, "The Owls" 280).[86] David compares the nearly mystical experience to being drunk and forgetful. He sees and feels in terms of this "imaginary" drunkenness and real discomfort. The shadow of a passing moment is represented in David's case by an intensive staring at the dots of television for half an hour. It reveals his desire to "[aims his car] more or less to the west" (*Americana* 125).

By the end of the first part of the novel, David decides to travel with three companions. For Paul Giaimo,[87] David's decision to leave his work and home is a way to defy his television network boss, Weede Denney (24). This is, however, not a journey against images as he is planning to learn the art of filmmaking. It could be said that David desires to perceive his essence from the other side of the lens. By going west, he is trying to go to the remotest places, where technology is not as strongly present as in the cities. It is his way to break free from the monotony of life and to seek a more hopeful future. He has beheld the weariness of his soul by the repetition of activities. The journey is ultimately an inner voyage, a way

46 *Don DeLillo's Technoculture*

to revive himself. He shares this feeling with his companions, as "they journeyed toward their own interior limits.... not hopeless in their flight" (*Americana* 203).

For DeLillo, the overt layer of technoculture, be it remote locations or television-rooms, is not devoid of meaning. It serves as a distraction from or a revelation of "a dull and unlocatable roar." The characters seen channel differently with the brightness of their environment. Nevertheless, even if their approach to a particular brightness differs, all the characters are held in a way or another by a particular aura, or "waves and radiations." Television, in particular, involves the viewer either in a passive or in an active state of interaction. As has been shown, Murray is fascinated by television's mythological symbolism. Jack channels with television through the senses of hearing and touching in order to be distracted from the eminence of death, and David is absorbed by televisual synesthesia. It is noticed that most of the characters are not interested in the content of television, except Jack who transfers his angst to images of natural catastrophes.

In contemporary technoculture, technology and transcendence are intertwined, either explicitly or implicitly, to reveal a new form of experience. If this intertwinement is not always acknowledged, it is still felt in the brightness and the "waves and radiation" of everyday life. DeLillo could have easily reworded Arthur Symons's famous quote "I write.... a literature in which the visible world is no longer a reality, and the unseen world no longer a dream."[88] Indeed, DeLillo seeks not only to describe a layered technocultural reality, but also to locate its concealed meanings. As seen in the first part of the chapter, individuals are woven together with technology. This entanglement does not mean that technology holds an uncanny power over individuals, as DeLillo attempts to avoid technological determinism. Rather, it means that individuals are always involved in a technocultural environment, characteristics of which is referred to as "radiance in dailiness."

DeLillo uses "radiance in dailiness" as an expression describing the obvious and the underlying connections between his characters and technoculture. The second part, as seen, explored the underlying layers of the characters' technocultural implication in dailiness. By doing so, DeLillo acknowledges the loosened boundaries between the seen and the unseen. Instead of lamenting the terrible consequences this provokes, DeLillo chooses to show that in "our time, a mythic time" (Haraway 150), "culture [remains] ordinary" (Williams, "Culture is Ordinary" 1). Our culture is a technocultural construct that breaks the boundaries between opposites. In order to understand how these boundaries are broken, it was necessary to locate the "radiance" involved in everyday exposure to brightness, especially the televisual one.

Not all of DeLillo's characters are disinterested in television broadcasts, as the author does not undermine the importance of the miscellaneous programs transmitted by image technologies. In an interview, DeLillo declares that the television viewer has developed a "sense of perform-ance" as regards televisual events.[89] Once televisual events have become live historical broadcast, viewers have started to feel a degree of related-ness to televisual content. As will be seen, the transition of image tech-nologies, including television, to real-time broadcasts has contributed to building one's consciousness. "In our culture and everywhere around us we are shaped-to some fairly important degree-by visual imagery," DeLillo declares.[90] For him, individuals are shaped by visual technologies because they are exposed to ongoing construction of history rather than to imper-sonal events. A larger interest in television, in particular, and image tech-nologies, in general, has emerged with the appearance of the broadcast of historical events.

Notes

1 Plant, Sadie. *Zeros + Ones: Digital Women + the New Technoculture*. London, Fourth Estate, 1997.
2 DeLillo, Don. "'An Outside in this Society': An Interview with Don DeLillo." Interview by Anthony DeCurtis. *Conversations with Don DeLillo*, edited by Thomas DePietro, Jackson, University Press of Mississippi, 2005, pp. 70–71.
3 DeLillo, "'An Outside in this Society': An Interview with Don DeLillo," p. 70.
4 Dewey, Joseph. *Beyond Grief and Nothing: A Reading of Don DeLillo*. Columbia, University of South Carolina Press, 2006.
5 See Heidegger, Martin. *The Question Concerning Technology and Other Essays*. Translated by William Lovitt, New York, Garland Publishing, 1977; Borgmann, Albert. *Technology and the Character of Contemporary Life: A Philosophical Inquiry*. London, University of Chicago, 1984; Williams, Raymond. *Television: Technology and Cultural Form*. 2nd ed., London, Routledge, 2003. See also Cooper, Simon. *Technoculture and Critical Theory*, p. 18; Shaw, Debra B. *Technoculture: The Key Concepts*. Oxford, Berg, 2008, p. 12; Davis, Erik. *TechGnosis*, p. 9.
6 Davis, Gregory H. *Means without End: A Critical Survey of the Ideological Genealogy of Technology without Limits, from Apollonian Techne to Postmodern Technoculture*. Lanham, University Press of America, 2006, p. 9.
7 Cooper, *Technoculture and Critical Theory*, p. 18.
8 The term "technoculture" has been coined by Henry G. Burger in early 60s to designate a new field of study that supports both technology and culture (Genosko 1).
  Genosko, Gary. *When Technocultures Collide*.
9 Roderick, Ian. *Critical Discourse Studies and Technology: A Multimodal Approach to Analysing Technoculture*. London, Bloomsbury Academic, 2016.

48 Don DeLillo's Technoculture

10 Laist, Randy. *Technology and Postmodern Subjectivity in Don DeLillo's Novels*. Frankfurt, Peter Lang, 2010.

11 "I'm just translating the world around me in what seems to be straightforward terms.... But I'm not trying to manipulate reality. This is just what I see and hear."
McCrum, Robert. "Don DeLillo: 'I'm Not Trying to Manipulate Reality–This Is What I See and Hear'." *The Observer*. Guardian News and Media, August 7, 2010. Accessed May 16, 2017.

12 Kavadlo, Jesse. *Don DeLillo: Balance at the Edge of Belief*. Frankfurt, Peter Lang, 2004.

13 Davis, *TechGnosis*.

14 Glavanakova, Alexandra K. "The Age of Humans Meets Posthumanism: Reflections on Don DeLillo's *Zero K*." *Studies in the Literary Imagination*, vol. 50 no. 1, 2017, pp. 91–109. *Project MUSE*, https://doi.org/10.1353/sli.2017.0007

15 McLuhan, Marshall. *Understanding Media: The Extensions of Man*. London, Routledge, 2001.

16 Umberto Eco points out that despite McLuhan's gift to give the reader an appealing version of that which is already known, he still has "this technique of nondefinition of terms" (238).
Eco, Umberto. "Cogito Interruptus." *Faith in Fakes: Travels in Hyperreality*. Translated by William Weaver, London, Vintage, 1998, pp. 221–238.

17 Hazard, Patrick D. *AV Communication Review*, vol. 13, no. 1, 1965, pp. 71–75. *JSTOR*, www.jstor.org/stable/30217185

18 Nel, Philip. "DeLillo and Modernism." *The Cambridge Companion to Don DeLillo*, edited by John Noel Duvall, Cambridge, Cambridge University Press, 2008, p. 13.

19 Veggian, Henry. *Understanding Don DeLillo*. Columbia, University of South Carolina, 2014, p. 34.

20 The importance that DeLillo gives to the occurrences of everyday life is well known. "As in Joyce's *Ulysses* and Malcolm Lowry's *Under the Volcano* (1947), another of DeLillo's favorites, DeLillo seeks the epic in the everyday" (Nel 14).

21

> Over the course of more than a half century of writing, Don DeLillo's fiction has communicated how characters, readers, and art experience media both old and new, doing so in ways that many consider to be unique in the history of American literary writing. DeLillo works through the implications of those technologies.
>
> (Veggian 18)

22 DeLillo, Don. "An interview with Don DeLillo." Interview by Thomas LeClair. *Conversations with Don DeLillo*, edited by Thomas DePietro, Jackson, University Press of Mississippi, 2005, p. 12.

23 Dewey, *Beyond Grief and Nothing*, p. 41. See also Osteen, Mark. *American Magic and Dread Don DeLillo's Dialogue with Culture*. Philadelphia, University of Pennsylvania Press, 2000, p. 63.

Don DeLillo's Technoculture 49

24 As described by Chris Shilling, motility does not designate motion without objective. "Motility accomplishes an extension of the body schema, through the incorporation of new skills and new objects, which enables us to expand the quantity and quality of our movements and to exercise agency" (Shilling 55). Shilling, Chris. *The Body in Culture, Technology and Society*. London, SAGE, 2005.

25 The body is "a source of, a location for and a means by which individuals are emotionally and physically positioned within and oriented towards society" (Shilling 11). Despite its frailty, the body is adjusted to the world through the necessary technologies that individuals build.

26 Borgmann, *Technology and the Character of Contemporary Life*.

27 See also Glavanakova, "The Age of Humans Meets Posthumanism," p. 96.

28 Roderick, *Critical Discourse Studies and Technology*, 2016.

29 "Metaphors are not simply flourishes or decorative devices but, instead, are crucial to how we come to define, experience, and act in our everyday life" (Roderick 68).

30 Barglow, Raymond. *The Crisis of the Self in the Age of Information, Computers, Dolphins and Dreams*. London, Routledge, 1994.

31 Ritual practices "bind and contain the anxiety of participants at the same time that they organize their behavior" (Barglow 144). Its main characteristic is that it is connective and exclusive to the real world.

32 Formal procedures are undertaken in an impersonal and an anonymous manner. They are in most cases executed by machines rather than by humans (Barglow 144).

33 Osteen, *American Magic and Dread Don DeLillo's Dialogue with Culture*.

34 DeLillo, Don, *Ratner's Star*. New York, Vintage, 1980, p. 17.

35 Kranzberg, Melvin, and Carroll W. Pursell, editors. *Technology in Western Civilization*, vol. 1. New York, Oxford University Press, 1967.

36 DeLillo, Don, *Zero K*. New York, Scribner, 2016, p. 236.

37 "Il s'agit de repousser les limites de ce que signifie être humain. La mort n'est plus envisagée de façon religieuse, comme un au-delà spirituel, mais de façon technologique" (38). DeLillo, Don. "Le Grand Entretien: Don DeLillo." Interview by François Busnel. *America: L'Amérique Comme Vous Ne L'avez Jamais Lue*, August 2017, pp. 25–43.

38 Noble, David F. *The Religion of Technology: The Divinity of Man and the Spirit of Invention*. New York, Alfred A. Knopf, 1998. See also Glavanakova, "The Age of Humans Meets Posthumanism," p. 99.

39 Plant, *Zeros + Ones*, p. 61.

40 Ibid., p. 66.

41 Haraway, Donna Jeanne. *Simians, Cyborgs, and Women: The Reinvention of Nature*. London, Free Association, 1991.

42 DeLillo declares in his interview with François Busnel that the Convergence is a project based on secrecy and novelty. "At that point, I understood that people [at the Convergence] hide because they wanted to conceal the biggest secret of our era. What would it be? Becoming immortal" [my translation]: "Là, j'ai compris que si ces gens se cachaient, c'est parce qu'ils voulaient cacher le plus grand secret de notre temps. Quel est-il? Devenir immortel" (38).

50 *Don DeLillo's Technoculture*

43 McLuhan, *Understanding Media*, p. 47.
44 DeLillo, *Zero K*, p. 238.
45 Transhumanist technoculture will be explored further in Chapter 5.
46 In this context, "intention" is to be distinguished from "intension," as it does not refer to the linguistic concept, which is usually contrasted to extension. Rather, "intention" is to be understood in terms of "intentionality," as understood by Augustine and John R. Searle. "Intentionality" refers to the directedness of many (but not all) mental states and events that refer to something (object or else) in the world.
47 Part six, "Arrangement in Gray and Black" covers the period from Fall 1951 to Summer 1952. This part is divided into eight chapters that revolve primarily around the lives of Nick and Matt Shay. As the rest of the novel, this part describes "a technological environment that has become so intrinsic and normative that, to cite Jacques Ellul, it 'shapes the total way of life' " (Russo 219). Russo, John Paul. *The Future without a Past the Humanities in a Technological Society*. London, University of Missouri Press, 2005.
48 DeLillo, Don. *Underworld*. London, Picador, 2011, p. 509.
49 Ibid., p. 780.
50 Osteen, *American Magic and Dread Don DeLillo's Dialogue with Culture*, p. 224.
51 See Wilcox, Leonard. "Don DeLillo's 'Underworld' and the Return of the Real." *Contemporary Literature*, vol. 43, no. 1, 2002, p. 125. *JSTOR*, www.jstor.org/stable/1209018; Osteen, *American Magic and Dread Don DeLillo's Dialogue with Culture*, p. 225; Kavadlo, *Balance at the Edge of Belief*, p. 124.
52 Wilcox, "Don DeLillo's 'Underworld' and the Return of the Real," pp.120–137.
53 Slack, Jennifer Daryl, and J. Macgregor Wise. *Culture and Technology: A Primer*. New York, Peter Lang, 2015.
54 See Kranzberg and Pursell, *Technology in Western Civilization*.
55 DeLillo traces the cause of this uncertainty to the disruption of the foundations of cause and effect. He believes that the manifestation of this disruption is the clearest in the assassination of J. F. Kennedy. He even declares that his books could not have been written "in the world that existed before the Kennedy assassination." This point is further explored in Chapter 2.
DeLillo, Don. "The Art of Fiction CXXXV: Don DeLillo." Interview by Adam Begley. *Conversations with Don DeLillo*, edited by Thomas DePietro, Jackson, University Press of Mississippi, 2005, p. 103.
56 Coale, Samuel. *Quirks of the Quantum: Postmodernism and Contemporary American Fiction*. London, University of Virginia Press, 2012.
57 DeLillo, "The Art of Fiction CXXXV: Don DeLillo," p. 103.
58 DeLillo, " 'An Outside in this Society': An Interview with Don DeLillo," p. 73.
59 DeLillo, "The Art of Fiction CXXXV: Don DeLillo," p. 107.
60 DeLillo, Don. Interview by William Goldstein. *Conversations with Don DeLillo*, edited by Thomas DePietro, Jackson, University Press of Mississippi, 2005, p. 48.
61 Hoffmann, Gerhard. *From Modernism to Postmodernism: Concepts and Strategies of Postmodern American Fiction*. New York, Rodopi, 2005, p. 338.

Don DeLillo's Technoculture 51

62 Each new novel "confirms the possibility of nothing less than the transcendence and authenticity for which DeLillo's characters have searched since David Bell headed west" (Dewey 138).

63 DeLillo, " 'An Outside in this Society': An Interview with Don DeLillo," p. 71.

64 McClure, John A. *Partial Faiths: Postsecular Fiction in the Age of Pynchon and Morrison*. Athens, University of Georgia, 2007.

65 DeLillo, Don. *White Noise*. London, Picador, 2012 [1985].

66 Conte, Joseph M. *Design and Debris: A Chaotics of Postmodern American Fiction*. London, University of Alabama Press, 2002.

67 Martucci, Elise. *The Environmental Unconscious in the Fiction of Don DeLillo*. New York, Routledge, 2007.

68 Bawer, Bruce. "Don DeLillo's America." *The New Criterion*, April 1985, www.newcriterion.com/issues/1985/4/don-delilloas-america. Accessed May 23, 2016.

69 Williams, Raymond. "Culture Is Ordinary." *Raymond Williams on Culture and Society: Essential Writings*, edited by Jim McGuigan, London, Sage Publications, 2014, p. 9.

70 DeLillo, Don. *The Names*. London, Picador, 2011 [1982].

71 Hesiod. *Theogony and Works and Days*. Translated by Catherine Schlegel and Henry Weinfield, Athens, University of Michigan Press, 2006.

72 Frow, John. "The Last Things before the Last: Notes on *White Noise*." *Don DeLillo's White Noise*, edited by Harold Bloom, Philadelphia, Chelsea House Publishers, 2003, pp. 35–72.

73 Passages from several authors investigating the role of the supermarket in Jack's life point to similar conclusions. See Osteen, *American Magic and Dread Don DeLillo's Dialogue with Culture*, p. 166; Duvall, John N. "The (Super) Marketplace of Images: Television as Unmediated Mediation in DeLillo's *White Noise*." *Arizona Quarterly: A Journal of American Literature, Culture, and Theory*, vol. 50, no. 3, 1994, p. 178. Project MUSE, https://doi.org/10.1353/arq.1994.0002; Laist, *Technology and Postmodern Subjectivity in Don DeLillo's Novels*, p. 67.

74 Osteen, *American Magic and Dread Don DeLillo's Dialogue with Culture*, p. 166.

75 Duvall, "The (Super)Marketplace of Images."

76 LeClair, Tom. *In the Loop: Don DeLillo and the Systems Novel*. Champaign, University of Illinois Press, 1987.

77 Williams, *Television*.

78 Kosinski, Jersy. *Being There*. New York, Grove Press, 2007.

79 Laist, *Technology and Postmodern Subjectivity in Don DeLillo's Novels*, p. 70.

80 Cecchetto, David, et al. *Ludic Dreaming: How to Listen Away from Contemporary Technoculture*. New York, Bloomsbury Academic, 2017.

81 In *Mythologies* (1957), Barthes suggests that as speech a myth is a message, be it seen, written, or heard and not only spoken, which forms itself upon

> material which has *already* been worked on so as to make it suitable for communication: it is because all the materials of myth (whether pictorial or

52 *Don DeLillo's Technoculture*

written) presuppose a signifying consciousness, that one can reason about them while discounting their substance.

(110; emphasis in original)

Barthes, Roland. *Mythologies*. Translated by Annette Lavers, New York, Hill and Wang, 1972.

82 Foster, Dennis A. "Alphabetic Pleasures: *The Names*." *Introducing Don DeLillo*, edited by Frank Lentricchia, Durham, Duke University Press, 1991, pp. 157–173.

83 DeLillo, Don. "An Interview with Don DeLillo." Interview by Maria Nadotti. *Conversations with Don DeLillo*, edited by Thomas DePietro, Jackson, University Press of Mississippi, 2005, pp. 109–119.

84 Cytowic, Richard E. *Synesthesia: A Union of the Senses*. 2nd ed., London, MIT Press, 2002.

85 DeLillo, Don. *Americana*. New York, Penguin Books, 1989 [1971].

86 "L'homme ivre d'une ombre qui passe / Porte toujours le châtiment / D'avoir voulu changer de place."
Baudelaire, Charles. *Les Fleurs du Mal*. Paris, Chêne, 2007.

87 Giaimo, Paul. *Appreciating Don DeLillo: The Moral Force of a Writer's Work*. Oxford, Praeger, 2011.

88 Symons, Arthur. *The Symbolist Movement in Literature*. London, W. Heinemann, 1980, p. 6.

89 DeLillo, " 'An Outside in this Society': An Interview with Don DeLillo," p. 57.

90 DeLillo, Don. " 'Writing as a Deeper Form of Concentration': An Interview with Don DeLillo." Interview by Maria Moss. *Conversations with Don DeLillo*, edited by Thomas DePietro, Jackson, University Press of Mississippi, 2005, p. 156.

2   Latent History and Techno-Progress

In his interviews, DeLillo remains usually vague about his definition of history, even if it is a recurrent theme in his fiction. His reluctance emanates from a feeling of ill-equipment for the task.[1] DeLillo uses history as main theme in *Libra* (1988) and *Underworld* (1997). He also develops theories on the postmodern shape of history in *Great Jones Street* (1973) and *Running Dog* (1978). Yet, DeLillo continuously rehashes his inability to elaborate on the historical aspect of his novels. When speaking about *Libra* in an interview, for instance, DeLillo states that even if *Libra* is "technically" historical in nature his first and foremost aim is to write a novel: "In a way *Libra* is about history. But it certainly is not history itself. I tell people, when they want to know what to call this book, that it's a novel."[2] Similarly to postmodern authors such as E. L. Doctorow and Robert Coover, DeLillo explores historical figures and events in a way that critics read closely or loosely in terms of historiographic metafiction. However, DeLillo finds it difficult to define the state of postmodern history outside his literary projects.

DeLillo's hesitation to articulate a bold statement on the definition of postmodern history derives from a common uncertainty. This uncertainty concerns the manner in which history is mediated in the technocultural era. It concerns particularly the proximity of the historical event to the postmodern historian who finds it difficult to distance him/herself from said event. In an attempt to locate history in postmodern world, Keith Jenkins argues that "[b]ecause post-modernists see nothing as fixed or solid this jeopardizes the sorts of attempts that they may make to define what they see themselves as part of" (71).[3] The proximity of history is provoked by the fast and easy access to the historical event through technocultural mediums.

As seen in Chapter 1, technoculture interrelates culture and technology in daily brightness. This chapter focuses on daily visual brightness of various

DOI: 10.4324/9781003407768-3

54 Latent History and Techno-Progress

audio-visual devices, referred to from now on as image technologies. According to Don Ihde, "[i]mage technologies belong as intricately to our contemporary ordinary lifeworld" (44).[4] Their manifestation in cultural life comes in the form of "television, the growing spectrum of perception-enhancing and reproducing devices such as camcorders, VCRs, cassette players, CDs, etc." (44). These devices represent what Debra B. Shaw calls "spectacular culture,"[5] which she develops from Guy Debord's *The Society of the Spectacle* (1967). Through image technologies, "spectacular culture" favors the sense of sight, which results in impoverishing the other senses. As Shaw explains, "[b]ecause television, film and advertising are concerned with projecting images, the sense of sight is elevated above other senses and becomes the measure of our experiences" (21). In this context, historical reality is jeopardized, as characters do not approach it with a sense of historical distance. In other words, characters' exposure to daily visual intake results in an alienation from their axiomatic understanding of history. As will be shown, characters redefine history because of the lack of a temporal distance between their living rooms and historical events.

In order to avoid semantic saturation of the word "history," DeLillo introduces the notion of "latent history" in his third novel *Great Jones Street*. As shall be demonstrated, latent history consists of two complementary aspects of history: possible past events and overlooked present events. The first aspect of history sheds light on events that might have happened in the past and the second focuses on present discarded or uncertain events. These aspects focus on imagining potential events, which redefines history both as past events and as events under construction. Moreover, latent history does not merely challenge historical causality; it also creates proximity between events and individuals through technology, which transforms history into a personal product.

Latent history is the postmodern manifestation of history as represented by image technologies such as film. John N. Duvall[6] posits that "DeLillo shows us nothing less than how America became postmodern," as the author is "aware that the twentieth century is the first to have been thoroughly documented on film" (2). The role of image technologies in redefining history as a postmodern construct implicates breaking free from grand narratives and opening history to imaginative possibilities. As Peter Boxall confirms,[7] "DeLillo's 1970s fiction is organized around the latent, inexpressible space of this unrealized possibility, this lost historical category" (82). Because latent history is mediated by technology, in general, and image technologies, in particular, the visual data it accumulates prevents relying solely on causality. As a result, latent history trades the causality of history for a wider range of possibilities. The aim of these possibilities varies with the desires of the characters. These desires are intensified by their sense of sight while they stare at screens.

Latent History and Techno-Progress   55

Despite his reluctance to voice his perception of history, DeLillo contests through his characters the exclusiveness of history to the past and to "valuable" events. The technocultural context within which history works nowadays prevents temporal distance. History, hence, becomes "the angle at which realities meet," in a world made a small village through technological advance (*End Zone* 10). It becomes a doorway to escape invisibility when "history means to merge" through the medium of televisual recognition (*Libra* 101). History also becomes a way to "own a fragment of the tangible past" in order to find "consolation in durable things"[8] (*Running Dog* 115). However, if "[t]hey made history by the minute in those days" (*Underworld* 141), and if it is "history measured in inches" (*Falling Man* 46), "[d]o we see ourselves living outside time, outside history?"[9] Is history possible at all, as DeLillo wonders in *Mao II* (157); or do we have to "roam freeways" in order to "rehearse the end of history" (*Underworld* 508). Finally, if "history is written on the commonest piece of paper in your pocket" (*Underworld* 354), has it integrated daily life so thoroughly that it cannot be distinguished from it?

The Implication of Image Technologies in the Rise of Latent History

"Latent History" in Great Jones Street *and* Running Dog

DeLillo first explores latent history in his third novel *Great Jones Street*.[10] Latent history is mentioned when the protagonist, the young rockstar Bucky Wunderlick, is forced by his partner, Opel, to organize a party in the room of his reclusion. While he sits in the middle of the living room, he hears various conversations, among which the words of a so-called Professor catch his attention. An unnamed Professor of Latent History at the Osmond institute contemplates contemporary history. It is revealed later in the novel that the Professor is Dr. Pepper. His camouflage talent allows him to change his appearance and to become unrecognizable under different circumstances. His transformations reflect his ability to bring to light different if not contradictory perceptions. For the Professor, history is not merely a set of recorded events; rather, it is a multitude of actual and imaginative possibilities. "It's axiomatic that history is a record of events. But what of latent history? We all think we know what happened. But did it really happen? Or did something else happen? Or did nothing happen?" (*Great Jones Street* 72).

The Professor believes that the agreed-on definition of history cannot explain the state of latent "accounts." Etymologically, the word history originates from Greek ἱστορία adopted to Latin "historia" which means "a learning by inquiry, information," connoting a vision of that which subserves knowledge (Partridge 1432).[11] More specifically, history refers

56   *Latent History and Techno-Progress*

to the recorded information, or the historiography, of known and valuable past events (1432). In this passage, the Professor questions the structure of traditional historiography in the postmodern context. He voices his skepticism about the Truth of amassed history. In this context, "Truth" could be read in terms of Hegel's notion of philosophical history.[12] This sort of history relates to the conception of reason. It implies that "the history of the world, therefore, presents us with a rational process" (22). Because this category is governed by reason, it leads to the absolute invariant Truth of the world. It rejects chance and focuses on the "True, the Eternal, the absolutely powerful essence" (23). In the light of this definition, history could be understood as the accumulated data of past events that were deemed worthy of being recorded because they represent Truth. The aim of this sort of history is to lead to absolute knowledge and to leave no space for chance and uncertainty.

Because of the nature of data-gathering that characterizes the postmodern world, selecting a set of events that contribute to strengthening established norms becomes difficult. The Professor believes that varied and even contradictory information is contained in latent history because of data-gathering possibilities. The logic of latent history is thus incompatible with absolute idealism. It accepts the bifurcation of interpretative daily tools used by the historian. Therefore, latent history refers to actual events that have not been necessarily recorded and that are still under construction. This kind of latent history will be referred to from now on as "actual possibilities." Latent history also refers to the events that emanate from fantasies and subjective deductions, referred to from now on as "imaginative possibilities."

Because of the nature of postmodern discourse, the Professor believes that rational historiographical productions are no longer positioned at the center of intellectual interest. He belongs to a category of thinkers who reject the rational finiteness of the past and the unanimity of historical accounts. His notion of latent history injects a degree of uncertainty in the postmodern representation of mediated happenings. "Latent history never tells us where we stand in the sweep of events" (*Great Jones Street* 73). Jenkins attributes the lack of a unified perception of contemporary history to the postmodernist's rejection of metanarratives, to the spread of skepticism, and to the triumph of the margins. As Jenkins words it, "what had previously been glimpsed somewhat intermittently and kept largely on the margins, not only now lies right across our culture, but is also variously welcomed" (76). The technocultural molds in which historical accounts are produced never cease to expand and to sculpt additional layers of interpretations. The infinite flow of actual and imaginative information produced about a particular historical event makes it difficult to accept polished and unhazy accounts.

Latent History and Techno-Progress 57

With the gradual expansion of image technologies, such as film, tape, and television, a psychological change seems to have occurred as regards history in general and historical figures in particular. In DeLillo's novels, the more image technologies are present in the characters' lives, the greater is their involvement in changing perception. Opening actual and imaginative possibilities of perception facilitates the immigration of historically located figures to latent history. *Running Dog* (1978)[13] is an example of such immigration. DeLillo's sixth novel, follows Lightborne, a dealer in erotic antiquities, who attempts to acquire a film suspected of being a pornographic footage of Hitler during his last hours. The footage, which is also referred to as the "unholy grail,"[14] has a double meaning. It is an example of latent history, and it attests to the technological advance that both exposes one's private life and incites others to develop voyeuristic tendencies.[15]

Running Dog adheres to one of the Professor's definitions of latent history. It concerns itself with questions such as "did it really happen? Or did something else happen?" (*Great Jones Street* 72). In other words, does the pornographic footage exists, or does it not? Does it contain "[t]he madness at the end. The perversions, the sex" (*Running Dog* 268), or does it show something else? The end of the novel reveals that the footage projects Hitler masquerading Charlie Chaplin in front of adults and children, gathered in the bunker under the Reich Chancellery during the last hours of their lives. Hitler reproduces Chaplin's *The Great Dictator*, becoming thus a "simulacrum's simulacrum."[16] Hitler impersonates his own figure as satirized by Chaplin to cheer up the children. Consequently, the "century's ultimate piece of decadence" (*Running Dog* 20) ends up being "Hitler humanized" (*Running Dog* 268).

To the question, "did it really happen?" which could be rephrased as "has there been perversion at the end of Hitler's life?" the answer is negative. Lightborne, as one of the characters who have been looking for the footage, is uninterested in this conclusion. The fire of revelation, which is fueled by imaginative possibilities throughout the novel, dies out at the end. Randy Laist[17] argues that in the technocultural era the main goal of individuals is to reify their fantasies: "Citizens of the technoculture are Victor Frankensteins, so furiously wrapped up in the fascinating project of monster-making that they abandon any conscious engagement with the nature of the thing they are tinkering into being" (173). The narration itself seems to have been affected by the disinterest, as the end of the footage is never revealed. Instead, the narrator spies on a nervous Lightborne who is thinking of alternative plans to sell the footage. The mystery thus revealed, the footage transitions to an "actual possibility;" as it *does* exist in the novel, and it *does* reveal something about Hitler's last hours even if the reader is not offered a full closure.

58   Latent History and Techno-Progress

An actual possibility, however, can still lead to uncertainty when the data around a particular historical event/figure is full of discrepancies. *Libra* (1988)[18] demonstrates the triumph of uncertainty through the gathered data on the assassination of John F. Kennedy. The advance noticed in image technologies brings forth more information about the event but less certainty about its minutiae. For instance, the Zapruder footage gives birth to myriads of accounts due to a lack of coherence with the official report of the assassination. As will be shown, DeLillo suggests that the uncertainty revolving around the assassination emanates from the emergence of conflicting data. Thus, the Professor confirms DeLillo's position when he voices his skepticism as regards the validity of exclusive historical accounts. He is aware that the "past and history.... are ages and miles apart. For the same object of inquiry can be read differently" (Jenkins 7).

In DeLillo's ninth novel, such object of inquiry is the Kennedy assassination, which comes in the form of mythologized tragedy. As expressed by Jesse Kavadlo,[19] "*Libra* is a postmodern novel, in its use of real people and history interwoven with fiction.... Yet at the same time, the secular tragedy of Kennedy's death in *Libra* becomes mythologized" (44). David Cowart agrees with this perception, as he advances that the "Kennedy assassination.... was always the stuff of myth" (106). The novel gives voice to several real and fictional individuals involved in the historical unfolding of the assassination.[20] We are introduced to multilayered images of Lee Harvey Oswald, Oswald's mother, Nicholas Branch, several conspirators from the Central Intelligence Agency (CIA), Jack Ruby, to name a few. These individuals offer different, if not contradictory, testimonies, which prevent *Libra* from defending a particular theory. As Cowart advises, "[readers] are ultimately to understand the book not in terms of this or that theory affirmed, nor as an argument for or against the lone-gunman hypothesis, but rather as a sense-making of history centered on the role of the irrational and its instrument" (102). The first instrument of this aspect of history seems to be the real and fictional individuals themselves. They are the mediated pictures, videos, and narratives presented to an audience that recreates them rather than accepts them as given.

The recreation of historical events in *Libra* is bequeathed by technocultural possibilities. This is represented by the daily work of Nicholas Branch, a retired senior analyst of the CIA. Branch is hired to write the secret and final version of Kennedy's assassination. The historian's "dailiness" is not filled with the brightness of television, but with "stacks of folders," "legal pads and cassette tapes," "a massive file cabinet stuffed with documents" (*Libra* 14). Branch also communicates with his document-provider who is known only as the Curator; "they talk on the telephone" so that the Curator can send the historian "the right document in an area of research marked by ambiguity and error, by political bias, systematic fantasy"

(Libra 15). The diversity of the technological apparatuses turns history into the "radiance" of daily intakes, especially regarding the data provided through visual technologies.

In this section, "radiance in dailiness" refers mainly to Branch's daily reception of material, especially photographs and tapes, to write a final version of the Kennedy assassination. Branch's dailiness, which is represented by his beliefs, behaviors, and activities, revolves around the event. The historian is so engulfed in his task that he is starting to feel bodiless. He is also bodiless to the reader, as the only physical detail given of him is his constant use of gloves (Dewey 100).[21] Branch conceals himself from the external world and surreptitiously grows old in "the fireproof room," with "paper everywhere" *(Libra* 14). His "radiance in dailiness" consists mainly of the various materials he receives, the speed by which he receives a multitude of data thanks to technological facilities, and the manner in which he interprets the material.

Exposure to the mediated historical event alters Branch's perception. As the "cases of cheap coincidence" grew numerous, Branch starts thinking that "someone is trying to sway him toward superstition" *(Libra* 379). He becomes, as he explores the assassination, filled with uncertainty. Throughout the novel, Branch receives the documents he asks for, and documents he is unaware of, for his historiographic task. He has access to "the data-spew of hundreds of lives" *(Libra* 15) in order to construct a conclusion of the historical event. Joseph Dewey suggests that, as a historian, "Branch seeks the convincing read, the unassailable solidity of plot, the harmonics of cause and effect, motivation and resolution" (100). Branch believes that the momentous data he has gathered would lead him to a final version of the real happenings of November 22, 1963. However, as he advances in his research, he realizes that his interpretation is not nearing Truth. On the contrary, he is unwillingly being immersed in an Epicurean context of chance.

Branch is gradually convinced that the conspired assassination of the president owes its success largely to hazardous occurrences: "the conspiracy against the President was a rambling affair that succeeded in the short term due mainly to chance. Deft men and fools, ambivalence and fixed will and what the weather was like" *(Libra* 441). The variety of material Branch receives prevents him from constructing the final reading of the Kennedy assassination. Even if Branch has been sitting for five years in the "room of documents, the room of theories and dreams" *(Libra* 14), he still "hasn't written all that much" *(Libra* 59). The historian is unable to write because the data keeps coming in, "[b]ecause new lives enter the record all the time. The past is changing as he writes" *(Libra* 301). Branch finds himself working on "answering the unanswerable" (Schuster 107).[22] Because history is a "shifting discourse," Branch discovers new readings

60   Latent History and Techno-Progress

that oblige him to "change the gaze, shift the perspective" (Jenkins 16). Consequently, his ambivalence increases as new material arrives, material that expresses the "fantastic burden"[23] of latent history. Leonard Wilcox[24] argues that "[p]erhaps more than any other American novel, *Libra* addresses the problems of historical representation in an age of image, sign and textuality" (339). The actual and imaginative possibilities, which this technocultural age elicits, lead to divergent conclusions. This enfeebles Branch's resolve to narrate *the* ultimate account.

When asked about Branch in an interview,[25] DeLillo answers that the historian reveals that having more material to analyze does not necessarily lead to more accurate answers. Indeed, the material is too "unruly and internally contradictory" (Cowart 97). DeLillo believes that Branch is defeated by "the enormous amount of material that the assassination generated" because "[h]e simply cannot keep up with it: the path changes as he writes."[26] Therefore, as the material grows, certainty decreases. Branch gradually "loses ground to a growing mountain of raw information" (96).[27] By the end of *Libra*, Branch is far less certain that the details of the tragedy concord. Coale confirms this view when he posits that "[Branch] is overwhelmed by facts, volumes, snippers of evidence, photographs, men who have mysteriously died, pyramids of papers, and scraps of facts" (78). The random richness of the material resembles the multilayered structure of technocultural dailiness. This may imply that Branche knows as much as any unconcerned person that happens to glimpse at the living-room TV before carrying on their everyday activities. The historian does not receive specific data about the assassination. He rather receives endlessly mediated references, loosely connected to the assassination. This historical obfuscation leads Branch to doubt the very possibility of a conclusion.

Branch and the Professor share their skepticism concerning the validity of the data that keeps coming (*Libra* 301). They demonstrate that the heart of postmodern historical confusion is produced by the overflow of information made possible by technology. The two researchers reach this conclusion through difference approaches. Branch is unwillingly immersed in postmodern aspect of history, which finds its roots in the recording of the Kennedy assassination. Whereas, the Professor "academically" explores this history by defining it as latent history. The actual and imaginative possibilities that technology proposes, such as the material Branch receives, lead to exhaustive information details, and yet, to a great deal of truth concealment. Jean Baudrillard argues in "Fatal Strategies" that such a paradoxical situation is possible because, in postmodern times, everything is mediated and simulated by screens. "To prove this," Baudrillard advances, "all you need to do is watch television, where real events follow one another in a perfectly ecstatic relation, that is to say through vertiginous

Latent History and Techno-Progress 61

and stereotyped traits, unreal and recurrent, which allow for continuous and uninterrupted juxtapositions" (187).

The practice of investigating history is ingrained in technocultural mediums. One of the files Branch receives from the Curator contains a computer-enhanced version of Zapruder film, a footage recording the assassination of President Kennedy. The historian believes that the film is "a major emblem of uncertainty and chaos" (*Libra* 441). Cowart advances that "[t]ruth remains elusive" in this footage, which leads to questioning the authenticity of epistemological perception and the reliability of representational systems (98). Whereas, Wilcox asserts that the footage is a symbol of technological efficiency, as the footage "looks ahead to the increasingly technologized examinations of the Kennedy assassination" (351). If the role of postmodern image technologies is to attempt abolishing uncertainty, the possibilities that they open defy this role. With each re-watch, the footage viewers come up with new possibilities. The footage, which is representative of postmodern film, offers, as will be demonstrated later, visual exactitude but different readings. These readings are not fixed in a singular Truth. Instead, they induce different, if not, contradictory possibilities.

From Truth to Technocultural Possibilities within History

It has been demonstrated so far that latent history does not aim to unveil Truth but rather aims to discover and rediscover possibilities within history. The reason behind this shift lies in the progressing technological efficiency. Particularly important is the technological tendency to validate different and even contradictory readings of one single historical event such as the Kennedy assassination. The actual and imaginative possibilities of latent history are driven by technological mediums. It is hereby essential to provide an adequate technocultural structure of these possibilities.

In *Great Jones Street*, the Professor welcomes the diversity of latent history because he believes that history offers possibilities rather than Truth. Michael Scriven defines the possibilities of history as "a number of possible subsequent turns of fortune, none of which would seem to us inexplicable" (qtd. in Ferguson 71).[28] With the vitality of technological possibilities, latent history conceals Truth unceasingly. Interpretation gains ground by validating different readings and by elevating none above the others.

DeLillo is particularly interested in this relativity when he investigates the Kennedy assassination. The assassination has changed the manner in which the American consciousness views truth and history. DeLillo's choice of a character such as Branch to examine the assassination celebrates postmodern possibilities. This point is strengthened by Marianne I. Rossi in her investigation of the structure of history in DeLillo's novels: "In many ways, [the Kennedy assassination] can be defined as a postmodern event,

62   *Latent History and Techno-Progress*

an occurrence that has defied closure by generating a mass amount of data without a narrative to structure it" (22).[29] Branch himself is compelled at some point to admit that "[t]here's always more to it. This is what history consists of. It's the sum total of all the things they aren't telling us" (*Libra* 321). Jenkins develops on this idea. He posits that because "[w]e are (our culture is) a-moral, sceptical, ironic, secular," we have become "partners with uncertainty" (36). It could be said that uncertainty has become part of a technocultural identity that, at times, perversely welcomes doubt as a door to fantastical interpretations.

In order to adequately function within uncertainty, the Professor suggests that it is better to work with possibilities than to work with Truth. His interest in imaginative possibilities emanates from his honest distrust of history. Indeed, the Professor believes that "[h]istory is never clean," because "[i]n some cases less happened than we suspect. In other cases we merely suspect that less happened" (*Great Jones Street* 73). The English historian Edward Hallett Carr agrees with this view. He posits that "the faces of history never come to us 'pure', since they do not and cannot exist in a pure form: they are always refracted through the mind of the recorder" (19).[30] The mind of the (postmodern) recorder is attracted to the interpretations born of stained data and personal inferences. The possibilities that postmodernism brought, at the level of technological advance and philosophical relativity, allow "as many people(s) as possible to make their own histories such that they can have real effects (a real say) in the world" (Jenkins 80).

DeLillo ascertains the shift from Truth to possibilities in *Libra*. He declares in an "Author's Note" at the end of *Libra* that "this book makes no claim to literal truth." Rather, he considers the novel as "a way of thinking about the assassination without being constrained by half-facts or overwhelmed by possibilities."[31] He believes that individuals should not be afraid of the "tide of speculation that widens with the years."[32] Investigating possibilities is a valid approach to history, as they infer probable events rather than seek Truth. In the same line, the Professor's ultimate goal is to "avoid a narrow purview" (*Great Jones Street* 73), so he dedicates his research to possibilities. Such openness decenters factual events and brings from the margins "events that almost took place, events that definitely took place but remained unseen and unremarked on.... and events that probably took place but were definitely not chronicled" (*Great Jones Street* 72). In Baudrillard's words, "[a]n example of this ex-centricity of things, of this drift into excrescence, is the irruption of randomness, indeterminacy, and relativity within our system" ("Fatal Strategies" 188). In an attempt to be freed from the centrality of narrative noticed in the postmodern history, the Professor distinguishes between two aspects of overlooked history. As will be delineated below, the Professor explores possible events and overlooked actual events.

Latent History and Techno-Progress   63

The Professor first points out the events that almost took place, which are a set of possibilities that speak to the imagination of the historian. DeLillo himself seems to address this aspect of a historian's work: the opened bridge between past and present leads to much conjecture. The imagination of the historian becomes central in acknowledging "holy moments,"[33] an undertaking that requires investigating possibilities rather than facts. As DeLillo elaborates, in *Libra*, holy moments radiate with a "kind of accidental holiness, a randomness so intense and surrounded by such violence that it takes on nearly a sacred inexplicability."[34] The randomness that emits almost a sense of the sacred could be correlated to an obsessive need to come across intense events that hold sway (Jack Gladney) and that provoke a "spiritual" experience.

The technocultural traffic between the randomness of broadcast events and the incited response indicates the prevalence of random possibilities in dailiness. Branch himself does not only focus on facts; he processes imagined spiritual moments as well. He processes these possibilities because the material under scrutiny includes unusual themes. Branch finds himself in a web of unusual themes occurring during the day of the assassination:

> We will build theories that gleam like jade idols, intriguing systems of assumption, four-faced, graceful. We will follow the bullet trajectories backwards to the lives that occupy the shadows, actual men who moan in their dreams. Elm Street. A woman wonders why she is sitting on the grass, bloodspray all around. Tenth Street. A witness leaves her shoes on the hood of a bleeding policeman's car.
>
> (*Libra* 15)

According to Dewey, the reason behind this thematic concern in *Libra* is to reach a "therapeutic energy of the imagination able to accept, rather than resolve, uncertainty, instability, and mystery" (96). This aspect of history can be understood in terms of Humphrey Jennings's *Pandaemonium* (1987).[35] The project derives new connections from past accounts, be they historical or artistic, within their technocultural contexts. Kevin Robins and Frank Webster argue that *Pandaemonium* is "the imaginative force of Surrealist 'coincidence': 'the exploitation of the chance meeting on a non-suitable plane of two mutually distant realities'" (27).[36] These two realities represent the technologically advanced time of the historian and the images of the investigated accounts.

Similarly to Jennings's *Pandaemonium*, Branch's work is better understood in terms of images that connect at the level of imaginative history to form an "unrolling film."[37] Instead of claiming Truth, these images "represent human experience" as they are "too varied, even contradictory" to overstep personal interpretations.[38] Through them, the "galactic is

64   *Latent History and Techno-Progress*

juxtaposed against the microscopic, the bizarre accompanies the mundane" (Robins and Webster 28). Correspondingly, DeLillo adheres to unusual connections that emanate from imagination. In *Libra*, these connections form a narrative that taunts Branch,[39] as the Curator begins to send far-fetched connections: "The Curator begins to send fiction, twenty-five years of novels and plays about the assassination. He sends feature films and documentaries. He sends transcripts of panel discussions and radio debates" (*Libra* 442).

At this point in Branch's research, facts are no longer favored over the imaginary. He undergoes a microscopic analysis of the imaginary, and he accepts the bizarre as much as the real. Another example of such juxta-position is the Warren Commission Report. The Warren Commission is an 888-page report on the assassination released on September 24, 1964. It is referred to in DeLillo's *Libra* as "the megaton novel James Joyce would have written if he'd moved to Iowa City and lived to be a hundred" (181). The Report connects relevant information with the activities of daily life. In an interview with Anthony DeCurtis, DeLillo elaborates on this view: "The first fifteen volumes [of the Warren Commission Report] are devoted to testimony and the last eleven volumes to exhibits, and together we have a masterwork of trivia ranging from Jack Ruby's mother's dental records to photographs of knotted string."[40] If the Report opens with an honest quest for Truth, such quest is soon overtaken by "a masterwork of trivia." The "photographs of knotted string" allegorically identify the role of images in creating unusual connections, that is, in opening possibilities and instilling uncertainties. For instance, during his research, Branch notices that several photographs "are overexposed.... suggesting things barely glimpsed despite the simple nature of the objects and the spare captions" (*Libra* 182). The technocultural function of the images exceeds their immediate use. They do not freeze a moment but suggest many possibilities.

Similarly, the Professor welcomes unusual connections to explore unlikely possibilities in his research. For instance, one of his academic goals is to reconstruct an imaginative scenario of the Reformation. He suggests that "the Reformation, as such, never took place. The Counter-Reformation was a response to something that never happened, as such" (*Great Jones Street* 73). The multitude of possible connections prevent a conclusion. In *Running Dog* (1978), one of the characters, who have been trying to find Hitler's footage, strengthens this idea by suggesting that history is a process under construction. "If you study the history of reform.... you'll see there's always a counteraction built in. A low-lying surly passion. Always people ready to invent new secrets, new bureaucracies of terror" (*Running Dog* 81). Even if the Professor's project is satirical, he makes a valid point. His project exem-plifies how imagination thrives through technological advance since imagin-ation reveals unseen possibilities rendered available by image technologies.

Latent History and Techno-Progress 65

History is no longer the sum of gathered truth about an event; it is latent history: an interpretation of incomplete data that offers ongoing technocultural possibilities.

This leads to the second aspect of history. The Professor advances that the actual or potential events that have been overlooked by historiography are more important than the recorded events. In the postmodern world, history becomes "a kind of museum or, better yet, a supermarket of human possibilities" (Cantor 53).[41] The technological advance gives the possibility to produce accounts and to emphasize events previously deemed unimportant. Still, events and individuals remain "unseen and unremarked on" when their immediate significance is not noticed.[42] For this reason, the Professor defines latent history in a way that includes actual events that are still under construction. The speed by which events are broadcast is particular to the postmodern technocultural living rooms, as image technologies continuously reveal the ongoing details of latent events. Christopher Coker interprets the use of the term "latent" as a feature of "risk age."[43] He suggests that "latent" refers to "the delayed symptoms that alert us to the fact that we can fall ill long after we have contracted a disease."[44] This view points to the unstable temporality of the actual possibilities taking place within latent history. "Actual" here is understood as "real" or rather as an event believed to be real even if it is still under construction. Incomplete events unfold in a technocultural context that fills the gaps through imaginative possibilities.

In an age when anything may be filmed and immediately broadcast, and in a time when events happen unexpectedly, history continually adapts to the spirit of multiple possibilities. The technocultural aspect of history blurs the boundaries between imagination and reality, facts, and possibilities. Latent history becomes "an argument between what actually happened, and what is going to happen next" (Arnold 18).[45] Therefore, past events are not the only events that could be recreated, actual events are continually being recreated and adapted to individual interpretations. While speculating on latent history, the scientist Maurice Wu, also referred to as the "intellectual potholer,"[46] elaborates on this point:

> Wu mused on latent history. Not the negative chronology of years B.C. but a class of intelligible events too fine to be collected in the sifting mechanism that determines which sets of occurrences are to be recorded and analyzed as elements in a definite pattern and which examined merely for their visibility as the coarser of the particles in the mesh.
>
> (*Ratner's Star* 387)

Wu suggests that there are events of latent history that are not eligible to be recorded and analyzed. Once a chosen set of occurrences is filtrated and

66   Latent History and Techno-Progress

determined in accordance with cause and effect, micro-events are broad-cast as fleeting images. Micro-events are "too fine," that is too vague to be thoroughly processed and too recent to be completely disregarded. Because of their visibility, they find a recipient in mediums such as television. By "the particles in the mesh," Wu means the images that succeed one another, on television for instance, without being deeply examined.

Latent history could be understood as a set of actual and imaginative possibilities whose aim is to seek a more appropriate understanding of a particular event, be it past or under construction, be it recorded or "lost historical categories." For DeLillo, the first signs of this historical mutation lie in the visual representation of events. In what follows, the role of image technologies in the postmodern technocultural age is investigated in order to clarify their implication in daily life. It is argued that this implication represents a decisive development in the postmodern technocultural age because it serves as a medium for latent history.

Historical Uncertainty and the Televisual Event in *Libra*

After Kennedy's filmed assassination, image technologies, especially film and television, have become a primary medium for latent history. This medium brings history to "the living room," which bridges the distance between historical events and individuals. This section zooms in the manner in which image technologies mediate historical events. More specifically, it focuses on the implication of image technologies in the Kennedy assassin-ation, and how the Zapruder footage represents "the seven seconds that broke the back of the American century" (*Libra* 181).

First, the section emphasizes the uncertainty that characterizes the American consciousness because of the insertion of filmed violence. The possibilities opened by Kennedy's filmed assassination conduce Americans' growing uncertainty not only about the event but also about who they are. Second, the section attempts to explain why and how Lee Harvey Oswald, a "zero in the system," succeeds in assassinating the President. Particular attention is given to his dailiness to demonstrate the manner in which his insertion in a postmodern technocultural context contributes to moving his actions. Oswald represents one of the last individuals who are believed to move straightforwardly. Not only does he symbolize the manner in which the "zero in the system" is brought to television, but he also attests to the growing involvement of image technologies, such as film, in dailiness.

Kennedy's Filmed Assassination: a Pioneer of Historical Uncertainty

In a casual conversation with James Axton, Frank Volterra remarks that the twentieth century is shaped by film (*The Names* 239).[47] Volterra is an

Latent History and Techno-Progress 67

unsuccessful documentary producer who tries to gain fame by filming a cult. The cult has been murdering children and old wanderers. The victims are not chosen at random. Rather, the victims' initials and the first letter of each word of a location have to concord. After they complete the rituals, the cultists move to a new location to find new victims and make new sacrifices. James and Volterra follow the movement of the cultists because the mystery they radiate attracts the two individuals. While James is mainly curious, Volterra desires to make a documentary that records the rituals. Volterra believes that the cultists "belong on film" because "the twentieth century is on film. It's the filmed century" (*The Names* 239). The internal structure of the cult cannot remain a mystery in a time when "the whole world is on film" (*The Names* 239). Volterra seeks to capture the cultists' "patterns, extreme forms, extreme ways of seeing" because the violence they are capable of seems "so natural to film" (*The Names* 239).

Similarly to Volterra, DeLillo is interested in film. However, for the author, film is not only about "figures in open space,"[48] as Volterra believes. Rather, DeLillo suggests that film encloses a complexity that has never before existed in the history of Man. "The last half century has been enormously complex period," DeLillo declares in an interview with Gerald Howard, "a strange spin-out experience, filled with danger and change" (124).[49] The spin-out refers to a new sort of violence brought to living rooms, initiated by the assassination of John F. Kennedy. Dewey explains that, "for DeLillo, the assassination marked the street-birth of the media age-specifically, of television news and the rush to bring catastrophe into living rooms" (93). The fact that the assassination belongs to the twentieth century implies that it is not only political in nature. It also marks an important turning point in the daily history of America. As Frank Lentricchia argues "assassination is one of the extreme but logical expressions of the course of daily life" (205).[50] Indeed, DeLillo is interested in film not only because it discloses violence and political distress, but also because it engenders historical uncertainty.

The moment that injects the American history with uncertainty is the assassination of President Kennedy. For Thomas Carmichael, "the Kennedy assassination is often read as the first postmodern historical event," both "[i]n the popular and professionalized discourses of contemporary cultural history" (207).[51] As previously seen, DeLillo believes that this contemporary cultural history, or latent history, is loaded with uncertainty. In *Libra*, DeLillo investigates the manner in which the uncertainty built around the assassination provokes "cultural disease,"[52] to put it in Kavadlo's words. Therefore, it could be said that the assassination triggers the postmodern atmosphere. Since the sixties, broadcast events have been shaking the very foundation of individual comfort and trust. DeLillo posits that the assassination gives "terrible dreams"

68 Latent History and Techno-Progress

because America's "most photogenic president is murdered *on film*" (104; emphasis added).[53]

The film that DeLillo refers to is the Zapruder film. This last is a 26-second silent video recorded by Abraham Zapruder, capturing the President's death. Since the "moment belongs to the twentieth century," it "had to be captured on film."[54] However, the significance of Kennedy's death lies not only in being filmed, but also in instigating uncertainty in the American consciousness. "[T]hat moment," Boxall declares, is "a moment which violently destroys the possibility of definition" (133). By resisting any sort of definition, the film provokes a dysfunction in traditional history, which aims to construct a coherent structure of causality. The film is the product of latent history by excellence. It could be understood as a precursor of the postmodern view of history, which does not adhere to causality and linearity.[55] Moreover, by being recorded and continuously broadcast on television, Zapruder film absorbs "historical time into a new cinematic temporality" (76). Boxall believes that this may create a sort of historical vacuum, as the film has the capacity to recover lost time (77). It seems that reliving past moments may unsettle history, as a retelling of past events; for the viewer may use imagination to unlock new possibilities, as seen previously. Thus, rather than strengthening the axiomatic definition of history, the film represents latent history as it is open to several interpretations.

DeLillo reads the Zapruder film in terms of the possibilities that characterize latent history. The author believes that the film has triggered two opposing outcomes. The film "represents all the hopefulness we invest in technology,"[56] but it also opens "a world of randomness, confusion, even chaos."[57] In an interview with Ann Arensberg, DeLillo specifies that the film deepens the realness of the assassination because it "has a bluntness that is unforgettable" (42).[58] However, the details of the assassination are not completely in accordance with "a reality that lends itself to an understanding of the fact."[59] Viewers replay the trauma in order to understand the "the primal trauma, through images and electronic representation" (Wilcox 349). However, the more the primal scene is revisited, the farther goes the truth of the event. Each time individuals proceed to a visual replay of the event they recreate it according to their mindset. As Jean Baudrillard observes, "we are so used to re-watching all films, fictional as much as our own.... that we are capable of reprocessing history as a reversed movie" [my translation].[60] History thus simultaneously gains fictionality and loses certainty.

The visual replay does not offer closure; instead, it gradually decreases the sense of certainty. The assassination investigation had officially ended in September 1964 with the release of the Warren Commission Report. The report concluded that Lee H. Oswald was a lone gunner. After the

Latent History and Techno-Progress 69

publication of the report, Americans accepted this conclusion. The attorney Vincent Bugliosi explains that a national poll succeeding the assassination shows that only 31.6 percent of Americans rejected the Commission's conclusion.[61] However, as time went by, more and more Americans began to believe in conspiracy theories.[62] Bugliosi argues that the increasing belief in conspiracy theories or a framed Oswald was the result of information technologies and informal or academic meetings:

> [T]hrough their torrent of books, radio and TV talk shows, movies, college lectures, and so on, over the years the shrill voice of the conspiracy theorists finally penetrated the consciousness of the American people and actually succeeded in discrediting the Warren Commission Report.[63]

For the attorney, the assassination is a relatively simple case, complicated by the medium's interpretations. He does not believe that there were multiple shooters, or that Oswald is part of a conspiracy. Rather, he supports the Warren Commission and even uses Zapruder film as supporting material.

The fact that Bugliosi supports the Warren Commission only confirms DeLillo's argument. The pro-Warren Commission group and the conspiracy theorists both use the film as supporting material but neither reach Truth. Despite the visual representation of the murder, the interpretation of the sequences of images that Zapruder shoots still stirs disagreements. As corroborated by DeLillo's following statement,[64] nobody agrees on the details of the assassination: "we still can't agree on the number of gunmen, the number of shots, the time span between shots, the number of wounds on the president's body, the size and shape of the wounds" (28). The uncertainty that emerges with the footage multiplies questions. Even if the advance in technology brings the assassination closer to the layman and the scholar, it also casts a great deal of doubt and confusion on this spectacular historical event.

The ambivalence created by film is produced by its capacity to simultaneously confuse and convince. The Zapruder recording, in particular, provokes uncertainty because even if "[f]ilm as a medium for showing history is appealing," it still "lacks accuracy and completeness" (Underwood 94).[65] Film reaches a larger audience, which implies that it is open to individual interpretations. Fredric Jameson[66] elaborates on this idea: "In modern North American history, of course, the assassination of John F. Kennedy was a unique event, not least because it was a unique collective (and media, communicational) experience, which trained people to read such events in a new way" (355). If they do not attain the ultimate Truth, these readings are still validated on a subjective level. This is so because film "manages to approximate and even to surpass real life by means of illusion"

70   *Latent History and Techno-Progress*

(McLuhan 317).[67] On the one hand, film makes use of illusion because it is edited and manipulated to provoke a particular response. Zapruder's film was not broadcast fully until the seventies; for years, the audience was shown only parts of the assassination.[68] On the other hand, film, as a "twenty-four frames per second, transcends "photography's 'frozen' reality by reproducing the movement that is such a recognizable and necessary part of the natural world" (Howells and Negreiros 208).[69]

Despite the missing "frames," film mediates the real world by offering visual realness but not reality.[70] Typical of technocultural uncertainty, the film invigorates a superstitious reading of the image. The viewer is capable of seeing real images; but instead of referring to one interpretation of the assassination, Zapruder film shatters factual linearity. This capacity amplifies the American desire to produce their own version of the truth, leading thus to the creation of endless possibilities. Since these possibilities are never complete, there are always new interpretations of events. This state contributes to creating a "culture of distrust and paranoia" loaded with a "sense of the secret manipulation of history."[71] DeLillo seems to believe that a technocultural shift was born with the uncertainty that instilled itself in America after the assassination. This uncertainty entered the American consciousness because of the mysteries that surrounded Kennedy's death. The loss of important documents, buried records, suspicious murders, and suicides all prevent a satisfactory closure. However, the uncertainty does not find its origins in the assassination itself but in a whole life's exposure to "radiance in dailiness," as will be argued below.

Oswald's Third Line of History: the Fall of Historical Causality

In *Visual Culture* (2012), Richard Howells and Joaquim Negreiros invite the reader to ponder on the role of image technologies in one's life. "Think of recent world events," they suggest, "and you probably think televisually: the open-topped limousines of the Kennedy motorcade in Dallas, the wide-eyed famine victims in Ethiopia" (2). The contrast that drawn is intentional. Howells and Negreiros aim to stress the contradictory nature of the images that reach one's living room. They are images absorbed by individuals such as Lee Harvey Oswald, who "stays home all day to watch TV" (*Libra* 11). While "Kennedy was an excellent TV image," a famine victim seems saddening and unappealing. While Oswald wishes to be the former, he finds himself in the position of the latter. In *Libra*, DeLillo suggests that Oswald seeks to transition from a state of being a "zero in the system" to merging with history. It is argued that such a transition is possible at all because Oswald lives within advanced technoculture. His daily visual intake conduces a third line of history. With this line, Oswald aims both

Latent History and Techno-Progress   71

to incarnate the image radiated by the president and to cease being a zero in the system.

Oswald's Dailiness: the TV Child as Underprivileged Cripple

Libra is made up of two parallel plots. Each chapter of the first plot is headed by a geographic place, and each chapter of the second plot is headed by dates. The first plot focuses on Oswald's dailiness. Indeed, in addition to Oswald's unstable political beliefs, the reader has access to Oswald's daily experiences and travels from America to Japan to the Soviet Union and back again to America. The novel carefully recounts his marriage, his relationship with his mother, his desire to enter history, and his exposure to television. The chapters of the second plot move toward November 22. This direction explores a conspiracy theory that makes of the retired CIA agent, Win Everett, the author of the assassination. After the Bay of Pigs disaster, a failure to invade Cuba, Everett is exiled in Texas to teach history and economics. Because he refuses to accept his fall, Everett plots a "spectacular miss" to redeem himself (*Libra* 51). He plans to frame Oswald and revive the political tension with Cuba. However, the spectacular miss becomes a real shot, for Everett was unable to control his own plot.

DeLillo dedicates an important part of *Libra* to Oswald's dailiness. The author aims to understand the manner in which Oswald, a "zero in the system," has become one of the best-known assassins in the history of America.[72] *Libra* maintains its focus on dailiness with its waves and radiations, and a particular sort of synesthesia. By describing the noises surrounding Oswald, for instance, DeLillo aims to show that before becoming an assassin, Oswald lived in an ordinary technocultural dailiness. However, contrarily to DeLillo's other novels, *Libra* focuses on a historical framework that sways between the real and the fictional. The novel starts, not with the President assassin, but with a young Lee Oswald. He is a child being raised poor and fatherless in the back alleys of the Bronx. The reader meets him during the year "he rode the subway to the ends of the city" (*Libra* 3). He does not watch the arrival of wagons, contrarily to Jack Gladney. He is the one riding and exploring the power of secrecy.[73] He does not gain synesthetic experience through television. His synesthetic experience comes from the train's noise; as he "could almost taste" the "iron in the sound of those curves" (*Libra* 3). In this context, Lee is just another child who does not make a difference between the " 'he' and 'you' in a shared experience of synesthesia, of tasting sound" (Kavadlo 55).

At home, the young Lee tastes the sound of television as he eats his "platter of chops," a sound marred with the bitterness of poverty and neglect. After being evicted by his brother, Robert, he moves with his mother to the basement,

72   Latent History and Techno-Progress

"where blue heads spoke to them from the TV screen" (*Libra* 4). Because his mother cannot afford living in a decent house, her "life became a dwindling history of moving to cheaper places" (*Libra* 5). As she takes her son with her, Oswald's life becomes a history of moving to smaller rooms.

Oswald becomes part of the legacy of "Men in small rooms"; it is the space of men reading and waiting,[74] men "struggling with secret and feverish ideas" (*Libra* 41). These ideas are fueled by technocultural variety. They are in themselves webs of images that never cease to expand. Oswald's definition of "ideas" evokes Gilles Deleuze's conception of ideas as multiplicities:

> every idea is a multiplicity and a variety.... multiplicity must not designate a combination of the many and the one, but rather an organization belonging to the many as such, which has no need whatsoever of unity in order to form a system.[75]

Oswald senses his destiny being constructed, as he dives into the multiplicity of latent history. He remains "locked in the miniature room, creating a design, a network of connections" (*Libra* 227). The birth of his ideas has no stable or fixed origins. His ideas are constructs fired with rational paths and splinters of belief, systematic research and a degree of superstition. These unusual connections evoke one's ability to construct ideas as multiplicities. As his room becomes smaller, Oswald's ideas become bigger. He finds solace in the propagation of a network of usual and unusual connections.

This network of connections could be understood as Baudrillard's technocultural perception of the vanishing point of the subject. Baudrillard believes that the multitude of connections capable of being created, thanks to various technologies, blurs the distinction between the self and the object-other:[76]

> Permeability to all images, to all messages, to all networks.... what gets lost in this new ritual of transparency and interaction is both the singularity of the self, and the singularity of the other. That is, the irreducibility of the subject, and the irreducibility of the object.

(113)

For DeLillo, this state allows Oswald to create "a second existence, the private world floating out to three dimensions" (*Libra* 227). Oswald's second existence matches "his pre-scripted double" (Knight 108).[77] This double disturbs a sense of reliance, for it construes Oswald as "a familiar, if troubling, text, the template for a subculture of disaffected misfits" (Dewey 94). The multiplicity of ideas he imbibes coupled with the gateway of technological possibilities contribute to building Oswald as a troubled "text" who gives voice to disaffection.

The disaffection Oswald experiences can explain his desire to serve history. As Samuel Coale argues, "[e]ver the outsider, [Oswald] hopes that history will define him, use him, find a role for him in some system of payback and revenge" (78). In addition to the narratives he studies, Oswald places his hope in media. In this context, media is understood as "devices that mediate experience by re-presenting messages originally in a different mode" (Marvin 39).[78] As his mother informs the judge, "[t]his is a boy who grins while they are beating him up and waits for national news on TV" (*Libra* 48). According to his mother, Oswald has always been familiar with the injustice of the world. It is for this reason that, since his early childhood, he has sought comfort, and even guidance, in front of television.

Through television, Oswald can develop imaged connections with other individuals without being physically harmed. However, television can be a "pervasive media of effortless communication at a distance" (Marvin 40), so young Lee seeks comfort and guidance in a technocultural medium that has a tendency at times of being misleading. Unaware of the misconception, maybe even deception, Lee is a boy who looks for scraps of hope in the bright fragments of American mediated images. These images are transmitted with "formless form and contentless content."[79] With time, they offer Oswald guidelines to approaching history despite their superficiality.

Oswald attempts to decipher the images he watches because he believes that they detain the key to overcoming the injustice to which he is subjected. For DeLillo, there is a narrow connection between a whole culture/image force and the "story of the disaffected young man who suspects there are sacred emanations flowing from the media heavens" (106).[80] Oswald has dedicated body and soul to media because it represents the world as a "series of images that we can buy into and this includes things like thoughts and feelings" (Shaw 21). Media represents for Oswald a spectacle of electric light. Carolyn Marvin distinguishes between several manifestations of the spectacle. Among these manifestations, she describes what would be called "domestic spectacle." This phrase suggests that to the "growing popularity of domestic illumination, partly stimulated by the demonstration effect of the spectacle, helped transfer certain features of those spectacles indoors to private audiences" (42). By reaching "indoor private audiences," the most eminent news of this spectacle has the capacity to be stored and remembered by individuals. They are thus fossilized in the form of history with the passage of time. Oswald believes, therefore, that becoming an image on television means having a chance to be drawn as an immortal emblem in history.

Oswald considers the images and media voices as a way to transition from a state of invisibility to a state of fame, a transition from being a

74   *Latent History and Techno-Progress*

"zero in the system"[81] to an emblem in history. Marc Schuster suggests that in order to gain a sense of value "the individual must concede to the overwhelming power of the system and adopt the position of the object in order to survive" (95). In this context, the objects Oswald desires to transition to, and with which he surrounds himself, are the images and sounds of television. Marshall McLuhan explains that the TV child, whom he describes as an "underprivileged cripple,"[82] grows to experience in depth the enhanced colors of mosaic images. In McLuhan's words,

> [t]he young people who have experienced a decade of TV have naturally imbibed an urge toward involvement in depth that makes all the remote visualized goals of usual culture seem not only unreal but irrelevant, and not only irrelevant but anemic.
>
> (366)

As a TV child, Oswald separates himself from content to be absorbed by the mesh of the image and the hypnotic voices.

Oswald expresses this idea differently. Instead of admitting the appeal in absorbing images and media voices, he declares that he would like to "experiment with remote hypnotism. Hypnotism over the phone or on TV" (*Libra* 314). Rather than studying hypnotism, Oswald is himself in a hypnotic state, as he is caught watching television, throughout the novel. Ultimately, the image "does not foster linearity in living"; it rather encourages multiplicity and "the inclusive image" (McLuhan 350). This allows Oswald to imagine improbable historical possibilities since he "attempts to leave evidence of having passed through the system" (Schuster 105). As will be shown, Oswald is fully involved in the image, for it represents the object by which he intends to merge with history.

By the medium of television, images, and voices, Oswald seeks a line of history that would permit him not only "to be remembered as a historical figure," but also "to prove his own existence" (Schuster 105). In order to achieve both goals, he exposes himself to "atoms that reveal the outside as inside in an endless adventure amidst blurred images and mysterious contours" (McLuhan 357). "Ever the particle," Oswald seeks his way to mesh with history, by the medium of the fame that can be offered through television. Therefore, Oswald develops a tendency to seek refuge and direction in front of television, after he is "beaten up."

DeLillo recounts that after returning from Russia, Oswald is an unstable and cruel man whose fate depends on his capacity to write his "Hollywood movie."[83] "The result," Wilcox resumes, "is a kind of postmodern bricolage" (342). This bricolage is best demonstrated by Oswald's photograph, taken by his wife Mariana. He poses in a corner with "the rifle in his right hand" and the Militant and the Worker magazines in his left (*Libra* 278).

Oswald aspires to reach an image grander than what he is offered. He learns from journalists and actors, and he tries to resemble great men. He would like to "get closer to John Wayne, say something authentic," and be as "doubly real" (*Libra* 93). This is DeLillo's Oswald, a technocultural construct of high hopes and televisual aspiration. DeLillo summarizes his character as an "Oswald watching TV, Oswald working the bolt of his rifle, Oswald imagining that he and the president are quite similar in many ways."[84]

The closeness that Oswald feels with heroic charismatic men pushes him to wish for an iconographic transition toward history. Similarly to Jack Gladney, Oswald is exposed to the random sounds of television. However, while Jack is content with merely watching television, Oswald makes his way toward the medium. In this way, "television's narcotic undertow soothes the Gladneys," while "Oswald [is] himself the unfortunate subject of the very disaster footage the Gladneys relish" (Kavadlo 52). Oswald attaches himself, as Jack does, to a "grand personality" with the objective of absorbing historical power (56). However, while Jack remains passive in his attachment to Hitler Studies, Oswald actively attaches his destiny to Kennedy's. Oswald's aim is to break free from the ordinariness of life and fight his way toward merging with "the greater tide of history" (*Libra* 87). For Dewey, Oswald attempts to enter history because he is tired of "tough-guy fantasies of television, paperback novels, and movies" (94). Conversely, Osteen believes that Oswald's desire "to merge with history signifies a desire to move from private-life secrecy to public-life secrecy" (154). Either way, Oswald believes that he is capable of choosing the historical role that is convenient for him. For this reason, Oswald's position in history is best defined through a "third line of history." Through this line, DeLillo sways between the theory of a lone-gunner and that of a group of conspirators, avoiding, in this way, to embrace a definite conclusion.

The Third Line of History

In *Libra*, the third line of history is conceived by the historical figure David Ferrie,[85] an anti-Castro homosexual pilot involved in the conspiracy against the president. In the novel, Ferrie recruits Oswald for the attempt on the president. In a conversation with Oswald about the attempt, Ferrie describes "two parallel lines" that would shape the assassination. The first is "the life of Lee H. Oswald," and the second "is the conspiracy to kill the President" (*Libra* 339). The two historical lines are yoked together by a third line that cuts through causality:

> It comes out of dreams, visions, intuitions, prayers, out of the deepest levels of the self. It's not generated by cause and effect like the other

76 *Latent History and Techno-Progress*

two lines. It's a line that cuts across causality, cuts across time. It has no history that we can recognize or understand. But it forces a connection.

(*Libra* 339)

The third line of history transcends cause and effect to embrace imaginative possibilities, which makes it compatible with latent history. This third line consists of transhistorical elements in which reside Oswald's "force of dreams, intuitions, prayers."[86]

Ferrie and Everett believe that they can control the third line by forcing a hidden connection between Kennedy and Oswald. The making of Kennedy's overt historical line responds to the rules of cause and effects, as it is a planned rational line, constructed by the conspirators. Everett particularly is someone who "fashions linearity, designs causality, and recovers accountability from the figures he manipulates" (Dewey 96). The conspirators believe that since Oswald is the "zero in the system," he can be molded into any shape. However, because he is more trained by television than by Everett, Oswald remains out of control, and therefore out of Everett's linear causality. *Libra* suggests, in part, that Oswald might have allowed "the deepest levels of the self," which do not conform to rationality but to iconographic compulsion, to guide his actions. Therefore, the third line might represent an indirect precursor to latent history. Because of the technocultural implication in creating connections between Kennedy and Oswald, the third line of history could be read better in terms of imagination and coincidence than in terms of causality.

The meaning of this line is differently interpreted by critics, as it accepts multiplicity. Peter Knight, for instance, suggests that the third line "connects coincidence and conspiracy" (108). This connection links the coincidence of finding the perfect "pasty" to a conspiracy in progress. It also links the coincidence of the proximity of the building where Oswald worked to the road by which the Kennedy motorcade passed through. Knight's reading could be understood in terms of Carl Jung's synchronicity.[87] Jung uses the term as "a coincidence in time of two or more causally unrelated events which have the same or a similar meaning" (25). Oswald's fate and the conspiracy mapping constitute an unexpected connection of unrelated events that find meaning in the same objective.

An instance of the fate/mapping construct is narrated in *Libra* shortly before the assassination. Oswald is reunited with his wife and daughter on his twenty-fourth birthday. That evening, he watches a (real) movie called *Suddenly* (1954). The plot of the movie consists of an attempt on a nameless President, whom Oswald believes to be President Eisenhower. While watching Frank Sinatra taking position to commit the assassination, "a stillness" was formed around Oswald, as he has "an eerie sense he was being watched for his reaction" (*Libra* 369). The movie and the

Latent History and Techno-Progress   77

assassination are connected through Oswald, and Oswald is the already shaped individual corresponding to the fictional pasty that the conspirators are constructing: "They wanted a name, a face, a bodily frame they might use to extend their fiction into the world" (*Libra* 50). In this technocultural context, the bond between imagination, coincidence, and conspiracy matches the historical line of unidentified or random connections.

Samuel Coale suggests that the set of unresolved connections emanates from a sort of "epiphanies" that open up a "wider sense and presence of mystery, self-doubt, and self-distrust" (77). In this way, Oswald's epiphanies become sudden scripted revelations that lead to compulsive decisions, ones inspired by the images to which he is exposed. In the same evening when Oswald is watching the movie with his family, he feels "connected to the events on the screen. It was like secret instructions entering the network of signals and broadcast bands, the whole busy air of transmission" (*Libra* 370). At that moment, he realizes that "they" were "running a message through the night into his skin" (*Libra* 370).[88] Whether the "they" refer to television's suggestion of a message, or to a spiritual calling remains unclear. The technocultural aura of interwoven television-mesh and superstition leaves Oswald "with no halo of private protection, not even his own body, to protect him anymore" (qtd. in Plant 168). He intently watches Sinatra setting up the rifle and getting ready for the assassination. Oswald does not know whether he is being encouraged or dissuaded from his own plans. On the one hand, the movie shows him what he has to do to become famous; but on the other, Oswald "knew he [Sinatra] would fail" (*Libra* 370).

Oswald's epiphanies contribute to making history, but they slip away from historical cause and effect. Because these epiphanies relate to the possibilities of latent history, they block a finite explanation of the assassination. They belong to a hidden facet of the third line of history, which is compatible with imaginative possibilities.[89] Paul Maltby[90] and Adrian Wisnicki[91] explore this facet. For Maltby, the third line of history constantly invokes the invisible, "the transhistorical forces that shape human affair" (82). While Wisnicki reads this line as a "Providential Hand," that is "a force that arranges and controls reality" (53). Both readings fasten history to an invisible force that bonds Oswald to a semi-plotted destiny. For DeLillo's Oswald, this invisible force partly relates to image technologies, which incite him to choose violence whether consciously or unconsciously.

Oswald could be said to accomplish a Deleuzian line, a line woven with the multiplicity of other lines: "Every origin is a singularity and every singularity a commencement on the horizontal line, the line of ordinary points on which it is prolonged like so many reproductions or copies which form the moments of a bare repetition" (Deleuze, *Difference and Repetition* 202). Oswald's line is a repetition of real and fictional ideas. The accumulation of

78   *Latent History and Techno-Progress*

ordinary and unusual points that form this line leads to his insertion in history. Therefore, either willingly or unwillingly, Oswald stands at the heart of the third line of history. Either through the conspirators' manipulation or through a compulsive call for action, Oswald shakes the historical line of causality.

Oswald as a Technocultural Construct of Latent History

In light of what has already been said, Oswald seems to stand as a postmodern historical figure. Oswald is not the object of a conspiracy, isolated from other aspects of his life. He is rather the product of a lifetime of image absorption, leading to a "change in attitude by means of relating [himself] to the mosaic TV image" (McLuhan 366). DeLillo's Oswald carries his own goals and plans, which do not solely originate from the conspiracy. These goals and plans emanate from Oswald's perception that feeds on image technologies.[92] They are also filled with coincidence, dreams, and uncertainty since, as Ferrie believes, they emanate from a "boy" who is "sitting on the scales, ready to be tilted either way" (*Libra* 319). DeLillo uses "Libra" as a title for his novel because it is Oswald's zodiac sign and, more importantly, because it expresses Oswald's tendency to topple either way. "Will Oswald go toward the left," DeLillo asks, "or the right?" In terms of the assassination, Oswald might have been "a man of the left who ended up carrying out the wishes of the right wing."[93]

After shooting the President, Oswald is captured and questioned. When he is returned to his cell, he reflects on his "life's work" (*Libra* 434). He believes that after his trial he will have time in jail to educate himself and to become stronger since "[e]everybody knew who he was now" (*Libra* 435). He is confident that his impact on history will grow as he attracts the attention of "the lawyers first, then psychologists, historians, biographers" (*Libra* 435). Because of this growing audience, "[h]is life had a single clear subject now, called Lee Harvey Oswald" (*Libra* 435). As the balance tilts to the left in his mind, he imagines that he is capable of entering history as a hero. "Historical figures," Boxall posits, "as much as historical plots, wheel into themselves, until they reach that mystical point at which they 'enter history'" (131). However, the concluding episode of Oswald's life is not controlled by his desires but by forces working beyond him. His personal identity merges with technocultural possibilities, which absorb and redefine him. For Raymond Barglow, "[p]ersonal identity is not a fixed ideal, but is historically constructed, in ways that are never entirely unproblematic in our culture" (37).[94] As will be concluded, this culture, or rather technoculture, deconstructs Oswald's personal identity by turning it into a televisual product through image technologies.

Latent History and Techno-Progress 79

Oswald fails to gain control over his fate because the image technologies that assist him in integrating history also disassociate him from his name. For Frank Lentricchia, after Oswald is caught, the question is no longer "who is this Oswald? It is, who is Lee Harvey Oswald?" (203). Before being murdered in his turn, Oswald hears his name on radios and televisions. His full name "sounded extremely strange. He didn't recognize himself in the full intonation of the name" (*Libra* 416). Schuster elaborates on the ambivalence provoked by Oswald's full name:

> Blinded by his own desire to become a historical figure himself, Lee fails to recognize that.... becoming Lee Harvey Oswald will render Lee an object within the matrix of history rather than a subject with the power to shape history.
>
> (102)

Instead of bringing him historical power, the full name "sounded odd and dumb and made up. They were talking about somebody else" (*Libra* 416).

Oswald's failure to recognize his name is due to the multiplicity of ideas he is turned into through media technology. Similarly to any other product, media technology has stripped him from his reality[95] and identity by denying his heroism. Schuster argues that "under the media's collective gaze," the assassination as a subversive act "becomes nothing more than a model for reproduction and exists only 'as a function of its reproducibility'" (145). In a way, the assassination becomes independent from Oswald. Media's collective gaze keeps Oswald's full name as a fictional attachment to the subversive act, but it conceals him as an active agent in the assassination. Kavadlo argues that Oswald fails to recognize his full name because he "ceased to be real long before DeLillo or anyone fictionalized him" (60). However, even if Oswald might have lost his identity to media culture prior to the assassination, he becomes fully absorbed by technocultural identity only *after* he is filmed.

Technocultural identity regroups a multitude of connections woven between human beings and technological implication. More specifically, technocultural identity deals with individuals' sense of self and the manner in which technology, image technologies in particular, reshapes their self-image.[96] In Oswald's case, his self-image is woven with media culture, which provokes his inability to "recognize himself in the full intonation of the name." Cowart supports this idea by suggesting that "Oswald" can be redefined endlessly: "It is ultimately inconsequential whether there is a separate, real-life Oswald, with his own political valences and aspirations. The dynamics of identity, history, and linguistic meaning share the same endless fluidity" (102). The dissociation created between the man and the name is the result of the open possibilities that

80   *Latent History and Techno-Progress*

characterize latent history. After the assassination, Oswald is continuously reread and recast in a new light. He is interpreted in myriads of ways, both fictional and real. Viewed from a structuralist approach, Oswald becomes a technocultural construct whose fixed signified (body) is no longer referred solely by an arbitrary but personal set of signifiers (descriptive characteristics, name). Oswald is deconstructed in a way that the language of media "simultaneously overturns and confounds the structure that makes the hierarchized terms [descriptive characteristics and name] intelligible" (Shaw 160).

By failing to recognize his full name, Oswald realizes that he has turned into a new and unrecognizable text without origins. As a text without origins, Oswald "furnishes the empty substance of a subsequent order, which, itself, no longer even knows the distinction between signifier and signified" (Baudrillard, *Simulacra and Simulation* 64).[97] It could be said that one of the reasons preventing Oswald from achieving the image of an authentic historical hero consists of identifying in him the mark of the simulacrum. He becomes a text open to the imaginative possibilities of latent history, which is compatible with the multiplicity of technocultural identity.

Another reason for Oswald's failure to materialize "the powerful world of Oswald-hero" consists of the emergence of his killer, Jack Ruby (*Libra* 46). Just as Oswald's iconographic compulsion contributes to invoking a third line of history, he is exposed to this line himself. Ruby robs Oswald from a future of "deep self-analysis and reconstruction" (*Libra* 435). It seems that by giving a voice to Oswald, DeLillo's aim is not to glorify him but to raise the question of his position in history. For Timothy Parrish, "*Libra* reimagines Oswald's story from Oswald's perspective not to tell a revisionist history but to reveal how futile his dream of controlling history is" (31).[98] The fact that his assassination is filmed attests to his loss of control.

If filming Kennedy's assassination is accidental, Oswald's is a live manifestation of history's power to twist plots and fantasies. Filming as a communication medium illustrates the capacity of technoculture to divert the traditional course of history. McLuhan supports this argument when he boldly argues that Oswald's guards failed to protect him because they "were paralyzed by television cameras" (366). The "fascinating and involving power of television"[99] distracts the guards from their role, which contributes to Ruby's success. As a result, Oswald becomes the object he himself used to consume.[100] He becomes "Lee Harvey Oswald" a name "with no discernable person behind it" (Schuster 109). Hence, Oswald's alteration into a simulacrum for television consumers ironically strips him from his identity and transforms him into a latent history product with multiple facets.

Latent History and Techno-Progress 81

DeLillo's Lee Harvey Oswald represents a technocultural construct, which could be considered the precursor of what Lentricchia calls "contemporary production." Lentricchia suggests that Lee Harvey Oswald is "a contemporary *production*, a figure who is doubled everywhere in *Libra*, even, most harrowingly, in strategic places" (203; emphasis in original). Before being an assassin, Oswald aims "to make some rough sense of the daily jostle" through attempting to merge with history (*Libra* 440). In the process, Oswald constructs a "lie that concealed small rooms [and] TV" (*Libra* 86). This lie conceals his second self, the conspirator. Because he carries the "lie" with him wherever he goes, it may have tilted his scale toward assassination.

Perhaps similarly to Tommy Roy Foster, Oswald is motivated by a voice telling him that, in order to go down in history, he has to kill the President. In *White Noise* (1985), Foster is a murderer who corresponds with Heinrich, Jack Gladney's son. When Heinrich inquires into the reason for killing six innocent individuals, Foster answers that his aim was to go down in history and that voices in television showed him the way (*White Noise* 53). Foster's reaction to the sounds he hears on television attests to the grip that image technologies, as technoculture's expression, have on the individual's psyche. The isolation of both Oswald and Foster estranges them from their actual selves, and "the more uncertain the status of the self becomes, the more we want to secure it" (Barglow 19). Foster attempts to secure the self by listening to television, as it replaces human interactions. Its "voices" suggest a way to go down in history. His psyche is touched by the power of technoculture, which replaces parental or environmental guidance by televisual suggestions.

Could Oswald have had a similar experience? The reason why asking this question is possible at all lies in the fact that "there is no inherent cause that could predispose Oswald for the role of assassin as an effect" (Kelman 63). Therefore, Oswald's real motive could have been anything. What is certain, for DeLillo, is that the American consciousness has known a transition of perception after Oswald:

> After Oswald, men in America are no longer required to lead lives of quiet desperation. You apply for a credit card, buy a handgun, travel through cities, suburbs and shopping malls, anonymous, anonymous, looking for a chance to take a shot at the first puffy empty famous face, just to let people know there is someone out there who reads the papers.
> (*Libra* 181)

For DeLillo, Oswald is a sort of prelude to the manner in which people started to behave after the assassination. DeLillo believes that Oswald and Ruby are always treated as individuals who would move in a linear

82 *Latent History and Techno-Progress*

manner.[101] In reality, they are the "last two men in the world who would ever behave in that way."[102] DeLillo believes that from the assassination onward, people are no longer considered as simple constructs with straight transparent plans and simple lives. Living in a technocultural world implies being open to actual and imaginative possibilities. It may also mean aspiring to new goals suggested by image technologies. Beyond the facade, there are schemes on the walls, pictures and twisted lines, and notes that reveal the presence of a hidden set of beliefs and ideas that lurk in the shadows.

Postmodern technoculture opens latent history to a multitude of actual and imaginative possibilities. Image technologies not only record events such as the Kennedy assassination, they also validate improbable scenarios, which leads to a degree of uncertainty. This uncertainty is the result of the stark representation of an event, which becomes coated with controversial maps of information. The Zapruder film, as an example of latent history, opens a door to myriads of interpretations even if it recorded the assassination directly. Therefore, events such as the Kennedy assassination are no longer expected to be clear and definite. They attest to the ability of a "zero in the system" to impact a whole nation. It has been argued that Oswald's path and success in killing the president is emboldened by the image technologies to which he has been exposed throughout his life. Oswald aims to live through history, which is captured by media. However, the same media absorbs him since it responds to a technocultural identity which transcends Oswald's aims, and which favors open possibilities.

DeLillo's goal in writing *Libra* does not seem to emanate from a desire to reproduce events as he believes happened. His goal is to point to the role and result of daily intakes of images. The manner in which image technologies have transformed history into an ongoing product of everyday feeds is further explored in later novels. Chapter 3 elaborates on the outcome of such implication. It is argued that reality itself is reconceptualized through the technological involvement in dailiness.

Notes

1 See the compilation of interviews with DeLillo entitled *Conversations with Don DeLillo* (2005), edited by Thomas DePietro, especially pages 31; 47; 64; 106; 158; 161.
2 DeLillo, Don. Interview by Kevin Connolly. *Conversations with Don DeLillo*, edited by Thomas DePietro, Jackson, University Press of Mississippi, 2005, p. 32.
3 Jenkins, Keith. *Rethinking History*. London, Routledge, 2004.
4 Ihde, Don. *Postphenomenology: Essays in the Postmodern Context*. Evanston, Northwestern University Press, 1993.
5 Shaw, Debra B. *Technoculture: The Key Concepts*. Oxford, Berg, 2008.
6 Duvall, John N. *The Cambridge Companion to Don DeLillo*. Cambridge, Cambridge University Press, 2008.

Latent History and Techno-Progress 83

7 Boxall, Peter. *Don DeLillo: The Possibility of Fiction*. London, Routledge, 2006.
8 This manifestation is not an attempt to return to the past. Rather, as Mark Osteen suggests, "[collectors] detach artifacts from the past and create a separate order that is both an elision and an emblem of history" (105).
 Osteen, Mark. *American Magic and Dread Don DeLillo's Dialogue with Culture*. Philadelphia, University of Pennsylvania Press, 2000.
9 This question, which is asked in DeLillo's latest novel *Zero K* (2016), brings the characters "back to earth," as it attests to the complexity of being conscious of reality (*Zero K* 65).
 DeLillo, Don. *Zero K*. New York, Scribner, 2016.
10 DeLillo, Don. *Great Jones Street*. London, Picador, 2011 [1973].
11 Partridge, Eric. *Origins A Short Etymological Dictionary of Modern English*. London, Routledge, 2009.
12 Hegel, Georg Wilhelm Friedrich. *Philosophy of History*. Translated by John Sibree, New York, Prometheus Books, 1991.
13 DeLillo, Don. *Running Dog*. London, Picador, 2011 [1978].
14 Osteen, *American Magic and Dread Don DeLillo's Dialogue with Culture*, p. 99.
15 Patrick O'Donnell confirms the latter when he suggests that "a film of Hitler in the bunker would confirm the pervasive intrusion of technology into private lives" (59).
 O'Donnell, Patrick. "Obvious Paranoia: The Politics of Don DeLillo's 'Running Dog'." *The Centennial Review*, vol. 34, no. 1, 1990, pp. 56–72. *JSTOR*, www.jstor.org/stable/23738950
16 Cowart, David. *Don DeLillo: The Physics of Language*. Georgia, University of Georgia Press, 2003, p. 64.
17 Laist, Randy. *Technology and Postmodern Subjectivity in Don DeLillo's Novels*. Frankfurt, Peter Lang, 2010.
18 DeLillo, Don. *Libra*. New York, Penguin, 2006 [1988].
19 Kavadlo, Jesse. *Don DeLillo: Balance at the Edge of Belief*. Frankfurt, Peter Lang, 2004.
20 Coale elaborates on the manner in which DeLillo approaches the novel. He explains that

> DeLillo's blend of historical and fictional characters blurs the focus even more as documentary and fiction bleed into one another, history's becoming fiction and fiction's becoming history, all cutting across causality helping to produce the quantum flux, the postmodern spell of uncertainty and skepticism.
>
> (79)

 Coale, Samuel. *Quirks of the Quantum: Postmodernism and Contemporary American Fiction*. London, University of Virginia Press, 2012.
21 Dewey, Joseph. *Beyond Grief and Nothing: A Reading of Don DeLillo*. Columbia, University of South Carolina Press, 2006.
22 Schuster, Marc. *Don DeLillo, Jean Baudrillard and the Consumer Conundrum*. New York, Cambria Press, 2008.
23 Jean Baudrillard argues that "the hypertrophying of historical research, the delirium of explaining everything, of ascribing everything, of referencing everything.... All this becomes a fantastic burden" ("Fatal Strategies" 189).

84 Latent History and Techno-Progress

24 Wilcox, Leonard. "Don DeLillo's *Libra*: History as Text, History as Trauma." *Rethinking History: The Journal of Theory and Practice*, vol. 9, no. 2–3, 2005, pp. 337–353.

25 DeLillo, Interview by Kevin Connolly, p. 27.

26 Ibid.

27 A view shared by Giaimo, Paul. *Appreciating Don DeLillo: The Moral Force of a Writer's Work*. Oxford, Praeger, 2011, p. 4; Dewey, *Beyond Grief and Nothing*, p. 100.

28 Ferguson, Niall, editor. *Virtual History: Alternatives and Counterfactuals*. Cambridge, Basic Books, 1997.

29 Rossi, Marianne Ingheim. "Constructing the Meanings of History, Identity, and Reality in Don DeLillo's *Libra* and *Mao II*." *MA thesis*, Oslo, The University of Oslo, 2008.

30 Carr, Edward H. "What Is History?" *Reading Architectural History*, edited by Dana Arnold, London, Routledge, 2004, pp. 14–23.

31 Mitgang, Herbert. "Reanimating Oswald, Ruby et al. in a Novel on the Assassination." *The New York Times*. The New York Times, July 19, 1988. https://archive.nytimes.com/www.nytimes.com/books/97/03/16/lifetimes/del-v-oswald.html?_r=2. Accessed June 16, 2018.

32 DeLillo, Don. "'An Outside in this Society': An Interview with Don DeLillo." Interview by Anthony DeCurtis. *Conversations with Don DeLillo*, edited by Thomas DePietro, Jackson, University Press of Mississippi, 2005, p. 55.

33 In his interview with Connolly, DeLillo declares that when Branch comes across an information concerning a misplaced pair of woman shoes, found in the scene of Oswald's arrest, it seems to the historian as a "holy moment" (35).

34 DeLillo, Interview by Kevin Connolly, p. 35.

35 *Pandaemonium* is the accumulation of historical and artistic texts that concern "the imaginative history of the Industrial Revolution. Neither the political history, nor the mechanical history, nor the social history, nor the economic history, but the imaginative history."
Jennings, Humphrey. *Pandaemonium, 1660–1886: The Coming of the Machine as Seen by Contemporary Observers*. Kindle ed., London, Icon, 2012.

36 Robins, Kevin, and Frank Webster. *Times of the Technoculture: From the Information Society to the Virtual Life*. London, Routledge, 2005.

37 Jennings, *Pandaemonium, 1660–1886*, Kindle ed.

38 Ibid.

39 Wilcox agrees that "as data piles up, it begins to mock the distinction between empirical data and text" (344).

40 DeLillo, Don. Interview by Anthony DeCurtis, p. 62.

41 Cantor, Paul A. "Adolf, We Hardly Knew You." *Don DeLillo's White Noise*, edited by Harold Bloom, Philadelphia, Chelsea House Publishers, 2003, pp. 51–72.

42 Mark L. Sample argues that Don DeLillo has been neglected by digital humanists. For Sample, DeLillo is himself subject to invisibility even if he has written extensively on the postmodern condition (187). The concept of "latent history" itself remains "unremarked on" even if it has the potential to shed light on the state of history in the postmodern technocultural era.

Sample, Mark L. "Unseen and Unremarked On: Don DeLillo and the Failure of the Digital Humanities." *Debates in the Digital Humanities*, edited by Gold, Matthew K. and Lauren F. Klein, Minneapolis, University of Minnesota, 2016.

43 Coker, Christopher. *War in an Age of Risk*. E-book ed., Cambridge, Polity Press, 2009.

44 Coker, Christopher. *War in an Age of Risk*, E-book ed.

45 Arnold, John. *History*. New York, Sterling, 2009.

46 Boxall, *The Possibility of Fiction*, p. 65.

47 DeLillo, Don. *The Names*. London, Picador, 2011 [1982].

48 The space Volterra refers to is the desert, which he considers as a space of violence. He aims to film the cultists while they perform a sacrifice. His ultimate objective is not to condemn the murder but to promulgate the cult's activities. See *The Names*, p. 237.

49 DeLillo, Don. "The American Strangeness: An Interview with Don DeLillo." Interview by Gerald Howard. *Conversations with Don DeLillo*, edited by Thomas DePietro, Jackson, University Press of Mississippi, 2005, pp. 119–130.

50 Lentricchia, Frank. *Introducing Don DeLillo*. Durham, Duke University Press, 1991.

51 Carmichael, Thomas. "Lee Harvey Oswald and the Postmodern Subject: History and Intertextuality in Don DeLillo's 'Libra', 'The Names', and 'Mao II'." *Contemporary Literature*, vol. 34, no. 2, 1993, pp. 204–218. *JSTOR*, www.jstor.org/stable/1208548.

52 Kavadlo, *Balance at the Edge of Belief*, p. 48.

53 DeLillo, Don. "The Art of Fiction CXXXV: Don DeLillo." Interview by Adam Begley. *Conversations with Don DeLillo*, edited by Thomas DePietro, Jackson, University Press of Mississippi, 2005, pp. 86–108.

54 DeLillo, "The Art of Fiction CXXXV: Don DeLillo," p. 104.

55 In "Adolf, We Hardly Knew You," Paul A. Cantor clarifies this idea. He suggests that "postmodernism finds itself forced to live in the posthistorical moment.... History loses its linear thrust into the present and beyond, becoming instead a repository of equally available styles and ideas" (53).

56 DeLillo, "The Art of Fiction CXXXV: Don DeLillo," p. 104.

57 Naughton, Jim. "Don DeLillo, Caught in History's Trap." *The Washington Post*, WP Company, August 24, 1988, www.washingtonpost.com/archive/lifestyle/1988/08/24/don-delillo-caught-in-historys-trap/48a5b0b1-8bd9-412f-8426-843a405896fe/?utm_term=.509cbae73bd9

58 DeLillo, Don. "Seven Seconds." Interview by Ann Arensberg. *Conversations with Don DeLillo*, edited by Thomas DePietro, Jackson, University Press of Mississippi, 2005, pp. 40–46.

59 DeLillo, "Seven Seconds," p. 42.

60 Baudrillard, Jean. *L'illusion de la Fin: Ou la Grève des Evénements*. Paris, Galilée, 1992.

Original quote: "Nous sommes tellement habitués à nous repasser tous les films, ceux de fiction comme ceux de notre vie.... que nous sommes bien capables, sous le coup du vertige contemporain, de faire redéfiler l'histoire comme un film à l'envers" (24).

86 *Latent History and Techno-Progress*

61 Bugliosi, Vincent. *Reclaiming History: The Assassination of President John F. Kennedy*. Kindle ed., New York, W.W. Norton, 2007.

62 Bugliosi analyzes the development of the American opinion regarding conspiracy theories. "The most recent Gallup Poll, conducted on November 10–12, 2003, shows that a remarkable 75 percent of the American public reject the findings of the Warren Commission and believe there was a conspiracy in the assassination."

63 Bugliosi, *Reclaiming History*, Kindle ed.

64 DeLillo, Interview by Kevin Connolly, pp. 25–39.

65 Underwood, Jr Robert Milton. *Musings of a Modern Man: Essays and Research Papers*. Lulu.com, 2014.

66 Jameson, Fredric. *Postmodernism, Or, The Cultural Logic of Late Capitalism*. Durham, Duke University Press, 2003.

67 McLuhan, Marshall. *Understanding Media: The Extensions of Man*. London, Routledge, 2001.

68 DeLillo, "The Art of Fiction CXXXV: Don DeLillo," p. 104.

69 Howells, Richard, and Joaquim Negreiros. *Visual Culture*. 2nd ed., Cambridge, Polity Press, 2015.

70 As Cowart concords, "[v]iewing the Zapruder film, one expects a simple factual record, surely real in some fundamental way. But in fact what one 'sees' is not reality but its simulacrum" (98).

71 Stephenson, Wen. "Oswald: Myth, Mystery, and Meaning." *PBS*. Public Broadcasting Service, November 20, 2003, www.pbs.org/wgbh/pages/frontline/shows/oswald/forum/. Accessed 18 Mar. 2018.

72 DeLillo states that he started *Libra* because of his interest in Oswald. The author desired to imagine "what he [Oswald] looked like, what he sounded like, where he lived" (*Conversations with Don DeLillo*, 48).

73 As Osteen states, "Lee Oswald discovers the power of secrecy early in his life, while riding the New York subways" (154).

74 The reader is informed that, as a child, Oswald "wanted subjects and ideas of historic scope, ideas that touched his life, his true life, the whirl of time inside him. He'd read pamphlets, he'd seen photographs in Life" (*Libra* 33).

75 Deleuze, Gilles. *Difference and Repetition*. Translated by Paul Patton, New York, Columbia University Press, 1994, p. 182.

76 Baudrillard, Jean. "The Vanishing Point of Communication." *The New Media and Technocultures Reader*, edited by Seth Giddings and Martin Lister, London, Routledge, 2011, pp. 110–117.

77 Knight, Peter. *Conspiracy Culture from Kennedy to The X Files*. London, Routledge, 2000.

78 Marvin, Carolyn. "Dazzling the Multitude: Original Media Spectacles." *The New Media and Technocultures Reader*, edited by Seth Giddings and Martin Lister, London, Routledge, 2011, pp. 38–47.

79 DeLillo, Don. "Unmistakably DeLillo." Interview by Mark Feeney. *Conversations with Don DeLillo*, edited by Thomas DePietro, Jackson, University Press of Mississippi, 2005, pp. 169–172.

80 DeLillo, "The Art of Fiction CXXXV: Don DeLillo."

81 DeLillo, *Libra*, p. 40.

82 McLuhan, *Understanding Media*, p. 363.

83 DeLillo, "The Art of Fiction CXXXV: Don DeLillo," p. 106.

84 Ibid.

85 Also referred to as the "student of coincidence," as he is the linking element between the conspirators and Oswald (Kelman 62).
Kelman, David. *Counterfeit Politics: Secret Plots and Conspiracy Narratives in the Americas*. Lewisburg, Bucknell University Press, 2012.

86 DeLillo, Don. Interview by William Goldstein. *Conversations with Don DeLillo*, edited by Thomas DePietro, Jackson, University Press of Mississippi, 2005, p. 48.

87 Jung, Carl G. *Synchronicity: An Acausal Connecting Principle*. Translated by R. F. C. Hull, New York, Bolingen Foundation, 2010.

88 As Schuster describes it, Oswald "bought into the ecstatic message of television hook, line and sinker" (104).

89 As Kavadlo affirms "*Libra* amounts to a fiction of transcendence" (46).

90 Maltby, Paul. *The Visionary Moment: A Postmodern Critique*. New York, State University of New York Press, 2002.

91 Wisnicki, Adrian S. *Conspiracy, Revolution, and Terrorism from Victorian Fiction to the Modern Novel*. London, Routledge, 2008.

92 Coale believes that DeLillo is primarily interested in the human perception. For him, the author "plumbs the depths of consciousness in which perception, imagination, and consciousness itself often seem to be different facets of the same process" (80). In Oswald's case, this process involves a desire to merge with history by means of image technologies.

93 DeLillo, "Seven Seconds," p. 43.

94 Barglow, Raymond. *The Crisis of the Self in the Age of Information, Computers, Dolphins and Dreams*. London, Routledge, 1994.

95 Schuster, *Don DeLillo, Jean Baudrillard and the Consumer Conundrum*, p. 104.

96 Radhika Gajjala et al. suggest that it is necessary to identify a

> continuum of possibilities along key dialectics of space/place, virtual/real, embodied/disembodied, membered/dismembered and voice/ voicelessness to talk about technocultural identity. These identities are produced at various online/offline and global/local intersections through visual performance and discursive self-representation, through dis- and multiply-embodied performativity, and through layered socio-cultural, linguistic and technical literacies, and access.
>
> (300)

> Gajjala, Radhika et al. "Layered Literacies and Nuanced Identities: Placing Praxis from Moo Space to Second Life." *Feminist Cyberspaces: Pedagogies in Transition*, edited by Sharon L. Collingwood, Alvina E. Quintana, and Caroline J. Smith, Newcastle upon Tyne, Cambridge Scholars, 2012, pp. 297–320.

97 Baudrillard, Jean. *Simulacra and Simulation*. Translated by Sheila Glaser, Ann Arbor, University of Michigan, 1994.

88 *Latent History and Techno-Progress*

98 Parrish, Timothy. *From the Civil War to the Apocalypse: Postmodern History and American Fiction.* Amherst, University of Massachusetts Press, 2008.

99 McLuhan, *Understanding Media*, p. 366.

100 Schuster reads Oswald's death as the ultimate event that turns Oswald into a commodity. As he brilliantly summarizes,

> "Lee Harvey Oswald" emerges from *Libra* as a mere ghost, the aftereffect of Lee's efforts to become a part of history.... Rather than subverting the system of signs that renders him a zero, Lee strengthens that system by giving birth to the "perfect" postmodern media figure.
>
> (109)

101 In his interview with Kevin Connolly, DeLillo declares that Oswald and Ruby were expected to "automatically move from spot A to spot B in the straightest possible line" (31).

102 DeLillo, Interview by Kevin Connolly, p. 31.

3 Reconceptualizing the Real

Building on the previous chapters, this chapter reads into DeLillo's *Mao II* (1991), *Underworld* (1997), *The Body Artist* (2001), *Falling Man* (2007), and *The Silence* (2020) to investigate the outcome of the unusual connections formed between the events of latent history and technocultural dailiness. In the first part of the chapter, such events uncover the connections between image technologies and two aspects of dailiness. The first aspect of dailiness is external; it concerns the growing tendency to record the unusual. The second aspect of dailiness is internal; it involves the manner in which recording violent events reconceptualizes the real in the mind. In the second part of the chapter, the reconceptualization of reality is elaborated on; as it is argued that this reality is not limited to the characters' interaction with technocultural space. It marks a transition of the characters' understanding of reality to a visual conception of personal and public events.

By describing unusual connections, DeLillo seeks to expose the concealed possibilities that technoculture contains. Joseph Tabbi[1] denounces critics' inattention to DeLillo's interest in such connections:

> DeLillo's fiction since *Libra*.... realizes certain possibilities for contemporary literature to contest not only with the raw material of the real, the actual, but with the more pervasive and culturally dominant media that are all too quick to turn this material into *story*.
>
> (175; emphasis in original)

For Tabbi, more attention should be paid to DeLillo's efforts to voice the technocultural construction of contemporary life. The critic argues that "DeLillo's approach requires a certain disciplinary fluidity, a degree of professional crossover" (176), in order to detect the connections DeLillo creates. Because the connections between image technologies and culture are evasive, DeLillo sunders their interconnectedness and manifestation throughout his novels. More specifically, DeLillo discreetly describes the

DOI: 10.4324/9781003407768-4

90 *Reconceptualizing the Real*

connections between reality and image technologies on a daily basis. In *Underworld*, particularly, DeLillo connects seemingly unrelated events to point out the manner in which reality is "undergroundly" influenced by the image technologies employed by media.

The Simultaneity of Recording and Receiving Events: *Underworld* and *Falling Man*

Visual Insertion of the Unusual in Dailiness

In order to explore the technocultural connections formed between unrelated events, *Underworld* relates the outcome of daily video recordings. These recordings unexpectedly change one's perception of reality. In *Underworld*, DeLillo brings back the legacy initiated by Lee Oswald.[2] Murder on tape finds its expression in *Underworld* with the Texas Highway Killer. This section deals with the connection created between the serial killer and both the Video Kid and Matt Shay. While the Video Kid is the medium between the killer and television viewers, television is the medium between the Texas Highway Killer and the video-viewer Matt. The involvement of the Video Kid attests to the manner in which daily life interconnects with image technologies, especially camcorders and television. The outcome of such interconnection may lead to witnessing random historical horror previously unrecorded. On the other side, Matt represents the murder viewer whose repeated exposition to the footage leads him to questioning and reflecting on mediated reality.

Keeping with a structure of connection, the novel brings together devices, which have deeply integrated the characters' dailiness and latent history. In this case, the questions are no longer "did it really happen? Or did something else happen?" (*Great Jones Street* 72). Rather, the questions are concerned with the visible aspect of latent history. This aspect indicates how technology breaks the distance between characters and actual events. Proximity renders history the product of everyday immediate exposure to happenings taking place anywhere in the world. Such exposure stresses the randomness of recorded events in the technocultural era. It will be therefore argued that the connection between characters' dailiness and the visible aspect of latent history, televisual events, injects a degree of randomness in society. Consequently, the very definition of the real is defied, as represented by the case of the Texas Highway Killer (from now on referred to as the THK).

The THK is introduced in Part Two of *Underworld*, entitled "Elegy for Left Hand Alone: from Mid-1980s to Early 1990s." In the first chapter of this part, the narrator reports one of the THK's crimes. A twelve-year-old girl accidentally videotapes the scene. The child, also called the Video Kid, is "neither the victim nor the perpetrator of the crime but only the means of recording it" (*Underworld* 155). She discovers the world through the camera by shooting random scenes. Recording a man driving a car is, for her, "doing something simple and maybe halfway clever" (*Underworld* 156).

After he depicts the role of the child in the scenario, the narrator zooms in the recorded murder and addresses the reader. The narrator takes on a televisual voice to enliven the sequence of images that the reader is supposed to visualize: "Now here is where he gets it," the narrator declares, "You see him jolted, sort of wire-shocked—then seizes up and falls toward the door or maybe leans or slides into the door is the proper way to put it" (*Underworld* 158). The narrator stresses particularly the randomness of the crime: "There is a crude power operating here. You keep on looking because things combine to hold you fast—a sense of the random, the amateurish, the accidental, the impending" (*Underworld* 156). The narrator then asks if this sort of crime has existed before camcorders or has been designed for "random taping and immediate playing" (*Underworld* 159).

This crime enacts the sequel of the legacy initiated by Zapruder's accidental recording of the Kennedy assassination. DeLillo aims to elaborate on the Zapruder film through the Texas Highway Killer. This last is connected to the atmosphere of murder that has marked the American society since the Kennedy assassination. In an interview,[3] DeLillo explains that the THK reproduces the scene filmed by Zapruder: "The Texas Highway Killer surely aims for the heads.... I think it has to do with the Kennedy assassination. Somehow this flows through the culture, and it flows through the book."

DeLillo recognizes the thematic connection between *Libra* and *Underworld*.[4] He confesses that *Underworld* revives the "experience of real events and historical characters, the power they carry, the aura they carry."[5] In this context, the aura of the THK is investigated. He represents all the successors of the last linear individuals, Oswald and Ruby. The produced aura could be therefore understood as the technocultural manifestation of randomness characterizing latent history. As DeLillo reminds the reader, the Kennedy assassination introduced the American consciousness to "a world of randomness and ambiguity."[6] This thought finds its expression in *Underworld* when the narrator declares that the encounter between the "victim, the killer and the child with a camera" provokes the connection of "[r]andom energies that approach a common point" (*Underworld* 157).

The threefold encounter confronts the viewer/reader with "forces beyond your control, lines of intersection that cut through history and logic and every reasonable layer of human expectation" (*Underworld* 157). Stripping the layers of history, logic, and reason from the viewer's perception devises a sense of paranoia. This thought is elaborated by Duvall:

92 *Reconceptualizing the Real*

> *Underworld* is nothing short of an attempt to account for the emergence of paranoia as a significant feature of American national identity during the Cold War. This is also, then, a novel about how the United States became postmodern, both culturally and aesthetically.
>
> (*Don DeLillo's Underworld* 22)

Paranoia finds its origins in the rise of the twentieth century filmed violence. The elements that inject randomness in the world also galvanize "what is uncertain and unresolved in our lives."[7]

In the first chapter of the novel's second part, an anonymous narrator, suspected of being Matt Shay, is watching the footage on television. The identity of the narrator is obscured on purpose because they represent every reader as a television viewer (Kavadlo 111). The unnamed narrator discloses three simultaneous movements connecting dailiness to technology. The first movement explains the involvement of the reader in the murder, the second focuses on the Video Kid and her camcorder, and the third explores the deep implication of image technologies in dailiness.

The narrator builds a connection between the footage that the viewer/reader watches on television, the means of recording the murder (the Video Kid's camcorder), and the whole culture of recording familial events. It is worthwhile to quote at length a passage that describes the link between these movements, as it clarifies how one's perception adjusts technoculturally to image technologies.

> And you keep on looking. You look because this is the nature of the footage, to make a channeled path through time, to give things a shape and a destiny....
>
> The girl got lost and wandered clear-eyed into horror. This is a children's story about straying too far from home. But it isn't the family car that serves as the instrument of the child's curiosity, her inclination to explore. It is the camera that puts her in the tale.
>
> You know about holidays and family celebrations and how somebody shows up with a camcorder and the relatives stand around and barely react because they're numbingly accustomed to the process of being taped and decked and shown on the VCR with the coffee and cake.
>
> (*Underworld* 157–158)

In this passage, the use of the second person narrative facilitates building a connection between individuals' comfort around image technologies, especially camcorders and footages, and the disquiet such technologies can suddenly provoke. These movements take place simultaneously to reveal the interconnectedness of unrelated elements.

Reconceptualizing the Real   93

In the first movement, the narrator involves the reader in the scene, as he believes that "you keep on looking" when the news reveals a crime footage. For Jesse Kavadlo, the second person narrative not only obscures the identity of the narrator, but it also "turns the reader into the 'you', making the reader complicit in the violence, the anger, and the spectacle" (111). The reader is assumed to be regularly experiencing such visual absorption through his/her own exposure to television, cameras, and footages.

The second movement concerns the Video Kid's involvement in the crime. Even if it is "the camera that puts her in the tale," the Video Kid's active decision to record caught the murder. Without her, there would be no footage, but the randomness of the crime is inappropriate for the setting the child expects to record. Through recording, the Video Kid is learning "to see things twice" (*Underworld* 155). However, this intimate device of learning does not solely help her understand her surroundings; it also exposes her to horror, to a "man shot dead as he drives along on a sunny day" (*Underworld* 160). In the third movement, DeLillo reminds the reader that recording scenes is part of his/her dailiness since "you know about holidays.... and how somebody shows up with a camcorder." Taped experiences are as much ordinary as lived experiences. Individuals "barely react because they're numbingly accustomed to the process of being taped." The ordinariness of a technocultural experience is inserted when individuals are "taped and decked and shown on the VCR with the coffee and cake."

The ordinariness of viewing footages during the most basic activities demonstrates the deep insertion of image technologies in dailiness. By being "the simplest sort of family video" (*Underworld* 155), the footage is easily propelled onto ordinary life. However, its particularity lies in reaching "living-rooms,"[8] as it loses its "family privacy" and becomes public goods. This transition gives the footage a new identity through television. It becomes a repetitive broadcast in hotel rooms,[9] in living rooms,[10] and in supermarkets.[11]

The footage is shown in a hotel room where Nick Shay is staying. Marc Schuster remarks that "Nick seems more or less comfortable with his (and humanity's) diminishing role in the world of objects" (139). Nick is so used to the objects around him that he considers them part of his dailiness. In the hotel room, he switches on television not to be informed of the latest news about the murder. Rather, he would like to listen to the "noise" of television itself. While he is looking at the "TV screen, where the tape was nearing the point when the driver waves," he was "waited for room service to knock on the door" (*Underworld* 209). Nick does not pay particular attention to the horror of the footage. He is "watching" the sound and presence of television. Nick seems to become indifferent to the footage because it has gained a degree of ordinariness and repetitiveness.

94 *Reconceptualizing the Real*

The narrator stresses the repetitiveness of the footage, each time adding "again," and "one more time." The narrator also stresses the availability of the footage broadcast. After announcing that the footage is being broadcast again, the narrator introduces the state of characters. For instance, "[t]hey were showing the videotape again but Nick wasn't watching" (*Underworld* 208), and "[t]hey were showing the tape again…. Matt came in, surprised to find the TV on" (*Underworld* 215). It could be said that the repetitiveness is an implicit indicator of the affirmed technological presence in daily life.

Matt's surprise reminds the reader of the television that is always switched on in the Gladneys' house, imposing a mythical authority that slips from the control of the viewer/listener. Television, as the house of myth, duplicates the event of the murder until it is turned into a personal fantasy-driven construct. As Joseph Boorstin confirms, the story behind the "making of our illusions—'the news behind the news'—has become the most appealing news of the world" (7).[12] In *Underworld*, as much as in *Falling Man*, such construct is born from the marriage of the screen/ TV news with the individual's inner turmoil, resulting in the emergence of fluid layers of reality. The viewer is thus captivated by their own hyperreal experience. In what follows, it will be argued that the full power of television lies in broadcasting footages that give the illusion of representing (remote) realness (*Underworld*), until television becomes the very house of recording proximate terror (*Falling Man*).

The Superreal and Underreal Aspects of the Televisual Event

The Proximity of Latent History and the Hyperreality of the Event

Similarly to Jack Gladney, Matt is captivated by the news that television broadcasts, but contrarily to him, Matt does not aim to escape death. Matt is captivated by the transmitted footage because of its professed realness and proximity. The footage exemplifies a latent history event, which transcends its pastness and keeps living in the present, as "history, our history, has collided with the wall of real time" [my translation] (Virilio 52).[13] History has reached its speeding limit because its collision with real time creates an unprecedented proximity to events. For instance, while waiting in line at the supermarket, Matt is distracted by the "nine monitors, ten monitors, all showing the tape" (*Underworld* 215). Finding television receivers in the supermarket is not odd, as television extends its presence beyond the living room. It is found in the corners of "offices, hotels, schools and hospitals," to mention a few (Howells and Negreiros 239). The proximity is not only ordinary but comfortable to Matt, as he switches his attention without confusion from shopping to watching the monitors.

Matt cannot ignore the monitors not because he is particularly interested in the murder but because the proximity of historical horror is temporarily attractive. Characterized by latent history's temporal flexibility, the footage epitomizes how "[t]hey made history by the minute in those days" (*Underworld* 141). For Jean Baudrillard, this proximity announces the end of the axiomatic definition of history. As he words it, "we have reached this limit where the sophistication of events and information has led to ending the existence of history as such" [my translation] (*L'illusion de la Fin* 17).[14] The murder Matt keeps watching is no longer a past historical event. Its ceaseless broadcasting attests to history's hyperreal "resurrection" in the screen as a continuous present historical event (Baudrillard, *Simulacra and Simulation* 31).[15] This resurrection is the result of living in a visual technoculture that breaks the distance between historical past, present, and future. DeLillo reads the technocultural reconstruction of temporality as "history in the microwave."[16] This sort of history speeds across monitors in supermarkets and living rooms. Consequently, the legitimacy or realness of a historical event is questioned since the speediness leaves no time to the viewer to process all that which an event contains. The footage of the crime, for instance, absorbs Matt's attention when it is broadcast because "it is realer than real" (*Underworld* 158), but it no longer exists once it ends as it becomes "underreal" (*Underworld* 158). Its realness is limited to the timespan of its appearance on screens.

The short moment of the footage broadcast creates much controversy in Matt's mind. The narrator remarks that "when [the footage] was running [Matt] could not turn away from it. When it wasn't running he never thought about it" (*Underworld* 215). The footage is concurrently an object that holds all attention and which keeps none. Matt wonders why the footage attracts his attention, so he attempts to assess the realness of the images it conveys. In order to understand the footage, Matt is caught by a repetitive irresistible urge to call his wife, Janet, to witness the driver's death.[17] The narrator involves Matt and addresses the reader again to explain the nature of the footage. "[The footage] shows something awful and unaccompanied. You want your wife to see it because it is real this time, not fancy movie violence—the realness beneath the layers of cosmetic perception" (*Underworld* 158). The footage encloses "something awful and unaccompanied" because it is characterized by a starkness that makes it "more real, truer-to-life than anything around you" (*Underworld* 157).

The footage is stripped from the glamour akin to filmic structure, which mirrors subjective reality. It seems that "the grain of the image, the sputtering black-and-white tones" of the footage exemplifies a "searing realness" (*Underworld* 157). It is a sort of realness that is incompatible with Matt's reality. Similarly to movies, "the things around you have a rehearsed and layered and cosmetic look" (*Underworld* 157). Contrarily

96 *Reconceptualizing the Real*

to movies, the footage is devoid of this layered glamour surrounding Matt. "You keep on looking," the narrator suggests, because the footage represents that which "lies at the scraped bottom of all the layers you have added" (*Underworld* 157). Matt creates a particular connection between the definition of the real (represented by the primitiveness of the footage) and a profound level of his mind (which lies beneath aesthetic layers).

This connection is involuntary because when he watches the footage, Matt finds himself "again, without wishing it, in the real, one of whose functions is precisely to devour any attempt at simulation, to reduce everything to the real" (Baudrillard, *Simulacra and Simulation* 16). However, the real, which is supposed to be unmediated, is "the traumatic kernel that cannot be integrated into imaginary and symbolic constructions" (Wilcox 346). Whereas, the violence of the mediated footage does not correspond to the real. Rather, it corresponds to Matt's "imaginary and symbolic constructions." To elaborate, since latent history encourages imaginative possibilities, it allows Matt to express the deepest uncanny feelings his mind harbors. The footage's lack of a "cosmetic perception" of reality gives it enough flexibility to be viewed either as "*superreal*, or maybe *underreal* is the way you want to put it" (*Underworld* 157; emphasis added). This choice or duality resists any reliance on objective truth. It gives the possibility of voicing a personal but possibly unethical version of reality. In its simplicity, and even primitiveness, the footage finds its way to "your hotel brain under all the thoughts you know you're thinking" (*Underworld* 156). It could be said that by penetrating Matt's deepest thoughts, the footage becomes a parasitic reconstruction of his conception of reality.

The conflicting composition of the footage, which encloses both the "superreal" and the "underreal," the true and the cosmetic, obscure its message. The footage's simplicity, which is supposed to disclose a degree of that which is real, may just be another product underlying "a symptom of a revolutionary change in our attitude toward what happens in the world, how much of it is new, and surprising, and important" (Boorstin 9). In this way, the footage does not dig up the truth about being, which is buried under layers of glamour. Rather, the footage represents a simulacrum among a series of simulacra brought by television to create an illusion of authenticity.

The simplicity of the footage does not stimulate the appropriate response to viewing murder because it seems to correspond to a change in attitude. This change is formed by a postmodern ability to "expect anything and everything.... the contradictory and the impossible" (Boorstin 4). Historical mediums no longer select or highlight the events that seem eligible to be shown to the public. Because of their collision with real time, brought by technological advance, historical events, such as the murder, are continuously broadcast. Furthermore, they are continuously required to

Reconceptualizing the Real   97

bring or *be* something new, as viewers are open to possibilities. Expecting anything and everything produces divergent emotional responses toward the footage. The viewer, such as Matt, does not necessarily sympathize with the victim or the Video Kid. Ethically, if there is anything real that the footage incites, it is Matt's mixed feelings and thoughts during its visualization. The narrator explains that the filmed crime "demonstrates an element of truth" but it also discloses "a note of cruel slapstick that you are willing to appreciate even if it makes you feel a little bit guilty" (*Underworld* 160). The footage is not broadcast to show the inhumanity of the murder but "because it exists, because they have to show it, because this is why they're out there, to provide our entertainment" (*Underworld* 160).

This idea is expanded from a technocultural level in *Players* (1977).[18] A terrorist, J. Kinnear, invites the protagonist Lyle Wynant to participate in his terror-mission. Kinnear suggests that violence in itself is just "another media event. Innocent people dead and mutilated. Toward what end? Publicize the movement, that's all. Media again. They want coverage. Public interest. They want to dramatize" (*Players* 180). Correspondingly, the footage is broadcast to entertain and not to teach the value of life. When analyzing *Underworld*, Duvall points out the aesthetic attractiveness of the footage, which disparages its ethical value: "In an age where television news is just another form of entertainment.... the viewer/consumer experiences not the tragedy and pain of human suffering but a set of slow-motion images stripped of all but formal aesthetic features" (50).[19] These aesthetic features cancel out more "humane" responses.

In a way, the tape contains its own "cosmetic" glamour, which does not so much reflect the real but the viewer's conspiracy with the murderer. As described in Plato's allegory of the cave, if an individual is used to seeing the shadow of an object all his/her life, when forced to see the object itself, the individual would "think that there was more reality in what he'd been seeing before than in what he was being shown now" (65).[20] In the technocultural context, the shadow of the object (the footage) could be read as the feelings and thoughts it invokes. For Matt, the footage invokes desired violence since violence is the sort of shadow that television usually broadcasts. In Kavadlo's words, "the Texas Highway Killer's violence expresses the viewer's own anger and potential violence" (111). He is incapable of seeing the object itself because it is endlessly repeated. He denies the unethical feelings provoked by the footage. The reality of the footage, therefore, seems to be linked with the daily televisual violence that simultaneously enthralls and confuses Matt.

The footage corresponds neither to reality nor to Truth. Rather, it reveals the "risk of existing" (*Underworld* 159) while stimulating in Matt a feeling of uncanny satisfaction. The protagonist feels that the victim "had it coming for letting himself be caught on camera" (*Underworld* 160).

98 Reconceptualizing the Real

Indeed, Matt is not so much concerned with the death of the victim as much as with the consequence of "allowing" exposure to recorders. In this scene, DeLillo creates a technocultural connection between the "risk of existing" and deserving death for allowing oneself to "be caught on camera." The author feels that such connection is natural in the postmodern world. Tabbi supports this idea when he posits that the author has always sought to bridge the gap between nature and technology: "the 'natural world' is one of created objects, and his fiction has always accepted the collapse of distinctions between nature and technology, and a consequent primacy and proliferation of reproductive images" (174). The footage is inescapably connected to the camcorder which mediates it as an event. Since the footage is able to reproduce itself infinitely, it becomes part of the ordinary. Consequently, viewers such as Matt increasingly form personal connections between their views and the footage, views that are not necessarily ethical.

Because the footage is taken out of context, and because it is continuously repeated, it gains a familiarity with the viewer that strips it from its original meaning. Consequently, its realness is shaped according to an endlessly repeated sequence of images. The footage integrates the televisual sphere, so it becomes "a sign of the mass media's power to produce and reproduce what we consider reality" (Schuster 145). M. W. Smith[21] builds on Baudrillard's hyperreality to argue that the familiarity of technocultural dailiness transforms life into a succession of scenes. "With its corresponding loss of context as a televised image, the real readily becomes a continuation of a previously existing 'scene' of television representations already familiar to us" (120). This familiarity encourages the mind to wander through imaginative possibilities.

Understanding the footage in these terms renders it not the object of truth but of fantasy. The footage affirms the transformation that historical tapes undertake once they are rendered public through television. Robert Lichter et al. argue that television provides "a shared fantasy world that merges with and sometimes replaces the more mundane world of real life of millions of Americans" (qtd. in Howells and Negreiros 249). The reason behind needing such fantasy relates to what Bill Kovach and Tom Rosenstiel call the awareness instinct. They argue that individuals need to "be aware of events beyond their direct experience" because knowing the unknown "gives them security, allows them to plan and negotiate their lives."[22] Shared fantasy not only feeds on the need to know new and dramatic events, but it also incites viewers to re-watch them. For Matt, "Taping-and-playing intensifies and compresses the event. It dangles the need to do it again" (Underworld 159).

Because Matt is caught by the need to re-watch the crime, he cedes to that which Boorstin calls "extravagant expectations." As he is re-watching

Reconceptualizing the Real   99

the crime, the news offers more information on the killer. Instead of being a silent footage, the black and white construct is accompanied by the voice of a caller who claims to be the Texas Highway Killer. Matt notices that "the voice was naked the way the tape was naked" (*Underworld* 215). According to Boorstin, bringing more information on an event such as this nourishes and enlarges extravagant expectations (5). The nourishment results from our "demand for the illusions with which we deceive ourselves. And which we pay others to make to deceive us" (5). The shared fantasy that viewers demand amplifies their desire for more. "This is reason enough," the narrator declares, "to stay fixed to the screen" (*Underworld* 159).

The footage becomes the product of the hyperreal, a simulacrum among a history of simulacra. It could be said that the footage represents the hyperreal because, similarly to the Zapruder film, it knows no beginning nor end once it is integrated to televisual broadcast. In this way, the footage does not elevate Matt to an enhanced perception of reality. Rather, the footage offers a fantasy of a "truer-to-life"[23] experience encouraged by technocultural possibilities.

The 9/11 Live Broadcast: Reality in the Age of Terror

If the footage opens a realm that feeds on fantasies and uncanniness, what would be said about live transmissions of events such as the 9/11 attack? In an interview, DeLillo suggests that the twenty-first century has officially started on September 11, 2001.[24] This date marks not only a renewed distrust of the American citizen in the government,[25] but also a return to "worries and fears that were thought to be lost."[26] The fact that the attacks were instantly broadcast brought raw material to the American living room. The event epitomizes how history unfolds minute by minute.[27] Its proximity reverberates the "superreal" and "underreal" interpretations being broadcast on "breaking news." Additionally, the proximity of the event seems to engender new fears that are amplified by illusory correlations. This raises the question concerning the manner in which the event reflects one's fears in a context of technocultural dailiness, as will be argued.

Three months after the attack, DeLillo published "In the Ruins of the Future."[28] In the article, he identifies how the event and the medium interact to create a degree of confusion in the minds of the viewers. The first reaction seems to be disbelief, which creates a degree of "underrealness" with regard to the event. For DeLillo, the fast broadcasting of the attacks should be juxtaposed to the slow and painful realization that the images the American citizen is viewing constitute the unfolding of his/her history:

> The event dominated the medium. It was bright and totalising and some of us said it was unreal. When we say a thing is unreal, we mean it is too

100   *Reconceptualizing the Real*

real, a phenomenon so unaccountable and yet so bound to the power of objective fact that we can't tilt it to the slant of our perceptions.[29]

DeLillo's description of 9/11 recalls the birth of latent history with the assassination of President Kennedy. In both cases, the images are so shocking that they seem unreal. During a moment of denial, the live broadcast of 9/11 seems to belong more to a scene from a movie than to reality.

The increasingly inclusive discourse of postmodern technoculture blurs the distinction between the real and the possibility, especially through "megaspectacles." In the preface of *Media Spectacle* (2002),[30] Douglas Kellner suggests that the beginning of the third millennium marks the interconnectedness of different discourses. Thanks to the wide broadcasting of "megaspectacles," the previously distinct spheres of existence, such as the global, cultural, technological, ethical, political spheres, merge in the "banal" setting of everyday life: "Sometimes megaspectacles such as September 11 and the Terror War take over the TV day in its entirety and dominate news, information, advertising, and entertainment for months on end."[31] September 11 particularly dominates the beginning of the third millennium in the American consciousness because of its simultaneity with the citizen's temporality. Sam George goes as far as to suggest that the "TerrorCulture" born from terrorism is concurrent with contemporary technoculture.[32] For DeLillo, this relationship was born decades earlier, but September 11 marks a painfully tangible re-actualization of forgotten fears. The author is particularly interested in depicting the manner in which terror seeps, once more, into the technocultural dailiness of his characters.

DeLillo investigates the proximity of the attack in his fourteenth novel, *Falling Man* (2007).[33] It describes the psychological state of Keith Neudecker, one of the surviving employees of the South Tower. The novel does not concentrate so much on the attack itself. It rather highlights how the victims and their families slowly adapt to post 9/11, or what Keith refers to as the "after-days." The "after-days" trigger different responses in the characters of the novel. Reality becomes connected to the technocultural representation of 9/11, be it spatial or televisual. The novel begins with an account of the commotion surrounding the falling towers. "It was not a street anymore but a world, a time and space of falling ash and near night" (*Falling Man* 3). The scene is seen from the viewpoint of a stupefied Keith. While he is walking straight ahead, a bottle of water is given to him, "shirts" are falling from the sky and his left arm remains unresponsive. He is unable to process the seriousness of the situation. All he can notice are irrelevant or mundane details: "There was something critically missing from the things around him. They were unfinished, whatever that means. They were unseen, whatever that means, shop windows, loading

Reconceptualizing the Real   101

platforms, paint-sprayed walls" (*Falling Man* 5). A truck driver offers him a ride, and Keith gives him the address of his estranged wife, Lianne Glenn.

Lianne has been watching the live broadcast on television meanwhile. The attack is underreal to her until Keith arrives to her doorstep. It seems to her that he has materialized from the medium. "When he appeared at the door it was not possible, a man come out of an ash storm, all blood and slag, reeking of burnt matter" (*Falling Man* 87). Similarly to the Video Kid, Keith and Lianne find themselves in an ordinary context with an unfamiliar event. The proximity of the attack creates an atmosphere of confusion and distress. Moreover, an unbalance is provoked because of the simultaneity of the televisual simulacrum and the realness of a constant threat. Lianne is unable to know the logical procedure in such situation as the "superrealness" of television merges with the "underrealness" of the man standing in ash and blood. "She turned off the TV set, not sure why, protecting him from the news he'd just walked out of, that's why" (*Falling Man* 87).

For DeLillo, the event marks the American disassociation with time and space; the event has particularly changed "the grain of the most routine moment."[34] As time passes, the characters in *Falling Man* readjust slowly to the electrifying atmosphere felt in the aftermath of the attack. Keith moves back with his wife and son. He develops new resolutions and perceptions. He reevaluates his irresponsibility born out of adultery and gambling, which had ruined his marriage previously. He is determined to become a better father and husband. He finds out that he cherishes the moments he is spending with his family. He tries to bond anew with his son, Justin. Reality itself becomes measured by the minute. "He began to think into the day, into the minute" (*Falling Man* 65). Being away from "all the streaming forms of office discourse" gives the daily reality a new meaning (65). The tasks that he has been performing at work seem distant and tedious. However, even if the reality in which he has been functioning seems robotic and hollow, he longs for the distraction that it used to provide. The fall of the towers symbolizes the ruin of a whole technocultural space, one that has shaped Keith's life for more than a year.

As he drives toward his apartment, which is located near the WTC, Keith realizes that everything looks strange and apocalyptic. "When he approached his building he saw workers in respirators and protective body suits scouring the sidewalk with a massive vacuum pump" (*Falling Man* 26). A feeling of uneasiness grips him as he climbs the stairs. The building is no longer a structure of refuge and protection. It becomes the very embodiment of danger. Mark Schuster relates Keith's newly gained awareness of danger to the loss of protection that he had been absorbing from the hyperreal codes of the towers: "Without recourse to the code embodied by the towers, the code that had allowed him to live as an archetype rather

102 *Reconceptualizing the Real*

than as a man, he is rendered vulnerable in his dealings with the world at large" (195). The archetype, thus, has fallen with the towers, leaving Keith exposed and unguarded.

Each part of the building represents a new threat that has been absent from Keith's previous perception of technocultural space. In addition to the stairs, Keith is "wary of the elevator.... He didn't want to know this but he did, unavoidably" (*Falling Man* 27). The fresh traumatic experience is felt in his every movement. When he reaches his apartment, Keith is unable to summon a sense of familiarity. He visualizes the man who has been living in "these two and a half rooms" after being chased by Lianne. As the glamour of the hyperreal dissipates, reality is clarified in the emptiness of the place. "He'd lived here for a year and a half.... finding a place close to the office, centering his life, content with the narrowest of purviews, that of not noticing" (*Falling Man* 26).

Keith is noticing everything now. Above all, he notices that the only reason he has returned to the apartment is to retrieve the "state papers of identity" (*Falling Man* 27). Similarly to the apartment itself, his possessions represent the "double" or the simulacrum that he has created to maintain self-estrangement. After he packs his documents and clothes, Keith locks the door of his apartment for the last time. He stands in the corridor and awaits a closure. A feeling of "underrealness" fills the air. He feels cheated from an epiphany that usually takes place in movies in such situations. "In the movie version, someone would be in the building, an emotionally damaged woman or a homeless old man, and there would be dialogue and close-ups" (*Falling Man* 27). Despite his new resolution to stay on the premises of the real, Keith cannot prevent himself from wishing a "superreal" epilogue as a victim of a terrorist attack. It could be said that the consumeristic technoculture that he has been absorbing all this time incites in him a desire to *feel* the way an actor would feel. In a way, he seeks consolation in imagining the attack as a fictional dream incapable of altering reality.

The "after-days" have gained a sharpness Keith has never noticed before. "He began to see what he was doing. He noticed things, all the small lost strokes of a day or a minute.... Only it wasn't so idle anymore" (*Falling Man* 65). However, this attitude seems to be a preliminary response to the trauma of "falling." The sudden change of his technocultural space seems to take its toll on him despite his efforts to conceal his disquiet. Keith is being unwillingly immersed in this reshaped reality, as it is a *forced* readjustment. Linda S. Kauffman[35] argues that "Keith is eager to skate on the surface of things, but the terrorist attacks defamiliarized the habits of everyday life, making ordinary occurrences seem surreal" (138). If the attacks defamiliarize Keith from a routine revolving around work, it re-familiarizes

Reconceptualizing the Real   103

him with his previous household. However, it also re-familiarizes him with his previous destructive habits, as he regresses to adultery and gambling.

Keith is as much a falling man as those who have jumped from the towers to avoid being burnt alive.[36] He indulges in an extramarital affair with another victim of the attack, Florence Givens. After noticing that the briefcase he has been carrying the day of the attack does not belong to him, Keith decides to return it to its owner. Givens is about his age and is also unemployed. She does most of the talking by relating her side of the experience. The detail that marked her the most is the infinite stairs. In addition to adultery, Keith falls back into his poker addiction. By the end of the novel, he estranges his wife and son yet again. "There was no language, it seemed, to tell them how he spent his days and nights" (*Falling Man* 197). Keith rebuilds the archetype that prevents a lasting reintegration to the real. He re-immerses himself into the superficiality of dailiness through the hyperreal atmosphere of Las Vegas.

If Keith lives in denial and returns to his old habits, Lianne is unable to distract herself from the attack. She witnesses the event in two ways. She encounters it first by the medium of television, and second, by the arrival of her husband covered in blood and ash. The "after-days" for her consist of trying to build her marriage anew and to come to terms with the notion of terrorism. She finds herself gradually engrossed in a quest to understand the event. "She read everything they wrote about the attacks.... She read stories in newspapers until she had to force herself to stop" (*Falling Man* 67). In this way, Lianne dives into the technoculture of spectacle as defined by Kellner:

> [M]edia spectacles are those phenomena of media culture that embody contemporary society's basic values, serve to initiate individuals into its way of life, and dramatize its controversies and struggles, as well as its modes of conflict resolution. They include media extravaganzas, sporting events, political happenings, and those attention-grabbing occurrences that we call news—a phenomenon that itself has been subjected to the logic of spectacle and tabloidization in the era of the media sensationalism, political scandal and contestation, seemingly unending cultural war, and the new phenomenon of Terror War.
>
> (2)

Lianne succumbs to the phenomenon of terror. "She was awake, middle of the night, eyes closed, mind running, and she felt time pressing in, and threat, a kind of beat in her head" (*Falling Man* 67). The event shadows Lianne's understanding, values, and struggles, as it is present everywhere, even when she tries to close her eyes.

104 *Reconceptualizing the Real*

Lianne is unable to stop herself from seeking additional information about the event because she needs to clarify the hazy "underrealness" and "superrealness" that have been confusing her since the fall of the towers. She also considers it a duty to keep up with the unfolding history of her country. "She read newspaper profiles of the dead, every one that was printed. Not to read them, every one, was an offense, a violation of responsibility and trust" (*Falling Man* 106). However, her sense of responsibility and loyalty are not the only reasons she keeps absorbing the media spectacle. She confesses that "she also read [the newspapers] because she had to, out of some need she did not try to interpret" (*Falling Man* 106).

Lianne's need to keep up with the news seems to be a coping mechanism against a new reality she does not fully understand. She becomes irritated by anything that reminds her of the attack. She starts to confuse imaginative possibilities with reality. These imaginative possibilities push her to believe that threat is not only constant but lies at the heart of the post-attack technoculture. This is manifested by the "illusory correlation" which she creates. Donald Kretz defines "illusory correlation" as a misjudgment of information:[37] "Illusory correlation, as the name implies, is a systematic error in perceiving an expected relationship between events, people, groups, behaviors, etc. when no such relationship actually exists" (116). Lianne's illusory correlations are revealed in daily technoculture. For instance, she is triggered when she hears "music located in Islamic tradition" (*Falling Man* 67). The music is played by her neighbor, known only as Elena. Hearing the music agitates Lianne; "she thought of knocking on the door and saying something" (*Falling Man* 67). Lianne notices the music only after the attack, and it keeps reverberating throughout the novel (*Falling Man* 68, 70, 96, 104, 119, 124).

Once Lianne detects the music technoculture, she is unable to "un-hear" it. In this context, music technoculture is understood as a "real" space of expression, one amplified by technology. As expressed by René Lysloff,[38] technology is "a cultural phenomenon that permeates and informs almost every aspect of human existence—including forms of musical knowledge and practice" (32). Not being simply a parasitic effect on the human's authentic or "real" experience, technology offers the means to experience music of different cultures and with different amplifiers. For Lianne, the "loud" music is an intrusion in her personal space and an attack in itself. She does not process the music as a cultural expression but as a reminder of ash and blood. When she finally knocks on Elena's door, Lianne is unable to contain her anger. "The music. All the time, day and night. And loud" (*Falling Man* 119). Elena informs Lianne that she is imbuing the music with "personal" wrath. "Of course it's personal," Lianne answers, "Anybody would take it personally. Under these circumstances. There are circumstances" (*Falling Man* 119). For Elena the music has nothing to do with any "circumstances," as it gives her peace. However, Lianne cannot understand the music as a "peaceful" message and becomes physically violent toward Elena.

Similarly to Elena, Keith believes that the music is neither a "message" nor a "lesson" (*Falling Man* 124). However, Lianne is not relieved, as the music keeps playing after her visit to Elena. The fact that Elena is not intimidated and keeps playing the music defeats Lianne. She feels that the neighbor has won. Keith tells her jokingly that Elena might be lying dead because of the slap, to which Lianne answers, "dead or alive, she wins" (*Falling Man* 124). It seems that Lianne is not referring to the music itself but to the after-days. Terror has won over her struggle to have an ordinary life. She remains unassuaged because she is overwhelmed by unidentified thoughts. "I wake up at some point every night. Mind running nonstop.... Thoughts I can't identify, thoughts I can't claim as mine" (*Falling Man* 124–125). Despite her efforts to convince herself that "[t]hings were ordinary in all the ways they were always ordinary" (*Falling Man* 67), Lianne realizes later that everything has changed. "Maybe nothing was [ordinary]. Maybe there was a deep fold in the grain of things, the way things pass through the mind, the way time swings in the mind, which is the only place it meaningfully exists" (*Falling Man* 105). Lianne finds out about Keith's affair. She is disillusioned about the success of the marriage. At the end of the novel, she is more or less still a single mother who tries to come to terms with the age of terror.

The "grain of things" that seems to be implanted in Lianne's mind reverberates through DeLillo's novels. Matt, Keith, and Lianne represent the individual's shift of perception after the integration of superreal and underreal events in their dailiness. In *Mao II*, DeLillo seems to provide a reading of how the subtle transition from physical reality to televisual reality happens. As will be argued, the manner in which reality is processed in postmodern technoculture partly depends on the visual encounter, or the gaze, as it reorients one's approach to reality.

The Reprogrammed Mind in *Mao II*, *The Body Artist*, and *The Silence*

The Emergence of a Third Reality

In the prologue of *Mao II*,[39] a young woman in her twenties, seeks to merge with the symbolic image of Reverend Moon. In a public Moonie mass wedding, she is ready to give in soul and body to her faith. She stands next to a husband she has never seen before in a stadium filled with brides and grooms taking part in the wedding ceremony. After the ceremony, the newlywed couple Karen Janney and Kim Jo Pak are separated for six months. Their eventual union depends on their devotion and on their ability

106 Reconceptualizing the Real

to spread faith. Karen is involved in the "truth of the body common" (*Mao II* 77). Her daily tasks consist of walking the streets, selling peanuts, and praying in unison with her sisters.

Karen clings desperately to the thought that she is content. However, wearing clothes of unidentified previous owners, and being stacked in a van with other young women makes asceticism increasingly harder to maintain.

> She believed deeply in Master and still thought of herself as a seeker, ready to receive what was vast and true. But she missed simple things, parents' birthdays, a rug underfoot, nights when she didn't have to sleep in a zipped bag. She began to think she was inadequate to the strict plain shapes of churchly faith. Head pains hit her at the end of the day.
>
> (*Mao II* 78)

Karen experiences unidentified headaches that symbolize existential discomfort more than body dysfunction. One night, as she feels stifled in the overpopulated van, Karen gets out for a breath of fresh air. She stands in utter disbelief as her cousin and two men in suits abduct her. She is taken to a motel where her father is waiting.

Unable to accept their daughter's choice, her parents decide to "deprogram" Karen. For eight days, she sits motionless for 18 hours as she hears and watches cases of the so-called deception of which she has been the victim. "They repeated key phrases. They played tapes and showed movies on the wall. The shades were drawn all the time and the door stayed locked. No clocks or watches anywhere" (*Mao II* 79). When she tries to drift to sleep, Karen keeps hearing the key phrases. "You were brainwashed. You were Programmed. You have the transfixed gaze" (*Mao II* 79). She is caught between conflicting resolutions. She is aware of her parents' love, but she also believes in her leaders and in her quest. She would like to go back to the comfort of a warm bed, but she fears that everything outside the church is "Satan-made" (*Mao II* 80).

As the deprogramming intensifies, the conflict deepens. "She couldn't figure out exactly who it was that lived in this body. Her name had broken down to units of sound and it struck her as totally strange" (*Mao II* 80). She is struck by a wave of "superreal" and "underreal" images. These images produce from her bipolar reactions. "Maybe you know the feeling of being deeply, as they say, conflicted, like you wanna stay but you wanna go, and they bring in a person you'd like to stab in the neck with something jagged" (*Mao II* 81). This person is Junette, a former sister with whom Karen performs "three weepy embraces" ironically. Junette tries to convince Karen that she has been indoctrinated (*Mao II* 81). The former leaves

Reconceptualizing the Real   107

with the conviction that Karen has been "awakened," but sometime later, Karen tries to escape.

After a failed attempt at escaping, Karen decides to become docile, "for the time being, because her parents loved her and she didn't want to do another winter in the van, she might just let them bend her mind a little" (*Mao II* 81). However, her mind seems to have succumbed to more influence than she realizes. "You were brainwashed. You were Programmed. You have the transfixed gaze" (*Mao II* 79). The narrator keeps repeating these expressions with insistence to stress the dehumanizing effect they have on Karen. The effect of repetitiveness to which Karen is exposed could be read in terms of the mechanical overload represented in Charlie Chaplin's *Modern Times* (1939). The Little Tramp, a production line worker, has to adjust continuously to the speed of the conveyor belt of the factory. The task of the Little Tramp is to tighten nuts on metal plates. The repetitive gestures performed by the worker with increasing speed leads him to a breakdown. His body becomes so accustomed to the mechanical gestures that he no longer distinguishes between everyday activities and his job. The wrenches in his hands start tightening anything that has the shape of a nut, even if they are buttons on a woman's dress.

The mechanical gestures implanted in the Little Tramp's daily habits could be correlated to Karen's repetitive mental processes. The way the two characters are reprogrammed is different in terms of embodiment and in terms of technological mediums. The Little Tramp is exposed to physical mechanical movements, while Karen is trapped in a mental rewinding of the same images and expressions. Still, they have much in common. Both characters start confusing everyday real life with mechanical and imaginary representations. They are overwhelmed with the overload and speed of technological representations. They are subjected to constant surveillance.

The incorporation of the same gestures and images for most of waking hours reprograms their sensory focus to the extent of alienation from real-life experiences. However, the effect of mechanical gestures is temporary for the Little Tramp while it is permanent for Karen. The deprogramming, which is supposed to cure her from the "transfixed gaze," ironically reprograms her nervous system. As a result, she is estranged both from church and from her parents. The visual reiteration of historical cases overwhelms her capacity to distinguish the difference between the superreal and the underreal. The constant repetition of these cases for a week contributes to decreasing her loyalty to the church, but they are not strong enough to send her back home.

As she is being escorted to the airport to go back home, Karen succeeds in escaping the vigilance of her captors. She does not return to her sisters and leaders, as she has lost her "link to the fate of mankind" (*Mao II* 82). She roams the streets until she meets Scott Martineau, the protagonist's

108 *Reconceptualizing the Real*

assistant and caregiver. Scott notices Karen "walking zigzag on a nearly empty street" (*Mao II* 83). She makes sure that Scott is not a part of the deprogramming scheme before giving him an account of everything that has happened to her. Finding herself torn between two worlds, Karen accompanies Scott to escape both. They make their way to the promise of a third reality, that is, Bill Gray's house. The latter is a famous ghost-author who has been hiding from public life for years. Karen acclimatizes herself to the new household until she becomes part of it.

Despite having the appearance of a transparent character, Karen might be one of the most problematic characters in DeLillo's novels. In her reading of *Mao II*, Stephanie S. Halldorson suggests that Karen is an empty shell that seeks a hero-narrative capable of submerging her:[40] "[Karen] needs to find or be given a system or a pattern that will offer protection, explanation, and belief in reality to relieve her of the constant reminder of her individual self" (160). Karen seeks to merge with crowds and authoritative figures to avoid developing a self. This claim is not devoid of validity. However, it is often neglected that, contrarily to the other main characters in the novel, Karen is not afraid of trading individuality for a wider perception. Prior to being abducted, Karen acknowledges the hardships she fights against daily, but she never thinks of abandoning her faith. As already quoted, "[s]he believed deeply in Master and still thought of herself as a seeker, ready to receive what was vast and true" (*Mao II* 78).

Karen seeks to maintain raw innocent belief and reliance on others, which makes her seek a third reality, one which would maintain her innocent belief and reliance. The power to which Karen tries to merge with seems to correspond to Emmanuel Levinas's conception of the absolute Other.[41] In *Totalité et Infini: Essai sur L'extériorité* (1961), Levinas suggests that recognizing the "Other" means "giving." Simply put, the Other (Autre, Autrui) refers to the separate infinity which transcends the "I" and from which one can gain ethical enlightenment. Karen does not abhor the effacement of her identity by the other's physical presence. Despite the continuous struggle that the other's "visage" brings, Karen seeks its truthfulness. In Levinas's philosophy, "visage" represents the uncontainable Other that, in its alterity, opens doors to infinity (221). Karen seeks to glimpse at this absolute Other through the face-to-face experience with the other, that is, with individuals whom she meets. She lives in the moment, and her dailiness is mainly constituted of various encounters with strangers. This is shown, for instance, during the mass wedding day when she looks at her husband's face for the first time and speaks to him. She tries to decipher something foreign and yet necessary despite all the layers that hides it (*Mao II* 8–9). Karen selflessly seeks the way to an invisible transcendental Other, distant but endlessly attractive. However, the interminable distractions put in Karen's way prove to be inescapable obstacles. The deprogramming plucks her up violently from a strong grounding.

Reconceptualizing the Real   109

If the hardships of a Moonie life fail to discourage Karen from abandoning her lifestyle, the deprogramming does succeed in alienating her from its protective aura. When Karen is subjected to the deprogramming, she loses her connection with the church. She reaches a point of no return. The deprogramming provokes what Jacques Lacan calls the "split." Lacan suggests that individuals are always divided between a state of dreaming and a state of reality.[42] The split is felt the most when the individual is snatched from a "dream" to face an unwelcome reality (Lacan 70). In this context, dreaming is understood as a somnambulant state, thinly separated from reality. The objective of the dream is not to create a perfect world but to veil reality, to veil trauma. It could be said that Karen's sudden weaning from the Moonie protection creates in her a split, which is the source of the creation of a third reality. This, however, implies that the genuine quest for truth in the Other has been an illusion. Karen creates this illusion not to deceive herself as much as to accomplish oneness with a community and its environment. For her, disembodiment represents the best way to achieve that oneness, even if it means being in a somnambulant state.

Dreaming, while being alert to surroundings, represents and covers trauma simultaneously. Karen's pre-deprogramming existence seems best described as a case of womb fantasy. Caroline Rupprecht suggests that the womb is the symbol of both a mysterious confusing space and a safe place.[43] On the one hand, the womb fantasy represents for Karen the hardships of sleeping in cold zipped bags and the lack of physical comfort. On the other hand, disappearing in a crowd and seeking the protective gaze of religious leaders cloak Karen and her sisters from the tumult of the world. The manner in which characters perceive the womb varies according to their gaze. Moreover, the structure of the womb fantasy takes various shapes in technocultural space: "As an imaginary image, the womb can be a cave, a room, a house, or a city; as well as a seemingly boundless geographic or architectural space" (13).

It could be said that the womb fantasy is molded by one's perception of technocultural space. In the case of Karen, this space seems to serve as a protective enfolding to counter traumatic experiences:

> In the van every truth was magnified, everything they said and did separated them from the misery jig going on out there. They looked through the windows and saw the faces of fallen-world people. It totalized their attachment to true father.
>
> (*Mao II* 13)

If the van is the closest representation of the womb, in a heavily technocultural world, the world outside becomes for Karen a rejected notion. Karen accepts to endure asceticism because she is convinced that the struggle which she imposes on herself counters the lies of "fallen-world

110   *Reconceptualizing the Real*

people."[44] However, the "underreal" connotation of her quest limits her perception of reality. After the deprogramming, the umbilical cord is severed. This throws her back into the reality from which she has been hiding. Once Karen is snatched out from the somnambulant state of the church-protection, she fails to reintegrate it. Nevertheless, she keeps trying to reconstitute it in new ways, specifically in filling the split through the construction of a third reality.

After "awakening" from the somnambulant state, Karen tries to weave her consciousness back with a familiar context. In this context, "awakening" refers to Karen's involuntary withdrawal from a protective ascetic life to see the fuller representation of the world. When Scott finds her, she is "walking zigzag" in the street. She is disoriented not because she has lost her way but because she is not fulfilling her Moonie tasks. She is not selling peanuts or spreading the faith in a nearly empty street. She is located in a familiar technocultural space, but she is not representing the Moonie church.

The vulnerability that ensues from this split renders her subservient to outside influence. It seems that Karen accompanies Scott, a stranger, because she is in need of a new host for her womb fantasy. However, thinking that she seeks protection and shelter from Scott or Bill would be undermining the magnitude of her alienation. It seems that she is not alienated only from the church, but also from a direct empathy with physical beings. Prior to the abduction, Karen is driven toward the physical presence of the other. After the abduction, Karen is lost and aimless. In Levinasian terms, this sense of aimlessness is the result of her alienation from face-to-face experience. It could be deduced from this that the deprogramming to which she has been subjected dissolves her commitment to unmediated relationships with others.

If Karen fails to attach a sense of reality to an unmediated person, she finds a host for it in a new technocultural space. Karen tries to revive a sense of protection, womb fantasy, by means of transference. In this context, transference means simply the act of rediscovering essence from a new or unfamiliar structure of technoculture. Even if she is being distanced from church life, Karen seeks to reproduce its essence. She transfers a sense of womb fantasy into her new surroundings, and she maintains a contact with face-to-face experience through televisual mediation. This is how her third reality emerges: she expresses her entrapment between two worlds by becoming a ghost figure that is always half-existing in a state of constant transference.

When the photographer, Brita Nelson, pays a visit, in order to take Bill's picture, she could not help noticing how Karen seems to be half-present. "[Karen] curled into a chair and played with a stray spoon.... [She] had the body lines of a teenager, the crooks and skews and smeariness, and a way of merging with furniture, a kind of draped indecision" (*Mao II* 56). As an

Reconceptualizing the Real   111

extension of the body, the "Womb Chair" that Karen curls into provides tangible comfort. In 1946, the architect and artist Eero Saarinen created a chair model called "Womb Chair," whose main purpose is to create a space of comfort and protection. He informs a client in a letter that the Womb Chair "was designed on the theory that a great number of people have never felt really comfortable and secure since they left the womb. The chair is an attempt to rectify this maladjustment in our civilization" (qtd. in Rupprecht 4). Even if the purpose of the chair seems idealistic and too ambitious, being tangibly "enveloped" in it has a positive psychological effect on individuals. For Karen, the chair takes up the role of the van, in a way. She feels gazed upon in the Womb Chair, a well-planted recollection of the once cherished aura of the Moonie faith. However, the more Karen merges with technocultural space, the less she bonds with human beings as she is caught in a "kind of draped indecision."

This indecision of being is what attracts Scott when he meets Karen. Scott believes that Karen molds perfectly with the household because she seems "a character out of Bill's fiction" (*Mao II* 80). The third reality, represented in the conflictual aura emanating from Karen, strikes Scott as "something out of Bill Gray.... The funny girl on the tumbledown street with an undecidable threat in the air, stormlit skies or just some alienating word that opens up a sentence to baleful influence" (*Mao II* 77). As will be seen, because the split that forms this indecision is never fully rectified, Karen seeks refuge in totally merging with her technocultural space.

Mediated Gaze: "the Virus of the Future"

One evening, as it usually happens, Scott tries to attract Karen's attention while she is watching television. "He looked at Karen, who was sitting up in bed watching TV. He stared, waiting for her to see him.... He stared until she turned and saw him" (*Mao II* 117). This triangular movement (from Scott to Karen, from Karen to television, and from television back to Scott) accomplishes an encounter with the real. For Lacan, the encounter with the real is an encounter that takes place regardless of one's intention and consciousness (54). It involves a technocultural space that is larger than the individual's perception, so it is always half perceived and it always has the potential to elude the individual. The encounter does not refer back to the act of *looking at* as much as *being looked at*, or having the feeling of being looked at. In this case, Karen sees only from one point, but she is looked at from all sides.[45]

Karen is gazed at both by technocultural space and by Scott before she realizes it. Lacan points out that "gaze" concerns things as much as human beings. The gaze is not only that which is comprehended but also that which remains unseen in the world.

112   *Reconceptualizing the Real*

In our relation to things, in so far as this relation is constituted by the way of vision, and ordered in the figures of representation, something slips, passes, is transmitted, from stage to stage, and is always to some degree eluded in it—that is what we call the gaze.

(73)

Much of the gaze that surrounds Karen alludes her, but if she feels Scott's eyes on her, she *delays* in acknowledging it. She seems attracted more to television's "gaze" than to Scott's, as the gaze of televisual images is requited:

There were times she became lost in the dusty light, observing some survivor of a national news disaster, there's the lonely fuselage smoking in a field, and she was able to study the face and shade into it at the same time, even sneak a half second ahead, inferring the strange dazed grin or gesturing hand, which made her seem involved not just in the coverage but in the terror that came blowing through the fog.

(*Mao II* 117)

Television camouflages a raw encounter with Karen's past. The trauma she has endured because of the deprogramming is countered with an oddly comforting vision field offered by television. However, Karen is not delighted in the other's plights. She is rather "involved" with the events of the screen.

Contrarily to Jack Gladney, viewing disasters does not give Karen a feeling of longevity. Television rather brings back the familiar, the face-to-face experience. Drawing on Levinasian exteriority, it could be said that Karen is being swamped up by the totality of the faces she sees on television. She is studying the outside representation of the faces. This traps her in an everlasting return to the self as she is using television, in general, and the faces, in particular, as distraction from the other (Scott, for instance). She is not seeing other people as much as unseeing herself. Simultaneously, when she is absorbed in the events of television, Karen reconnects with the other: "she was able to study the face and shade into it at the same time, even sneak a half second ahead." She looks at the movement of the images, but she is being looked at and she is shown images to which she relates. By predicting the course of the images, Karen is not a passive viewer. She is involved in a sort of perception that blurs the distinction between the real and the virtual.[46]

Karen's level of attention varies with the sort of perception she establishes with the third reality that constitutes her environment. Jean-Paul Sartre[47] suggests that a subject, Karen in this case, molds her environment in a way that "everything is in place."[48] As a "privileged object" of foreign nature, it

Reconceptualizing the Real   113

(Scott) "appears" in her field of vision. For Sartre, when an object appears in one's field of vision, a moment is required to process it as a privileged object and subsequently as a human being (343). At first, Scott is indistinguishable from the objects set around Karen. He, then, appears as a privileged object because he is not part of the static space; a vague sense of familiarity accompanies him. "Thus suddenly an object has appeared which has stolen the world from me. Everything is in place; everything still exists for me; but everything is traversed by an invisible flight and fixed in the direction of a new object" (343). This privileged object shares Karen's space and even tries to take it from her. There is an aperture of one's space toward the not yet visible human being.

Karen attempts to maintain, as long as possible, an undisturbed emersion in her technocultural space, which explains *her* delay in acknowledging Scott's gaze. However, the strong presence of the privileged object, expressed by Scott's look,[49] compels her to "bend" her third reality to include him:

> She watched the set at the foot of the bed. There was a woman on an exercise bike and she wore a gleaming skintight suit and talked into the camera as she pedaled and there was a second woman inserted in a corner of the screen, thumb-sized, relaying the first woman's monologue in sign language. Karen studied them both, her eyes sweeping the screen. She was thin-boundaried. She took it all in, she believed it all, pain, ecstasy, dog food, all the seraphic matter, the baby bliss that falls from the air. *Scott stared at her and waited.* She carried the virus of the future. Quoting Bill.
>
> (*Mao II* 119; emphasis added)

Karen is absorbed in an environment of virtual objects and faces. It could even be said that, to her, the faces that she studies are realer than Scott. They are familiar constructs that attest to her "thin-boundaried" perception. Karen's fixation on television could be described as "a near obliteration of self-awareness" (*Players* 205). She sets on an unplanned journey to what is to become "home." She also seeks to adjust to a new perception of reality through the most comforting medium, that is, television. Her easy belief in the televisual event is an attempt to be fully immersed in a third reality, a reality that maintains distance with a "foreign" but privileged object.

If Karen delays acknowledging Scott, his gaze eventually brings her back to the physical world. "He stared until she turned and saw him" (*Mao II* 117). Scott remains a dangerous object that weakens her control. His gaze threatens to dissolve her safe universe by bringing her back to "stark" reality. However, what if it is the medium itself, rather than

114 *Reconceptualizing the Real*

privileged objects, that dissolves the safe universe? What if television stops functioning and, consequently, puts the character face-to-face with their unmediated environment?

DeLillo answers this question 29 years later in *The Silence* (2020).[50] The author seems to suggest in his latest work that if the medium suddenly stops functioning, it would be difficult for the gazed upon watcher to break free from the enchantment of the medium. *The Silence* invokes a world, realer than real, in which the televisual becomes reality and the real shrinks to empty screens. A sudden electricity failure unsettles drastically the normal unfolding of Super Bowl LVI. Nothing "super" about "Super Sunday" is supposed to happen other than the final game of the American football season. Yet, power failure happens while a building inspector, Max Stenner, is sitting impatiently in front of a giant TV screen waiting for the game to start. His wife, Diane Lucas, a retired physics professor, is switching between watching her husband and watching one of her guests, a former student named Martin Dekker. Martin, a physics teacher, watches neither of his hosts; his vision is populated by Einstein's work, an abstract realm of infinite quotes that he tirelessly recites.

The trio is awaiting the arrival of two other guests, Jim Kripps and Tessa Berens. The couple, which the reader meets first, walk to the hosts' apartment after a near plan crash, caused by the same power outage, and after a detour to the hospital where Jim gets head-stitched. The plot seems barren as the fulfillment of the apocalypse is interceded by episodes of intimacy (Jim and Tessa) and by what seems to be stale dialogues. For Ron Charles, the staleness of the plot is reflected on how the characters react to the lack of television and light: "these characters swing erratically from domestic banality to absurdist spectacle. Never have five people reacted with such existential dread to missing the Super Bowl."[51] Critics rightly identify the central role of technology in the dailiness of the characters. The misfunction of a set of apparatuses does unsettle their lives. However, viewing the power of technological resources chiefly in terms of negative effects on the individual reduces the layered reality of technoculture to technological determinism.

The behaviors of the characters toward the "catastrophe" are reversed from those of *Falling Man*. In *The Silence*, the first reaction is that of "superreal" imagination. The sense of doom and paranoia are strong; the characters start giving voice to "extraterrestrial" and "Chinese" narratives as causes for the power outage. Soon the sense of "underreal" disbelief fills the room, particularly for Max if not for the other characters. Max Stenner finds it difficult to detach from his "Womb Chair." When the TV goes blank, he acknowledges Martin only to ask "What is happening to my bet?"[52] He does not seem to ask this question to anyone in particular, although he looks at Martin then at Diane.

Reconceptualizing the Real   115

Being suddenly "banished" from his third reality, Max struggles to communicate with his physical surroundings. Even if he mechanically interacts with his wife, Martin, the neighbors, and his friends, he is half-present, existing in "a kind of draped indecision" (*Mao II 56*). Similarly to Karen, Max is attracted more to the televisual gaze. When this gaze "goes blank," Max loses his grip on the familiar. Even if he is not alone in the living room, Max makes sense of others more "accurately" when the screen completes the triangular encounter. The moment the screen fails to complete the encounter, the privileged objects, Diane and Martin, overwhelm Max's space. More than this, the power outage obliges Max himself to go back to the physical reality and to be *seen*. Once the realm of bets, advertisement, and football is obsolete, he is left to acknowledge himself. In order to *delay* acknowledging his physical reality, with everything that it comprises, he becomes, in his immersion, the very televisual set.

Max tries to summon the third reality, by reproducing the "gaze" of the televisual event. As a result, he embodies the voice of television, hoping it would bring the screen back to life. It is worthwhile to quote at length a passage that depicts the manner in which Max is "trying to induce an image to appear on the screen through force of will:"[53]

Max said, "*Avoids the sack, gets it away—intercepted!*" It was time for another slug of bourbon and he paused and drank. His use of language was confident, [Diane] thought, emerging from a broadcast level deep in his unconscious mind, all these decades of indigenous discourse muddied up by the nature of the game.... Half sentences, bare words, repetitions. Diane wanted to think of it as a kind of plainsong, monophonic, ritualistic.... speaking from deep in his throat, the voice of the crowd. "*De-fense. De-fense. De-fense.*" He got up, stretched, sat, drank.... He said, "*These teams are evenly matched more or less. Punting from midfield. A barn burner of a game.*" Diane was beginning to be impressed.... He kept on talking, changing his tone, calm now, measured, persuasive.... Then, singing, "*Yes yes yes, never fails to bless bless bless.*" Diane was stunned. Is it the bourbon that's giving him this lilt, this flourish of football dialect and commercial jargon. Never happened before, not with bourbon, scotch, beer, marijuana. She was enjoying this, at least she thought she was, based on how much longer he kept broadcasting. Or is it the blank screen, is it a negative impulse that provoked his imagination.

(Emphasis in original)[54]

The "decades of indigenous discourse" provide Max with memorized diction. By reproducing the "superreal" voice of the screen, which is stressed by the emphasized language, Max summons the "plainsong, monophonic,

116 *Reconceptualizing the Real*

ritualistic" multiplicity of the TV programs he absorbs daily. The fact that this intensified behavior has never occurred before leads Diane to suspect that something about the blank screen is pushing him to disassociate completely, for a moment, from the physical world. He "broadcasts" the very content that he is supposed to receive.

In *The Silence*, as much as in *Mao II*, the virtual context of the screen offers the sort of proximity that the physical world can no longer provide. If Karen needs the proximity of the mediated Other, Max craves the mediated gain and loss of money, the "commercial jargon," and the "ritualistic" thrill of football games. Even if the two characters differ in the reason for their screen-need, they share the unrectified split that makes it difficult to connect with the unmediated physical presence of other human beings. The intensified behavior displayed by Max seems to have its origins decades earlier, with the thin-boundaried responsiveness of Karen.

In *Mao II*, Scott advances the theory of "the virus of the future" to explain Karen's split from unmediated reality. Scott brings up his theory when he is discussing with Brita the state of individuality in contemporary technoculture. Brita informs Scott that the new tide of speed compels people to eat in a hurry. People are not only forced to eat food they have not prepared, but they also have to eat in locations with which they are not familiar. Not only do they have to eat standing up but they are also forced to look directly into a mirror while eating (*Mao II* 88). Whereas Brita reads this phenomenon as "total control of the person's responses, like a consumer prison" (*Mao II* 88), Scott views the proximity of the mirror as a protective reflection for hiding in a familiar space (*Mao II* 89). "You use it to hide. You're totally alone in the foreground but you're also part of the swarm, the shifting jelly of heads looming over your little face" (*Mao II* 89). Mass weddings embody this need to blend and disappear into one congruous body. For Scott, the grim vision of the future could be countered by coagulating into such community. However, this community seems to have migrated to the virtual world, and it follows new rules.

The spatial change that the world has undergone because of the advance of technology contributes to shifting the form of the virtual community. Scott suggests that the new technocultural space provokes a collapse of the traditional order of time and space:

> We've gone too far into space to insist on our differences.... This isn't a story about seeing the planet new. It's about seeing people new. We see them from space, where gender and features don't matter, where names don't matter. We've learned to see ourselves as if from space, as if from satellite cameras, all the time, all the same. As if from the moon, even. We're all Moonies, or should learn to be.
>
> (*Mao II* 89)

Reconceptualizing the Real 117

As time becomes a perpetual present in the virtual world, space breaks out from physical lived experience. As seen with Max, physical space gives way to the summoned technocultural spirit of televisual image. The virtuality of this image is present even when its physical manifestation is absent. In this way, space no longer refers solely to the physical world; it also refers to the gaze of virtuality.

This mediated gaze is expressed, in *The Body Artist* (2001),[55] through a virtual personification of the protagonist's grief. After the suicide of her husband, Lauren Hartke retreats to the house which they have been renting. At some point, her main occupation consists of watching a live-streaming video from a town in Finland. Lauren spends hours looking at the real-time broadcast of a two-lane road. The proximity of time and space fascinates Lauren even if she fails to understand fully its significance.

> She set aside time every day for the webcam at Kotka. She didn't know the meaning of this feed but took it as an act of floating poetry. It was best in the dead times. It emptied her mind and made her feel the deep silence of other places, the mystery of seeing over the world to a place stripped of everything but a road that approaches and recedes, both realities occurring at once... and she sat and watched, waiting for a car to take fleeting shape on the roadway.
>
> (*The Body Artist* 38–39)

The death of Lauren's husband provokes a disassociation with her physical world. She seeks to be "emptied" from the memory of loss. It could be said that Lauren allows the virtual reality to submerge her mind. This is confirmed when she ventures to interpret the appearance of an undistinguishable young man, Mr. Tuttle, as an aperture by which virtuality flows out of her screen. "She amused herself by thinking he'd come from cyberspace, a man who'd emerged from her computer screen in the dead of night. He was from Kotka, in Finland" (45). The narrator never divulges the nature of Mr. Tuttle's appearance in Lauren's house. The superreal/ underreal aura radiating from him suggests that he is part of Lauren's attempt to overcome the void left by the death of her husband.

The unexpected appearance of the unfamiliar young man and the intensity of the deserted road constitute a cloak of protection. They also teach Lauren to see herself "anew," as Scott would suggest. Lauren rediscovers herself "from satellite cameras." This rediscovery distances her from the real world, which is her way of dealing with grief.

Seeing the self "as if from satellite cameras" may be interpreted as becoming foundationless.[56] Characters such as Karen, Max, and Lauren are prone to be swamped up by the medium's images. An aura of power emanates from these images, especially when they are portraying imposing

118   *Reconceptualizing the Real*

historical events and figures. In Karen's case, Reverend Moon becomes a symbol of oneness with which she needs to merge. For Lauren, oneness comes in the form of healing; and for Max, oneness is represented by multi-layered and miscellaneous intake of ads, football, and gambling. However, is this kind of oneness with the virtual body necessarily groundless?

Halldorson argues that DeLillo demarcates his characters' identity to a "playacted image" because that is all they have left in a commodified world (161). If this is the case, the three characters trade a full-fledged identity to adapt to a commodified world. However, their interaction with virtuality is identified more from a split than from an impulsive identification with a superficial realm. This point can be elaborated through Karen's experience. After the deprogramming, Karen relearns to be a Moonie without going back to ascetic activities. In this new approach to oneness, Karen's face-to-face experience is indistinct. The Other becomes for her a self-referring virtual construct, but she does not seek a new superficial identity through this construct. She rather seeks new ways to *maintain* her identity through it. In this way, it could be said that the virus of the future refers to the severed relationship of the individual with the direct interaction with human face, but it also implies the appearance of the virtual gaze encountered in a third form of reality, mediated but not necessarily inauthentic.

The new way of seeing the virtual event explains why Karen, as a symbolic indicator to the third form of reality, is absorbed in her interaction with television. DeLillo devotes seven pages (187–193) on one of Karen's daily televisual interactions. After the inexplicable disappearance of Bill Gray, Karen temporarily moves in with Brita. During the day, Karen roams "blank-faced in Manhattan,"[57] and when night comes, she returns to Brita's apartment and loses herself in front of television. "She had no sense of time,"[58] as she watches with Brita the funerals of Ruhollah Khomeini. Brita's presence seems distant to Karen but the mourning of the crowd seems to be her own: "Karen could go backwards into their lives, see them coming out of their houses and shanties, streams of people, then backwards even further, sleeping in their beds, hearing the morning call to prayer" (*Mao II* 188). She absorbs the burden of loss as the mourning intensifies: "Karen's hands were over her mouth," as "[t]he living were trying to bring the dead man back among them" (*Mao II* 189). The longer Karen watches the funeral, the closer she becomes to the virtual crowd.

Karen connects to the televisual crowd in a way that cannot be limited to an abstract distance. She could not sustain the notion that there are people watching the funerals rather than *living* the pain. As she mourns "among" the crowd, she realizes that she might be the only one feeling this way.

It was possible to believe that she was the only one seeing this and everyone else tuned to this channel was watching sober-sided news

Reconceptualizing the Real 119

analysis delivered by three men in a studio with makeup and hidden mikes. Her hands were pressed against her temples.... She turned and saw Brita leaning back on the far arm of the sofa, calmly smoking. This is the woman who talked about needing people to believe for her, seeing people bleed for their faith, and she is calmly sitting in this frenzy of a nation and a race. If others saw these pictures, why is nothing changed, where are the local crowds, why do we still have names and addresses and car keys?

(*Mao II* 190–191)

The questions that Karen asks bring disillusionment to the notion of the physical community to which she has been holding. The community with which she forms a sense of belonging has immigrated to the virtual world. The boundaries between the real and the virtual gradually collapse, as she quietly lives the pain of the crowd. Halldorson contends that Karen's need to belong to a crowd remains an image that never steps onto reality. "Karen wants to be in the troops, but as much as she wants the image, the image is not a narrative. It advertises a dream; it allows her nothing but the chance to dream" (161). However, the crowd does seem to offer her a pattern of belief. Her desire to reunite with her sisters and Master is revived despite the unpromising environment.

Early in the morning the next day, Karen is filled with a new resolution. She is determined to bring back into reality the image of a "single family." She tries once again to reconnect with the physical face-to-face experience. She is soon found in a park preaching to the homeless. She scans the crowd of stacked shapeless forms, "searching for bodies with open eyes" (*Mao II* 193). She even tries to transcend her limitations in order to reach the hearts of the lost and abandoned. "She had Master's total voice ready in her head" (*Mao II* 194). No matter how hard she tries, however, the mass of individual shapes remains irresponsive, as no one acknowledges the other.[59] "Stale air holding close, the old dead smell of bedding and sweat and pee and slept-in clothes. She talked in the intimacy of first light with sleeping people all around" (*Mao II* 193). This encounter only deepens the split formed by her disassociation with the Moonie church. The unmediated face remains veiled and unreachable.

Karen returns to the gaze of the only person who acknowledges her existence. She returns to Scott and to the only technocultural space with which she can merge. Back home, she is "looking not so different from the first time [Scott had] ever seen her" (*Mao II* 218). She brings with her the pictures that Brita has taken of Bill. At this point, Bill has died on a ferry to Jounieh, but Karen declares that she keeps "seeing him.... But not really" (*Mao II* 219). The pictures she has brought with her keep Bill's image alive. She resumes her imitation of "speech machine"[60] while

120 *Reconceptualizing the Real*

maintaining her "thin-boundaried" state. Her transition to a mediated life is thus complete.

After having been torn away from the technocultural space of Moonie asceticism, the manner in which Karen approaches the world changes. Despite several attempts at regaining a connection with the other, Karen struggles to reconstruct a healthy relationship with physical individuals. This is problematic because, as has been shown, it is not her conscious choice to be distanced from her fellow-believers. The deprogramming has a parasitic effect on her mind. In her confusion, she returns to the closest point of familiarity she has known pre-deprogramming. Karen's technocultural space becomes an alternative for protection. In her (new) third reality, the household becomes the van and television becomes the window through which she watches the world living "in misery." She becomes part of furniture the way she has sought to become part of a larger body. In Karen's new technocultural space, a space that gains larger proportions for Lauren and Max, boundaries are broken between the real and the virtuality of the screen.

DeLillo seems to suggest that historical reality is being reshaped in terms of technoculture, more specifically technocultural space. This breaks the immediate connection between the individual and reality. Still, as Edward Hall words it, "[t]he screens that one imposes between oneself and reality constitute one of the ways in which reality is structured" (102).[61] Characters rely on image technologies in order to access a reality they can comprehend, in a world where the "simplest of our extravagant expectations concerns the amount of novelty in the world" (Boorstin 7). The speed by which information is conveyed through technologies changes the approach of DeLillo's characters to history, in particular, and reality, in general. With a larger technocultural space, the characters are able to adapt and to adjust to ambiguous changes. Since technocultural space plays a major role in DeLillo's novels, Chapter 4 examines the implication of technocultural space in the characters' self-understanding.

Notes

1 Tabbi, Joseph. *Postmodern Sublime: Technology and American Writing from Mailer to Cyberpunk*. Ithaca, Cornell University Press, 1996.

2 As Duvall confirms, "[t]he Zapruder video installation finds its eerie double in the novel in another piece of video, the film of the Texas Highway Killer shooting a victim" (*Don DeLillo's Underworld* 50).

3 DeLillo, Don. " 'Writing as a Deeper Form of Concentration': An Interview with Don DeLillo." Interview by Maria Moss. *Conversations with Don DeLillo*, edited by Thomas DePietro, Jackson, University Press of Mississippi, 2005, pp. 155–168, especially p. 162.

Reconceptualizing the Real 121

4 DeLillo, " 'Writing as a Deeper Form of Concentration': An Interview with Don DeLillo," p.162.
5 Ibid.
6 DeLillo, Don. "American Blood: A Journey through the Labyrinth of Dallas and JFK." *Articles by Don DeLillo*, 1983, www.perival.com/delillo/ddarticles. html. Accessed June 5, 2018.
7 DeLillo, "American Blood."
8 Joseph Dewey points out that, for DeLillo, "the assassination marked the street-birth of the media age-specifically, of television news and the rush to bring catastrophe into living-rooms" (93).
9 "They were showing the videotape again but Nick wasn't watching" (*Underworld* 208).
10 DeLillo, Don. *Underworld*. London, Picador, 2011, p. 215.
11 "Then [Matt would] get on line at the supermarket back home and there it was again on the monitors they'd installed to keep shoppers occupied at the checkout—nine monitors, ten monitors, all showing the tape" (*Underworld* 215).
12 Boorstin, Daniel Joseph. *The Image: A Guide to Pseudo-events in America*. New York, Vintage, 1992.
13 Original quote: "l'histoire, notre histoire, vient de percuter le mur du temps reél" (Virilio 52).
   Virilio, Paul, and Philippe Petit. *Cybermonde la Politique du Pire*. Paris, Les éditions Textuel, 1996.
14 Original quote: "nous avons franchi cette limite où, à force de sophistication événementielle et informationelle, l'histoire cesse d'exister en tant que telle" (Baudrillard 17).
   Baudrillard, Jean. *L'illusion de la Fin: Ou la Grève des Evénements*. Paris, Galilée, 1992.
15 Baudrillard, Jean. *Simulacra and Simulation*. Translated by Sheila Glaser, Ann Arbor, University of Michigan, 1994.
16 DeLillo, Don. "The Power of History." *The New York Times*, 7 September 1997, https://archive.nytimes.com/www.nytimes.com/library/books/090797a rticle3.html. Accessed May 7, 2018.
17 See DeLillo, *Underworld*, p. 158 and p. 217.
18 DeLillo, Don. *Players*. New York, Vintage, 1989 [1977].
19 Duvall, John N. *Don DeLillo's Underworld: A Reader's Guide*. New York, Continuum, 2002.
20 Plato. "Republic Excerpts." *The Norton Anthology of Theory and Criticism*. Edited by Vincent B. Leitch, William E. Cain, Laurie Finke, John McGowan, T. Denean Sharpley-Whiting, and Jeffrey Williams, New York, W.W. Norton, 2018, pp. 49–80.
21 Smith, M. W. *Reading Simulacra: Fatal Theories for Postmodernity*. Albany, State University of New York, 2001.
22 Kovach, Bill, and Tom Rosenstiel. *The Elements of Journalism: What Newspeople Should Know and the Public Should Expect*. Ebook ed., New York, Three Rivers Press, 2014.
23 DeLillo, *Underworld*, p. 157.

122 *Reconceptualizing the Real*

24 DeLillo, Don. "DeLillo Interview by Peter Henning." Translated by Julia Apitzsch, *Perival*, 2003, www.perival.com/delillo/interview_henning_2003. html. Accessed December 19, 2018.

25 As worded by John Carlos Rowe, DeLillo predicts "a searching criticism of our national failings without a complementary understanding of the global forces we have helped to produce and yet have exceeded our cultural, political, and military control" (134).
Rowe, John C. "Global Horizons in *Falling Man*." *Don DeLillo: Mao II, Underworld, Falling Man*, edited by Stacey Michele, New York, Continuum, 2011, pp. 122–134.

26 DeLillo, "DeLillo Interview by Peter Henning."

27 "They made history by the minute in those days" (*Underworld* 141).

28 DeLillo, Don. "In the Ruins of the Future." *The Guardian*, Guardian News and Media, December 22, 2001, www.theguardian.com/books/2001/dec/22/fiction. dondelillo. Accessed November 5, 2018.

29 DeLillo, "In the Ruins of the Future."

30 Kellner, Douglas. *Media Spectacle*. London, Routledge, 2003.

31 Kellner, *Media Spectacle*, pp. viii–ix.

32 "Since the events of September 11, 2001, the culture of terrorism has been etched in the minds of people worldwide.... [TechnoCulture and TerrorCulture] are not 'either/or' features but a concurrent reality of the global youth populace" (35).
George, Sam. "Emerging Youth Cultures in the Era of Globalization: Technoculture and Terrorculture." *One World or Many?: The Impact of Globalisation on Mission*, edited by Richard Tiplady, Pasadena, William Carey Library, 2003, pp. 33–54.

33 DeLillo, Don. *Falling Man*. London, Picador, 2011 [2007].

34 DeLillo, "In the Ruins of the Future."

35 Kauffman, Linda S. "Bodies in Rest and Motion in *Falling Man*." *Don DeLillo: Mao II, Underworld, Falling Man*, edited by Stacey Michele, New York, Continuum, 2011, pp. 135–151.

36 The symbolic representation of the falling man concerns many characters of the novel. In her essay "Bodies in Rest and Motion in *Falling Man*," Kauffman suggests that the title is not directed only to the victims who preferred to throw themselves from the buildings to meet a quick death. Rather, the novel "portrays many falling men—and women" (135). Keith is falling in the sense that he goes back to his destructive tendencies. His wife, Lianne, "spirals downward" when she accepts him back. Individuals with terminal Alzheimer fall out of a recognizable world. In short, each character fails to maintain an organized and peaceful life. The chaotic characteristic of existence reveals itself to them when their technological context malfunctions.

37 Kretz, Donald R. "Experimentally Evaluating Bias-Reducing Visual Analytics Techniques in Intelligence Analysis." *Cognitive Biases in Visualizations*, edited by Geoffrey Ellis, Cham, Springer, 2018, pp. 111–136.

38 Lysloff, René T. A. "Musical Life in Softcity: An Internet Ethnography." *Music and Technoculture*, edited by René T. A. Lysloff and Leslie C. Gay, Middletown, Wesleyan University Press, 2003, pp. 23–63.

Reconceptualizing the Real   123

39 DeLillo, Don. *Mao II*. London, Vintage, 1992 [1991].
40 Halldorson, Stephanie S. *The Hero in Contemporary American Fiction: The Works of Saul Bellow and Don DeLillo*. New York, Palgrave Macmillan, 2007.
41 Levinas, Emmanuel. *Totalité et Infini: Essai sur L'extériorité*. Paris, Kluwer Academic, 2017.
42 Lacan, Jacques. *The Four Fundamental Concepts of Psychoanalysis, the Seminar of Jacques Lacan Book XI*, edited by Jacques-Alain Miller. Translated by Alan Sheridan, London, W. W. Norton 1998.
43 Rupprecht, Caroline. *Womb Fantasies: Subjective Architectures in Postmodern Literature, Cinema and Art*. Evanston, Northwestern University Press, 2013.
44 Žižek poses this question in the introduction of *Living in the End Times*. He wonders,

> if truth has to be lived, why need this involve a struggle? Why not rather a meditative inner experience? The reason is that the "spontaneous" state of our daily lives is that of a lived lie, to break out of which requires a continuous struggle.
>
> (xii)

45 Rephrasing Lacan's thought on "The pre-existence of a gaze—I see only from one point, but in my existence I am looked at from all sides" (72).
46 In this context, the virtual is understood simply as the other side of the screen. Though this "other side" is virtual, it is still real. The second part of Chapter 5 elaborates on this point.
47 Sartre, Jean-Paul. *Being and Nothingness: A Phenomenological Essay on Ontology*. Translated by Hazel E. Barnes, New York, Washington Square Press, 1992.
48 Sartre, *Being and Nothingness*, p. 343.
49

> With the Other's look the "situation" escapes me. To use an everyday expression which better expresses our thought, I am no longer master of the situation. Or more exactly, I remain master of it, but it has one real dimension by which it escapes me, by which unforeseen reversals cause it to be otherwise than it appears for me.
>
> (Sartre 355)

50 DeLillo, Don. *The Silence*. Kindle ed., London, Picador, 2020.
51 Charles, Ron. "Don DeLillo's 'The Silence' is an absurdist look at our technology dependence," *The Washington Post*, 2020, www.washingtonpost.com/entertainment/books/don-delillos-the-silence-is-an-absurdist-look-at-our-tec hnology-dependence/2020/10/12/01b656ea-0beb-11eb-b1e8-16b59b92b36d_story.html
52 DeLillo, *The Silence*, Kindle ed.
53 Ibid.
54 Ibid.
55 DeLillo, Don. *The Body Artist*. London, Picador, 2011 [2001].

124 *Reconceptualizing the Real*

56 John Johnston argues that characters such as Karen are groundless. "For these characters, floating in a medium of images in which everything seems detached from both their physical and emotional needs.... announce the alpha and omega of social reality" (176).
Johnston, John H. *Information Multiplicity: American Fiction in the Age of Media Saturation*. London, Johns Hopkins University Press, 1998.

57 DeLillo, *Mao II*, p. 141.

58 DeLillo, *Mao II*, p. 187.

59 In Halldorson's words, "[t]hese people, living in tents and cardboard boxes, do not see themselves as masses of the homeless. They have nothing in common but a desire to protect their own cultivated space" (160).

60 DeLillo, *Mao II*, p. 220.

61 Hall, Edward Twitchell. *Beyond Culture*. New York, Anchor Books, 1989.

4 The Phenomenology of Technocultural Space

This chapter is concerned with the manner in which technocultural space reorients the perception of characters. Building on the previous chapters, "technocultural space" refers to the inward and outward methods of spatial understanding. The mutation of temporal distance into real time has been accompanied by the mutation of the perception of space. Characters do not only appropriate the image technologies of latent history; they also appropriate the informational characteristic of the space within which they exist. It is argued that the postmodern space of dailiness is a technocultural milieu, both as a material world and as a tele-visual realm.

The tele-visual aspect of technocultural space is particularly important. This tele-visuality does not refer solely to image technologies, as it does not disappear with the lack of exposure to screens. Tele-visuality is an intrinsic component that adapts to different environments. For this reason, the first task of this chapter is to demonstrate how space incites tele-visuality despite the lack of image technologies. In *End Zone* (1972), it is noticed that the protagonist's ability to form visual images does not depend on image technologies. Even when he moves to the desert, the protagonist, Gary Harkness, views the world as a televisual narrative. This poses a phenomenological question of perception. It will be argued that Gary adopts the method of image technologies even when they are scarce because space itself is informational in nature.

The phenomenological question of perception is also tested in an advanced technocultural space. If scarceness allows the mind to construct its own visual understanding, how does the mind react to a technologically enhanced space? The second part of this chapter will try to answer this question mainly through *Players* (1977). The novel reveals that technocultural space is implicated in the individual's behaviors. The individual can respond to her/his environment either by adapting to it or by yielding to its grandeur. Investigating material environment clarifies the role of the phenomenology of space in the structure of ontological perception.

DOI: 10.4324/9781003407768-5

126   *The Phenomenology of Technocultural Space*

Technocultural space, be it as barren as the desert or as complex as a metropolis, invites the characters to adapt. The hermeneutical processes of the characters seem to correspond to the space in which they are found. This shows that characters are not indifferent to technocultural space.

"Technocultural Space" in *End Zone*

Perception at the Margins of Civilization

Perhaps more than any other novel, *End Zone*[1] details the role of minimalistic technocultural space in building perception. DeLillo's second novel narrates the dailiness of a young American football player, Gary Harkness. Gary's aim to become a successful football player is often interjected with his fascination with mass murder. Gary fails several times to graduate from respectable universities because of his inability to adapt to a healthy environment. He is expelled from Syracuse University because of his inappropriate conduct within academic premises. Gary barricades himself with a classmate in an empty room for a whole day to help her "hide from the world" (*End Zone* 18). He then moves to Pennsylvania where he studies rigorously and plays football well. The endless repetitiveness of days, however, proves to be aimless and un-theological. "I tripped on the same step on the same staircase on three successive days" (*End Zone* 19). This incident brings Gary awareness about the futility of team-bound movements. Indulging in repetitive training is not the sort of "oneness" he seeks. Oneness "could not be truly attractive unless it meant oneness with God or the universe or some equally redoubtable super-power" (*End Zone* 19).

Even if Gary is unable to give up football, he fails to accept its shallow atmosphere. He quits the university to seek significance between "the blankest of walls, found only in dull places" (*End Zone* 20). In order to break free from a graver repetition he develops at home, Gary enrolls at the University of Miami. Repetitiveness is transformed into simplicity. However, during a course on nuclear war, Gary finds himself reluctantly enjoying books on all sorts of calamities. "I liked dwelling on the destruction of great cities" (*End Zone* 20). A thrill of excitement runs through him when he reads words such as "thermal hurricane, overkill, circular error probability, post-attack environment" (*End Zone* 21). His shock at the elation of reading about disasters provokes a mental breakdown. His inability to stop going to the library for more books on disasters compels him to leave yet again. He returns home to resume a routine of eating lunch in his bedroom and taking the dog for walks. After a few months, he is granted another chance at East Lansing. This time, Gary departs after a football game. He could not bear being partly responsible for the death of an opponent.

The Phenomenology of Technocultural Space   127

After another hibernation at home, Harkness receives a sudden call from Emmett Creed, a coach at Logos College in Texas. Gary finds, at last, an uncanny harmony between the mercilessness of the Texan desert and his developing perception. He bounds his love for football with deeper meanings inspired by the desert. In this context, the desert is not defined as the wilderness that stands untouched by man. As will be shown, DeLillo seems to define the desert in particular and nature in general as an informational slate extending the thoughts of his characters. The desert represents complementary element of Gary's perception rather than passive unattainable wilderness. This idea is relatively compatible with Raymond Williams' definition of nature as the mirror of human perception.[2] Nature has gradually changed from being a supreme deity, to God's creation, to a passive other, to a "selective breeder" with a historical background (67). Man's relationship with nature changes according to the way it represents itself and according to the way it is perceived by man.

DeLillo employs nature as a technocultural space extending Gary's perception, which redefines nature to include technological properties. Debra B. Shaw borrows Latour's conception of nature as a plural environment that is undistinguished from culture. She points out that nature "is deeply affected by cultural change and by its insertion into the very multiple and differing contexts which give rise to 'matters of concern'" (73).[3] Since nature cannot be separated from culture, it is also inseparable from the technologies functioning within culture. In this way, technocultural space is not limited to urban areas. It extends to the natural environment that seems untouched by man. The Texan desert stirs in Gary a feeling of familiarity involving repetitiveness and simplicity. The barren technocultural space fuses the religious oneness he has sought in Pennsylvania, the simplicity to which he has become acclimatized in Miami, and a spatial protection he could not find in East Lansing.[4] Gary believes that exiling in the Texan desert may offer a refuge from visualizing a history of random violence and from partaking in unethical perusal of disasters. For Tom LeClair, this exile is a response to "the need to stay within his approved but reductive American form of entertainment and the desire to withdraw, to find some authentic self" (59). In the desert, Gary finds a meeting point between "a form of entertainment" and his quest to steer away from personal history.

The desert symbolizes for Gary a tabula rasa of advanced forms of historical representations. The advanced visual history found in *White Noise* and *Underworld* turns to dust in *End Zone*. One of the main goals of DeLillo's second novel is to accentuate the manner in which the flatness of the Texan desert repositions history in Gary's mind. Mark Osteen[5] suggests that flat structures "represent for DeLillo an almost irresistible urge to create sterile spaces, to destroy history by demolishing its architectural symbols" (34). In the ascetic atmosphere of the desert, Gary finds himself in an "end

128   *The Phenomenology of Technocultural Space*

zone"[6] that apparently can free him from the "complexities of meaning and choice."[7] Such complexities lie in the visual enhancement of latent history. As already seen, the screens found in advanced technocultural space, such as supermarkets, living rooms, and hotel rooms, incite relishing on unfortunate events. Gary repudiates, or *tries* to repudiate, any sort of exposure to broadcasts on screens to avoid visual dependence on or addiction to violence.

The stillness of the desert remolds Gary's perception of time and space. Gary seeks to use and to subject time to the service of space. The goal of this utopian vision of postmodern space is to avoid being swamped up by a history of random violence rendered personal. Gary seeks to develop his own perception through the mediation of barren lands:[8]

> Exile in a real place, a place of few bodies and many stones, is just an extension (a packaging) of the other exile, the state of being separated from whatever is left of the center of one's own history. I found comfort in west Texas. There was even pleasure in the daily punishment on the field. I felt that I was better for it, reduced in complexity, a warrior.
>
> (*End Zone* 31)

The structure of the narrative as much as Gary's choices show an honest attempt at asceticism. However, Gary's struggles prevent him from maintaining the long-sought harmony, which leads him to endure a perpetual fight against the overload needs of the mind.

In a way, Gary's retreat to the desert is not so much an escape as much as a quest to develop self-understanding. Gary seeks to understand why he is drawn to destruction. In the desert, DeLillo places Gary in a space for reflection, a space that can stimulate his imagination in order to gain a better perception. In Texas, he finds himself in an atmosphere advocated by his father. "It paid, in his [father's] view, to follow the simplest, most pioneer of rhythms.... the mellow rocking of chairs.... Beyond these honest latitudes lay nothing but chaos" (*End Zone* 17). Similarly to Matt Shay, Gary secretly enjoys destruction and gore; and similarly to the Video Kid, he witnesses an unexpected random death. The chaos described by Gary's father could summarize the uncertainty and randomness seen in Chapter 2. Chaos then would refer to the events and imaginative possibilities that Gary fails to control. Because he cannot prevent himself from exploring and enjoying destruction and death, Gary retreats toward "eternal work cycle."[9]

In his quest to relinquish personal history, Gary espouses a ritualistic dailiness in a minimalist "zone." Only in the desert can Gary ascribe to a "diminished existence,"[10] an existence reduced to "[s]implicity, repetition, solitude, starkness, discipline upon discipline" (*End Zone* 30). It seems that

The Phenomenology of Technocultural Space   129

life in the desert is a diminished existence because it restitutes a symbolic distance with the unprecedented proximity of historical events. Gary trades the televisual repetitiveness of events for a ritualistic pristine repetitiveness. He is neither distracted by monitors nor lost in the collision of history with real time. Henri Lefebvre argues in *The Production of Space* (1974) that space and time are inseparable, so a change in the perception of space is inevitably followed by a change in the perception of time (339).[11] Gary is found in a space that restores the succession of past, present, and future. Therefore, in *End Zone*, time is not absorbed by the perpetual present of latent history. It dilates with the atmosphere of the desert. Gary's vision extends to "few bodies and many stones" (*End Zone* 31). Consequently, his reality is uninterrupted by intrusive superreal and underreal images, or so he would like to believe.

Even if the minimalistic space of the desert reduces the visual enhancement of latent history, it is still not an empty space. During a school break, Gary ventures in the land where there "is no water but only rock / Rock and no water and the sandy road."[12] Gary notices in the seemingly dead land the presence of movements. "Something sudden, a movement, turned out to be sunlight on paint, a painted stone, one stone, black in color, identifiably black, a single round stone, painted black, carefully painted" (*End Zone* 42–43). Gary repetitiveness expresses his surprise in discovering that the desert is not as deserted as it seems. Later in the novel, it is revealed that the "Stonepainter," the "Metaphorist of the desert," is his roommate Anatole Bloomberg. Bloomberg explains that painting the stone is an action against historical violence. The stone is the memorial of his Jewish mother, who has been shot by a lunatic (*End Zone* 188).

By painting the stone, Bloomberg attempts to "leave behind the old words and aromas and guilts" (*End Zone* 188). In this way, the desert is not as empty as it is believed; it contains profound human symbols and analogies. This does not mean that nonhuman entities are reduced from the equation either. Rather, it means that the desert as a natural space is not devoid of human implication. As highlighted by William Cronon:[13]

> This is not to say that the nonhuman world is somehow unreal or a mere figment of our imaginations—far from it. But the way we describe and understand that world is so entangled with our own values and assumptions that the two can never be fully separated.
>
> (30)

Elise Martucci completes this thought when she looks at nature and culture as facets of the same coin.[14] "If we understand that nature is a culturally constructed concept, and sometimes even objects, we must also recognize that 'nature' does not have an absolute definition" (19). The painted

130   *The Phenomenology of Technocultural Space*

stone attests to the entanglement of nature and culture/history. If the city is the very expression of the individual's values and expressions, the desert inscribes and transmits a larger symbolic construct of human information.

Martucci posits that Gary, among other characters, does not acknowledge the physical environment of the desert. For her, Gary journeys toward "the myth of the American West"[15] rather than toward an actual "stony" place. This confusion, Martucci concludes, leads Gary to a "placeless" destination, for he is journeying toward an inexistent concept (20). However, the black stone points out the possibility of experiencing a significant moment in barren lands. When Gary notices the stone, it divulges the presence of history in the desert.[16] This presence could be symbolically read in terms of the presence felt in "The Wasteland."

Who is the third who walks always beside you?
When I count, there are only you and I together
But when I look ahead up the white road
There is always another one walking beside you.[17]

Up ahead lays the black stone which becomes not only an emblem of history but also a point of familiarity. Since it provides a better sense of location, the stone is sought by Gary whenever he returns to the desert.[18] As corroborated by Curtis A. Yehnert,[19] "DeLillo portrays the individual as inseparable from the environment, the relationship mutually constitutive and interdependent" (359). It is thus probable that the interaction born between the desert and Gary deters a feeling of placelessness.

By attempting to reduce the layers of perception that characterize latent history, Gary does not relinquish the outer world altogether. He rather interacts with the presence felt in the desert. This interaction is possible because Gary does not find himself in a space devoid of symbolism. As expressed by Henri Lefebvre, "[w]hen it comes to space, can we legitimately speak of scarcity? The answer is no" (*The Production of Space* 330).

The Ontological Internalization of Outer Space

To the question "[w]ho is the third who walks always beside you?" Gary answers "[t]he sun. The desert. The sky. The silence. The flat stones. The insects.... The west and east. The song, the color, the smell of the earth. Blast area. Fire area. Body-burn area" (*End Zone* 89–90). The spiritual aura of the desert accompanies him with every step he takes and so do his thoughts. The vastness of the desert expands Gary's apocalyptic fantasies. The young man is unable to limit his thoughts to a "that terrain so flat and bare, suggestive of the end of recorded time" (*End Zone* 30). Gary's thoughts wander to images of "Blast area. Fire area. Body-burn area"

The Phenomenology of Technocultural Space 131

because the desert reflects his perception. The desert is, therefore, Gary's point of interaction between nature, culture, and technology. Ontological phenomenology is used as an approach to demonstrate the manner in which technocultural space contributes to the development of Gary's perception. The influence that European writers and existential philosophy have on DeLillo is well known (Veggian 38). This approach is compatible with the aim of the section not only because it is adequate for reading Don DeLillo, but also because it sheds light on the material and intrinsic manifestations of technoculture.

Before demonstrating the manner in which the desert contributes to Gary's perception, it is important to clarify the technocultural relationship between nature and technology. The natural and technological spheres of Gary's life are intertwined. Technology is inevitably immersed in nature, and nature is inevitably part of technology. Nature is not an empty space that is passively subjected to the changes brought by Man. Technology is not the neutral set of tools used to concretize changes. Rather, the nature–technology intermingling represents an "ambiguously natural and crafted" hybrid space.[20]

For Donna Haraway, the separation of nature and technology advocated by the western tradition is no longer functional in postmodern times (*Simians, Cyborgs, and Women* 150). This stands true for Gary's position in the world; he is particularly conscious of the way his body is shaped by angles and points in space, such as a small dorm room:

I believed it mattered terribly where we were situated and which way we were facing. Words move the body into position. In time the position itself dictates events.... What you [Bloomberg] and I say this evening won't add up to much. We'll remember only where we sat, which way our feet pointed, at what angle our realities met.

(*End Zone* 45–46)

While dialogues might have an immediate but fleeting importance, the experience of space is ingrained in memory. Gary retains how, back to the wall, he is facing Bloomberg, who is lying on his own bed. The "situatedness" or the "placing of bodies"[21] is not an optional device of description. As remarked by Martucci, "DeLillo keeps the material world at the forefront of his novels, and thereby emphasizing the lasting significance of place to our consciousness" (2). DeLillo continually returns to the role that space plays in the dailiness of his characters because it is an integral part of the human being.

Gary's "situatedness" is not limited to a consequential architectural structure, such as the dorm room. It holds true for scarcer spaces as well. During one of his walks in the desert, Gary declares that nothing else is

132 *The Phenomenology of Technocultural Space*

moving other than his feet. "Nothing else stirred, not even waning light folding over stone and not the slightest flick of an insect at the perimeter of vision" (*End Zone* 88). Yet, shortly after this statement, a vehicle makes its way toward him. It disturbs the silence and stasis of the desert, "a small murderous hum, as of unnamed sounds at the end of a hall" (*End Zone* 89). The unexpected motion allegorically reveals the intermingling of nature and technology, and it is correlated to the familiar space of a hall. It seems that even when no sign of a living being is noticed in the desert, the technological is still heard and felt.

For DeLillo, as for Haraway, this intermingling of nature and technology attests to a "confusion of boundaries"[22] that characterizes technocultural space. In an interview, DeLillo refers to space as a landscape, "whether it's a desert, a small room, a hole in the ground."[23] The author does not define the natural and the technological spaces differently. Any sort of landscape, or space, reflects the characters' perception. Therefore, "technocultural space" could be defined as the environmental product of a nature–culture equation expressed through technology.

Technocultural space encompasses the material environment within which DeLillo's characters exist. In this context, "environment" does not refer to nature only. Rather, as Martucci posits, the "environment is an integration of culture and nature" (2). "Technocultural space" refers also to the spatial dailiness that is constituted of the "brightness" and "waves and radiations" of technoculture. "Brightness" denotes the image technologies seen in the previous chapters. "Waves and radiations" encompass the invisible energies that carry information in space. Space contains the technological material that mediates the characters' hermeneutical processes. The interpretation of the characters' beliefs, behaviors, and activities depends partly on technocultural space. DeLillo, therefore, views technocultural space as an interactional environment. Such environment stresses the phenomenological interactions created between nature, culture, technology, and beings.

Throughout the novel, Gary meticulously describes the phenomenological aspect of technocultural space. He focuses not on the daily reception of events, but on what Maurice Merleau-Ponty calls "bodily space."[24] As a practical system, Gary's "bodily space" is defined as "the matrix of his habitual action.... his body is at his disposal as a means of ingress into a familiar surrounding, [and as] the means of expression of a gratuitous and free spatial thought" (119). Gary perceives space not in terms of distance but in terms of proximity. His actions depend partly on his bodily space. As he walks barefoot under the burning sky of the desert, Gary is anchored in its atmosphere. "The thing to do, I thought, is to walk in circles. This is demanded by the mythology of all deserts and wasted places" (*End Zone* 42). Gary's body does not dictate movement as much as participates in a

The Phenomenology of Technocultural Space   133

primitive and inclusive practice. This practice involves but is not limited to the identity of space. Similarly to buzzards, Gary "circles" a goal that consists of being able to merge with the scarceness of desert. Such amalgamation is supposed to distance him from latent history and to ingrain in him the atmosphere of the desert.

By distancing himself from skyscrapers, supermarkets, and hotel rooms, Gary experiences a state of "ascetic ideal." Friedrich Nietzsche[25] distinguishes several representations of ascetic ideals. One of them describes a temporary need for scarcity sought in the desert. Nietzsche advances that ascetic actors withdraw in what he calls "stage desert" in an attempt to avoid the technocultural magnitude of the city.[26] In Nietzsche's words, "stage desert" means:

> a voluntary obscurity perhaps.... a dislike of noise, honor, newspapers, influence.... an occasional association with harmless, cheerful beasts and birds whose sight is refreshing; mountains for company, but not dead ones.... perhaps even a room in a full, utterly commonplace hotel, where one is certain to go unrecognized and can talk to anyone with impunity.
>
> (109)

The atmosphere of the stage desert is felt during Gary's walks near campus. Gary explores the desert during school breaks without venturing too far. He seeks seclusion from the noise of latent history but he still cannot bear the silence of the desert (*End Zone* 48). He tries to be emptied from his morbid thoughts. Yet, he continuously finds himself exposed "to an unintentional cycle in which pleasure nourished itself on the black bones of revolution and dread" (*End Zone* 43). Hence, the stage desert is a field not only of heat and stones but of suggestions as well. "There were profits here," Gary reflects, "things that could be used to make me stronger; the small fanatical monk who clung to my liver would thrive on such ascetic scraps" (*End Zone* 30).

Such scraps refer to Gary's humble bodily space, humble but not devoid of "the black bones of revolution and dread." Despite his aim to seek isolation and scarcity in the desert, Gary cannot relinquish his ontological inclination toward violence. Gary's state-of-mind as an externalization of violence in barren lands is best described by Lefebvre. For Lefebvre, as inherent qualities in space, violence, and knowledge clash. Violence is a power that has the capacity to divide and/or reunite elements of knowledge. Arming himself with violence, Gary feels powerful in the desert. "Nowhere is the confrontation between knowledge and power, between understanding and violence, more direct than it is in connection with intact space and space broken up" (Lefebvre, *The Production of Space* 358).

134   *The Phenomenology of Technocultural Space*

The stage desert, as "intact space and space broken up," informs Gary's encounter with his being. This encounter is almost never devoid of violence, as it always seeks to form ontological enlightenment.

The stage desert stimulates particular reactions in Gary because it responds to vague sense of *being*. As he walks barefoot on the dry burning playa, Gary makes sure to remain within a technocultural horizon. "I was careful to keep the tallest of the campus buildings in sight. This was a practical measure, nonritualistic, meant to offset the saintly feet" (*End Zone* 42). Even if the purpose of this precaution is to unsettle the ascetic atmosphere, it is not an inauthentic gesture. John A. McClure confirms this idea when he suggests that DeLillo's successful characters seek oneness with "earthliness."[27] They seek to be "reconnected to a viscerally experienced, sacramentally infused world that is neither secular nor spiritual in the common sense of these terms" (65). Gary's precaution reveals the intermingled space of nature and technology in which he is "thrown," as Martin Heidegger would word it.[28] In Heidegger's view, thrownness "belongs to an entity which in each case is its possibilities, and is them in such a way that it understands itself in these possibilities and in terms of them, projecting itself upon them" (225). Simply put, thrownness means that individuals find themselves in a factual context that they have not chosen but within which they have to advance.

Because Gary is "thrown" into the world, he does not perceive the buildings and the stage desert as neutral or negligible spaces. Both spaces are part of a larger environment within which his "state-of-mind" works (Heidegger 174). State-of-mind refers to a state prior to the psychological manifestation of a mood. This "fallow" state allows individuals to build connections within the world. The connections built in this context are more primordial than the connections built between the external and internal aspects of existence. They do not split in a shallow relationship between subject and object. Rather, they are the possibilities that emerge from an indirect encounter with state-of-mind, by means of projection. In the process of thinking or perceiving, the human being, as Dasein, always builds connections by projecting possibilities. In this way, the human being is conscious of something as something rather than as an empty object (174–176). Gary projects his state-of-mind onto external possibilities. Even if state-of-mind is generally not perceived directly, DeLillo still gives a constructive reading of its presence. This reading points to a primordial process of thought that is constructed in the technocultural space of the desert.

The nature of Gary's thoughts shows that even if he is physically located in the desert, he does not relinquish his morbid fantasies. On the contrary, the Texan desert seems compatible with his "pleasure principle."[29] Gary leaves the city to avoid being exposed to the advanced technology that

The Phenomenology of Technocultural Space   135

overwhelms his perception. However, the distance he takes from latent history does not strip him from the capacity to view the world tele-visually. Gary finds in the desert a bodily space that extends his imagination. He looks down at the dry road, and an image arises from the ashes of the dead. "I thought of men embedded in the ground, all killed, billions, flesh cauterized into the earth, bits of bone and hair and nails, man-planet, a fresh intelligence revolving through the system" (*End Zone* 89). The space of perception (the desert) and the mode of perception (imagination) stimulate imaginative possibilities. These possibilities are not provoked by the advanced technology of latent history. They emanate from Gary's state-of-mind in barren lands.

The desert reorients Gary toward a perception which is not dictated by image technologies. The desert itself extends his perception. Space and perception are inseparable; they help Gary develop an understanding not only about the world but also about his very being. "Space and perception generally represent, at the core of the subject, the fact of his birth, the perpetual contribution of his bodily being, a communication with the world more ancient than thought" (Merleau-Ponty 296). In this way, Gary's retreat to the desert is also a retreat to "the virtual reality of his imagination" (Dewey 29).

Tele-Visuality in the Desert

Through the intermediary of language, DeLillo discloses Gary's process of thought in the technocultural space of the desert. At some point, Gary eases himself on the steps leading to dormitories. He closes his eyes in order to move to the "biblical phase of the afternoon, the peak of [his] new simplicity" (*End Zone* 54). The desert and the stairs of the building are implicated in his spiritual goal. Gary prepares himself "to think of night, desert, sorrowful forests" (*End Zone* 55). Instead, Gary's state-of-mind is manifested through a process of thought that sways between the technocultural and the instinctive.

Gary notices two young women walking toward a dormitory. In this moment, Gary has a similar reaction to his ancestor, Stephen Dedalus. "He felt a subtle, dark and murmurous presence penetrate his being and fire him with a brief iniquitous lust" (Joyce 126).[30] The "dark and murmurous presence," a visual one, shatters down his resolve to seek asceticism and simplicity. It is worthwhile to quote at length a passage that illustrates this point:

I thought of flaming limbs, a moody whore's mouth, hair the color of bourbon. Quietly I sweated, motionless on the steps. A girl in a cotton dress on a bed with brass posts. A ceiling fan rubbing the moist air. Scent

136   *The Phenomenology of Technocultural Space*

of slick magazines. She'd be poorborn, the dumbest thing in Texas, a girl from a gulf town, moviemade, her voice an unlaundered drawl, fierce and coarse, fit for bad-tempered talking blues. I listened to Bobby hum. I had forgotten to add a new word to my vocabulary that day and I resolved to do it before nightfall. I tried to get back to the girl again. It was a different one this time, roundish, more than plump, almost monumental in her measureless dimensions. She removed her tessellated bluegreen sweater. It was all happening in a Mexico City hotel. I heard Bobby stir. The girl became the hotel itself, an incredible cake of mosaic stone. I continued to perspire quietly.

(End Zone 55)

In this passage, DeLillo enacts a complex narrative construct to stress the movement between outer space and inner responses. This sort of narrative is characterized by the intermingling of visual and linguistic tools to build a certain atmosphere. This is the result of DeLillo's exposure to a diverse and rich heritage. As elaborated by Veggian: "DeLillo has often noted modern European authors such as James Joyce or film directors such as Michelangelo Antonioni, artists whose works explore similar emotions, as inspiration for [estranged] moods" (9). Such heritage contributed to formulating Gary's experience through what could be understood as a tele-visual narrative.

"Tele-visuality" is defined in this context as a visual externalization of Gary's fantasies. Gary's fantasies are being spread out on the landscape. His "tele-visuality" is a semi-transparent imaginative film that remolds itself to be compatible with physical space. It is worthwhile to explore the lengthy passage quoted above to demonstrate how DeLillo produces a tele-visual multilayered narrative. Taking apart the multilayered narrative can disclose the implication of technocultural space in Gary's layered state-of-mind. However, before exploring this state-of-mind, it is important to take a short detour to clarify the roots of the multilayered narrative technique used by DeLillo.

In order to depict Gary's state-of-mind in the dailiness of the stage desert, DeLillo uses a multilayered narrative. It could be said that DeLillo seeks to catch the spirit of a multi-referential framework of daily experience by using a narrative technique that is appropriate to it. He borrows James Joyce's narrative method to reach that aim. For DeLillo, Joyce belongs to a category of authors who write in the mode of "world narrative." In an interview, DeLillo declares that "Joyce turned the book into a world with *Ulysses* and *Finnegans Wake*. Today, the world has become a book—more precisely a news story or television show or piece of film footage."[31] This technique is multilayered because it fuses the spontaneity of the stream of consciousness with the structure of cinematic narrative.

The Phenomenology of Technocultural Space 137

Indebted to the modernist form, DeLillo borrows the stream of consciousness technique to experiment with visual narrative. He seeks to lay bare the spontaneous flow of perception, which emanates from the borders of Gary's consciousness. Gary sways between his physical sensations and the internal pictorial units that come to his mind. In order to stress the intermingling of Gary's technocultural space and his state-of-mind, DeLillo uses short sentences. These sentences convey two sorts of stream of consciousness. The first describes Gary's sensations. Even if he is captivated by his fantasies, Gary feels the perspiration that both his thoughts and the warm weather provoke. "I thought of flaming limbs.... Quietly I sweated, motionless on the steps." He is also aware of his teammate, Bobby Luke, sitting next to him. He does not see Bobby but he senses his presence. "I listened to Bobby hum.... I heard Bobby stir."

Gary remains responsive to his external world as a spontaneous flow of images arises in his mind. These images form a pictorial stream of consciousness. Benjamin Lee demonstrates that modernist authors, specifically Virginia Woolf, have developed a particular method to convey their view of the self, consciousness, and unconsciousness.[32] They use a "cinematographique technique" in order to "zoom in" on a specific occurrence (387). DeLillo was inspired by this technique most probably, as it is evident in his novels.

DeLillo zooms in to the smallest pictorial unit that forms in Gary's mind. In order to achieve this, DeLillo seems to fuse the stream of consciousness technique with cinematic *montage*. Veggian supports the idea that DeLillo uses a cinematic narrative technique, insisting that "[a]fter literature, cinema is the most important source of narrative technique, as well as affect, in DeLillo's fiction.... He will at times combine literary language with visual-cinematic narrative technique in his fiction, and to spectacular effect" (19–20). Weaving these distinct structures lead DeLillo to integrate cinematic technique within a linguistic form. James Gourley suggests that DeLillo experiments with non-linguistic technocultural mediums employed *within* language.[33] The experiment results "in representation that communicates, whilst also creating a metalinguistic discourse commenting on the problem of representation itself" (224).

In *End Zone*, this metalinguistic construct is manifested through the connectedness of Gary's internal and external aspects of life. This idea is supported by several critics. LeClair skillfully parallels the way the connectedness of the abstract and the concrete is built by DeLillo and the way it is lived by Gary:

While Harkness oscillates between simplistic extremes of the abstract and concrete or attempts to fuse them in one Word, DeLillo creates a

138 *The Phenomenology of Technocultural Space*

system that shows the reciprocal relations between abstract and concrete, codes and lives, ideas and talk, both in the novel and in the world.

(LeClair 60–61)

Technology is implicated not only in Gary's external dailiness but also in his internal processes. Gary conveys tele-visual scenes in a linguistic form. For Gourley, the technological motif "emphasizes the ability of language to conduct a transformation, where the visual in a text is foregrounded and becomes a successful act of aesthetic creation" (224). Veggian inverts this perception in a way that it emphasizes the role of language. For him, "the movement of characters through a metalinguistic narrative space is allegorical in that it approximates the reader's movement through the novel's language. It is a physical experience of the texture of words" (44). What is important is that the critics acknowledge DeLillo's experimental kinesis. This last involves the interaction of DeLillo's characters with their technocultural world through a metalinguistic discourse.

Gilles Deleuze's[34] description of the structure of a scene seems compatible with the manner in which DeLillo uses cinematic montage. What is particular about DeLillo's use of cinematic techniques is that he adopts the spirit of cinematic representation. Even if Deleuze is mainly concerned with film, there are important affinities between his reading of film and DeLillo's use of cinematic stream of consciousness. For Deleuze, "the plane of movement-images is a mobile section of a Whole which changes, that is, of a duration or of a 'universal becoming'" (68). An image succeeds the next in an incessant state of becoming. In the passage given earlier, each scene is constituted of shots separated by commas, and each cut of the scene is represented by a full stop thus giving grammar a particular function.

Benjamin Lee explores the grammatical significance in modernist subjective narratives. Even if he is not concerned with cinematic narrative techniques, he makes a valid point as regards the role of grammatical patterns in enriching the imaginative reading of ontological images. Lee systematically explains that "cultural ontologies of 'what exists' are referential projections of the categorical structures of interlocking grammatical patterns and can sometimes override these primary subjective experiences" (366). In this context, the role of grammatical patterns and punctuation is not limited to structuring the sentence or conveying a subjective state. Their role consists also of highlighting the sequence of the *images* themselves in their involvement in Gary's stream of consciousness. These scenes form a Whole that seems unconnected, but they are meticulously arranged by DeLillo. The author cuts Gary's visual representation of thoughts into shots and rearranges them in a way that includes technocultural space. Gary first imagines "flaming limbs," which recalls his inclination to morbidity.

The first shot is followed by two close-ups depicting Gary's sexual fantasies.[35] "I thought of flaming limbs, a moody whore's mouth, hair the color of bourbon." The close-ups are a virtual conjunction that add affects to Gary's arousal by the female body.

For Deleuze, affects are connectors that do not aim merely to picture shallow representations of individuals and things. "They have singularities which enter into virtual conjunction and each time constitute a complex entity. It is like points of melting, of boiling, of condensation, of coagulation" (103). As already explained, the positioning of bodies is important to Gary. The shot that is constituted of a "girl in a cotton dress on a bed with brass posts" represents Gary's arousal. The equivalent of the close-ups in the external world is Gary's quiet sweating. The scene is followed by a "girl in a cotton dress on a bed with brass posts." The inclusion of the bed's description is not invasive. It recalls Gary's awareness of the positioning of bodies in technocultural space. In a condensed scene, the female body is captured in a specific position to stimulate Gary.

Gary does not remain physically neutral to the scenes he imagines, and the scenes that he imagines are not unrelated to his bodily needs either. Gary pictures "[a] ceiling fan rubbing the moist air." This close-up not only describes the larger context in which Gary puts "the dumbest thing in Texas," but it also refers to Gary's need for fresher weather. "Sunlight covered everything. I smelled casual sweat collecting under my arms and soon the soreness in my body began to ease just slightly" (*End Zone* 54). Gary's ascetic imposition is weakened with the imagined cool air of a ceiling fan.

A reminder to add a word to his vocabulary interrupts the succession of images. When he tries to return to the "poorborn," "moviemade" girl, Gary fails to resuscitate her. The interruption reminds Gary of his pledge to abandon physical urges. He is caught between carrying on his erotic scenes and seeking scarcity of thought. DeLillo succeeds in constructing such entanglement because he brings together language and embodiment.[36] The entanglement that Gary experiences leads to the (involuntary) invocation of surreal sequences.

> It was a different one this time, roundish, more than plump, almost monumental in her measureless dimensions. She removed her tessellated bluegreen sweater. It was all happening in a Mexico City hotel. I heard Bobby stir. The girl became the hotel itself, an incredible cake of mosaic stone. I continued to perspire quietly
>
> (*End Zone* 55)

DeLillo's use of a surrealist genre[37] accentuates the manner in which Gary pictures his sexual fantasies in terms of his surroundings. James Giles argues

140   *The Phenomenology of Technocultural Space*

that this surreal anti-eroticism is an attempt to dehumanize the imagined female partner.[38] It could be added that in such case Gary uses the image of his surroundings as an escape from the female sexual partner.

The interpretation given by Giles remains one possibility among others. Gary is not indifferent to his surroundings. He finds all around him an expression of his inner thoughts. The evolution of the surreal shots calls attention to Gary's ability to imagine unrelated scenes that are still connected on some level. Such connections are possible because what Gary primarily *sees* is the representation of an invisible flow of information through space. Information, as a set of diverse data, destabilizes the unity and order that Gary seeks to find. Gary would like to be "de-multiplied"[39] from the chaos of latent history. However, multiplicity does not subside. It is rather transformed according to the technocultural space of the desert.

The surreal image born in Gary's mind does not refer to one single facet of his state-of-mind. Gary is conflicted between maintaining anti-eroticism and giving in to uncontrollable desires. In this way, the building that emerges from the roundish young woman could refer to the dormitory toward which the two young women are walking. It could also refer to Gary's girlfriend, Myna Corbett, whom Gary describes as "an explosion over the desert" (*End Zone* 68). This image pertains not only to Gary's interest in mass murder, but also to his violated asceticism.[40] It could be said that Gary does not eliminate erotic images represented by the transformation of a roundish young woman into a building. He delves deeper into the erotic through the expansion of the female body. The contradiction that emerges from this reading stresses the struggle that ceaselessly grows in Gary's mind.

Gary does not visualize simple and linear images. Images of various complexities, structures, and meanings rush into his mind. His memorized technocultural space becomes part of the layers of his interpretation of the world and the self. The deeper he dives into the sequences of images, the darker and more surrealist the environment of his desires becomes. Buildings in particular are molded to fill gaps in Gary's stream of consciousness. His imagined scenes, therefore, imply that the role of his environment is not limited to passive outer representations. Gary is part of his environment and his environment is part of his thoughts either consciously or unconsciously.

Technocultural space is neither neutral nor inconsequential. It is an environment that contributes to the character's developing perception. However, characters react differently to the structure of technocultural space when this last is itself too complex. If Gary's mind is submerged by "an incredible cake of mosaic stone," which is imagined tele-visually in barren lands, what happens when the enormous building is real and imposing? DeLillo answers this question in *Mao II* and *Players*. The two

The Phenomenology of Technocultural Space 141

novels explore the manner in which the body is dwarfed physically and symbolically by the metropolis.

Encounters with Technocultural Parallax in *Players*

The Complexity of Postmodern Architecture

Charles Jencks[41] argues that the late twentieth century has known drastic architectural changes. Familiar structures were demolished and a sense of identity fell with them (51). Against the backdrop of multiplicity and complexity, the new buildings uphold infinite layers of meaning and references. One recalls, for instance, the layers of meaning enclosed in living rooms, supermarkets, and hotels seen in the previous chapters. Jencks believes that the postmodern space, skyscrapers, in particular, encompasses layers that have not made "effective links with the city and history" (52). Becoming themselves mini-cities,[42] skyscrapers call into question their inhabitants' ability to adapt to the new technocultural era that they represent. Fredric Jameson[43] suggests that this technocultural space has already transcended the capacity of the human body to locate itself (44). The alienation that ensues puts in conflict the new forms of buildings and the individual's familiar bodily space. This raises a question regarding the individual's response to her/his new environment. Since individuals are used to simpler forms of technocultural space, how do they adapt, if at all, to the new imposing architectural structures?

DeLillo explores this question in *Players* (1977) and *Mao II* (1991). He tests the claims proposed by Jencks and Jameson by putting his characters within the context of skyscrapers. For the author, buildings such as the Twin Towers[44] are both self-referential and open to a "multiplicity of function."[45] This multiplicity can either strengthen the individual's agency or refer back to the buildings themselves. When the Twin Towers are understood in terms of their technocultural grandeur, they seem to contribute to creating self-alienation in characters, as is the case for Keith Neudecker, prior to their fall. Instead of reflecting each individual's sense of being, the Towers seem to scatter the self and absorb it within their mirrored walls. Nevertheless, it would be erroneous to believe that DeLillo blames buildings for the phenomenology of alienation. He rather propounds a reading of the characters' mode of adaptation, or lack of adaptation, to the sort of tower that "soars to heaven and goes unpunished by God."[46]

Skyscrapers symbolize a transitional complexity that has been too sudden to be fully absorbed. In DeLillo's conception of the Towers, the first transition consists of the fast actualization of the buildings themselves, as he shows in *Mao II*. This transition epitomizes that which Jameson calls "a mutation in built space" (38). The Towers' enormity was a mutation

142 *The Phenomenology of Technocultural Space*

that represented a new limit reached by technology. In DeLillo's view, this mutation indicates the attainment of a revolutionary structure orchestrated by the advance of technological methods: "The World Trade towers were not only an emblem of advanced technology but a justification, in a sense, for technology's irresistible will to realise in solid form whatever becomes theoretically allowable. Once defined, every limit must be reached."[47] This passage could be read in terms of Aristotle's definition of potentiality and actuality. In the case of the Towers, potentiality and actuality refer to a state of rational change in time. A potential construct (theoretical Tower) has been actualized into a concrete building.[48] However, the limit of this mutation, reached in the 1970s, has been too fast. As echoed by Jameson, "we ourselves, the human subjects who happen into this new space, have not kept pace with that evolution" (38). Individuals have not been able to adapt adequately to the Towers because of the speed by which they have been constructed.

If the fall of the Twin Towers revives and deepens the uncertainty born with the Kennedy assassination, their construction had not been without confusion. In *Mao II*, the proximity of the World Trade Center to the renowned photographer Brita Nilsson creates a phenomenological disquiet in her dailiness. She is unwillingly catenated to the elevation of the Twin Towers, buildings that gradually shadow her environment. She observes the transition of the comfortable space of her technocultural neighborhood into a foreign construct.

> Where I live, okay, there's a rooftop chaos, a jumble, four, five, six, seven storeys, and it's water tanks, laundry lines, antennas, belfries, pigeon lofts, chimney pots, everything human about the lower island— little crouched gardens, statuary, painted signs. And I wake up to this and love it and depend on it. But it's all being flattened and hauled away so they can build their towers
>
> (*Mao II* 39)

Brita depends on simple structures because she does not perceive them passively. She lives them, takes them up, assumes them, and discovers their immanent significance.[49] The movement of the Twin Towers to actuality displaces Brita's familiar bodily space. Her "lower island" does not constitute a landscape to which she is indifferent. Rather, the simple and humanly neighborhood functions on a deeper level of her being. She depends not so much on the environment she grasps with her senses. Brita depends on the implied space represented by the "lower island." This last is part of her identity as much as her environment.

Brita formulates a (partial) understanding of the Twin Towers once they are constructed and rented, that is, once their transition to actuality is

The Phenomenology of Technocultural Space 143

complete. "The size is deadly. But having two of them is like a comment, it's like a dialogue, only I don't know what they're saying" (*Mao II* 40). Brita seems to realize that the Towers are a provocative comment. Not only do they attest to the fast transition from potentiality to actuality, but they also reflect their own meaning. "If there was only one tower instead of two.... they interact. There is a play of light" (*Mao II* 40). This "play of light" could be understood in terms of Slovaj Žižek's "architectural parallax."[50]

> "Parallax," according to its common definition, is the apparent displacement of an object (the shift of its position against a background), caused by a change in observational position that provides a new line of sight. The philosophical twist to be added, of course, is that the observed difference is not simply "subjective," thanks to the fact that it is the same object existing "out there" which is seen from two different points of view. It is rather that, as Hegel would have put it, subject and object are inherently "mediated," so that an "epistemological" shift in the subject's point of view always reflects an "ontological" shift in the object itself.
>
> (245)

Architectural parallax is insightful for understanding the postmodern technocultural space as long as the subject/object duality is avoided. The Towers are not passive constructs. Their play of light is, for instance, the result of the interaction of their mirrored walls with the light of the moving sun. The Towers seem to be a provocative comment because their enormity offers myriads of possibilities. These possibilities reflect back to Brita, who is a viewer more than a subject. Brita understands the suggested movements of the Towers from her viewpoint, and the Towers' inherent shifts send messages that are open to interpretation. Brita, however, has the impression that the interaction taking place between the Towers is closed off and exclusive. She feels displaced by the Towers not only because of their grandeur, but also because of their presumed inaccessibility.

Either closed off or accessible, the Towers are in any case a comment about technological advance. In "The Ruins of the Future," DeLillo stresses the centrality that technology is gaining in the postmodern dailiness: "Technology is our fate, our truth. It is what we mean when we call ourselves the only superpower on the planet. The materials and methods we devise make it possible for us to claim our future."[51] The fall of the Twin Towers is irrelevant to this context, as they still represent postmodern architecture. They embody the concretization of technological advance. DeLillo believes that technology, as the fate and truth of the American dailiness, is not limited to the visible world. As will be argued,

144 *The Phenomenology of Technocultural Space*

its implication in dailiness contributes to the shaping of one's conception of the self and the world.

Pammy's Phenomenological Mode of Being

"Boxing in" the Self

If Brita feels displaced by the construction of the Towers, Pammy Wynant is completely destabilized by their enormity. Pammy, one of the two main protagonists of *Players*, works for a Grief Management firm, located at the North Tower of the World Trade Center. With the objective of understanding and assimilating grief, the firm as much as the rest of the novel is built as a "quasi-cinematic crosscutting."[52] This crosscutting reflects the shallowness of characters that are overwhelmed by an alien bodily space. In *Players*, DeLillo highlights the individual's lack of the appropriate mechanisms to adapt to fast technocultural changes. The reader is faced with empty selves that are too surpassed by their technocultural space to try tidying their realities (Dewey 50). The narrative describes Pammy's environmental encounters in particular as depthless. Similarly to her husband, Lyle Wynant, Pammy is a linear character. She tries to contain "what for most could be a considerable anxiety" (51). Similarly to Karen, Pammy avoids developing a personal history by maintaining a degree of order and simplicity in her dailiness. Pammy keeps a safe distance from her sense of self through becoming completely immersed in technocultural space. Even if the complex technocultural space within which she is "thrown" proves to be challenging, she finds a protective atmosphere in its enormity.

Tired of exploring "the palest limits of the city," Pammy turns her life into a set of repetitive activities and trajectories. However, her routine is constantly being challenged by her inability to adapt to a complicated technocultural space. Even if she spends an important amount of time in her workplace, she keeps confusing the Twin Towers "Pammy stood in the sky lobby of the south tower of the World Trade Center.... She wanted to go down, although she worked on the eighty-third floor, because she was in the wrong building" (*Players* 14). Pammy is incapable of identifying the Towers even if she goes to work five days a week. To use Merleau-Ponty's expression, she is incapable of transferring her "center of gravity" "into the new spectacle" of the Towers (293). Pammy's bodily space has not adapted to the Towers' "tyrannic grandeur" (*Players* 24). She feels that their architectural parallax transcends her. "Four times a day she was dwarfed, progressively midgeted, walking across that purplish-blue rug" (*Players* 24). The Towers represent "an imperative to grow new organs, to expand our sensorium and our body to some new, yet unimaginable, perhaps ultimately impossible, dimensions" (Jameson 39). Because Pammy has been unable to

The Phenomenology of Technocultural Space 145

develop the "new organs," she has recourse to the available option. She attempts to understand her environment by becoming part of it.

Pammy attempts to adapt her sensorium to the Towers by defining lobbies as "spaces" and elevators as "places" (*Players* 24). The "space" of a lobby is a sort of universal connector that helps her make sense of offices and individuals. The lobbies of the Twin Towers seem to be familiar "spaces" from which Pammy obtains comfort.[53] Conversely, as "places," Pammy is wary of elevators because they are too large to be "enclosures." She needs to remind herself that they could trap her if they ever stop working (*Players* 23). Her wariness is further accentuated by the fact that they have different doors for entering and exiting, "certainly a distinguishing feature of places more than of elevators" (*Players* 24). However, these "gigantic kinetic sculptures"[54] are not only the means by which Pammy rises and falls. They bring about a daily transition in the psyche of their riders. As Jameson insists, "elevators here henceforth replace movement but also, and above all, designate themselves as new reflexive signs and emblems of movement proper" (42). Not merely the result of engineering and architectural progress, lobbies and elevators reflect the movement toward a physical trajectory of various narratives.[55] Such narratives underline the reification of the individual by the mediation of architectural structures.

Even if Pammy tries to give definitions to particular parts of the Twin Towers, she still fails to understand the Towers as a whole.

> If the elevators in the World Trade Center were places, as she believed them to be, and if the lobbies were spaces, as she further believed, what then was the World Trade Center itself? Was it a condition, an occurrence, a physical event, an existing circumstance, a presence, a state, a set of invariables?
>
> (*Players* 48)

It could be said that Pammy cannot assimilate the context of the Towers because she does not have a "prehistory" of their conception. In other words, the process of their construction has been too fast for her to process. Merleau-Ponty suggests that "my first perception and my first hold upon the world must appear to me as action in accordance with an earlier agreement reached between x and the world in general" (296). Pammy has not had the time to develop an understanding of the World Trade Center. There has been no "earlier agreement" between her perception and the construction of the Towers.

Despite her inability to identify the Towers' essence, Pammy eventually understands the importance of their grandeur. After spending time writing brochures for Grief Management, Pammy realizes that only a building as grand as the Towers can encompass all the data. "Where else would you

146   *The Phenomenology of Technocultural Space*

stack all this grief? Somebody anticipated that people would one day crave the means to codify their emotions" (*Players* 18–19). The Tower's function does not stop as an information gathering for clients. It also maintains the emotions and actions of the workers, actions that are not necessarily related to work. This is best portrayed in *Americana*. While walking the corridors, David Bell decides to open the office doors one by one:

> Jones Perkins was down on one knee, golf club in hand.... Walter Faye was reading the Kama Sutra to his secretary. Mars Tyler was at his desk, running a strand of dental floss between his teeth. Reeves Chubb was in the process of changing his shirt. Richter Janes and Grove Palmer were pitching quarters to the wall. Quincy Willet was having his shoes shined by the freelance bootblack. Paul Joyner sat on his royal blue sofa, bare-foot, in the lotus position.
>
> (*Americana* 101)

Akin to the lenses of a camera, David zooms in to the everyday random practices of the employees. None of the employees is working. They are rather indulging in activities that are too disperse to be contained within one single category. David has the impression that he obtains a glimpse that simultaneously evokes a prison, an aircraft carrier and a home for the insane (*Americana* 101). This cacophony points to a building's multiplicity of function. It seems that the very structure of the building invites miscellaneous actions from the employees.

In *Players*, the Twin Towers' multiplicity of function entails hermeneutical architecture. The Towers become simultaneously "a physical event, an existing circumstance, a presence, a state, a set of invariables" (*Players* 48). Their internal parallax does not comment solely on the advance of technology. It also comments on the implication of architecture in the individual's struggle to develop understanding. Osteen suggests that "Pammy defines her world architecturally" (145). This statement is reinforced by Martucci who argues that the ontological aspect of DeLillo's characters is often linked to their phenomenological milieu.[56] However, Pammy renounces her agency in favor of an uncomplicated existence. Her understanding processes take the form of rigid blocks, which provokes a reification of her sense of self. Pammy is "boxed in"[57] the grandeur of the Towers. It could be said that the Towers become themselves the architecture of her understanding processes. Žižek describes consequential buildings such as shopping malls and the Towers as a whole world. They are boxed worlds "separated from the outside by a plain grey wall or by dark glass panels which just reflect the outside, providing no insight or hint of what goes on within" (263). Pammy's superficiality could be read in terms of this description. Her self-alienation forms a "plain grey wall" around her mind.

The Phenomenology of Technocultural Space   147

Pammy only sees the "outside" of who she is. She is neither attracted to self-exploration nor interested in gaining "insight or hint of what goes on within" herself.

Contrarily to Gary, Pammy is uninterested in imaginative possibilities. She rather channels her understanding to the external world. The rise and fall of the elevators, for instance, not only guide her physically four times a day, but also structure an uncomplicated approach to her self-estranged life. When describing Pammy in an interview, DeLillo declares that she is "prone to be affected by the shallow ideas drifting through her world."[58] An example of mechanical perception is Pammy's tap dancing. "Tap was so crisp when done correctly, so pleasing to one's sense of the body as a coordinated organism able to make its own arithmetic" (*Players* 79). Ironically, immediately after this statement, Pammy's coach, Nan Fryer, advises the dancers to unblock their systems in order to allow movements to turn into force, force into energy and energy into peace (*Players* 79). Instead of freeing her body from all tension, Pammy resumes "the intermediate routine" of mechanical steps (*Players* 79). These mechanical steps are not limited to dancing. Pammy's ontological sense of location depends on the places she schedules daily.[59]

By channeling to structures and strict movements, Pammy fails to develop deep connections with other people. Her "pseudo[life] of structured order"[60] reflects the linearity of an elevator. Her life itself is a succession of "transient" crossings with her husband, friends, and herself (Osteen 144). It is no surprise that she considers the Towers themselves as transient structures. "To Pammy the towers didn't seem permanent. They remained concepts, no less transient for all their bulk than some routine distortion of light" (*Players* 19). Pammy could have said that "the secret of being me is that I'm only half here" (*Mao II* 135). In this context, the quote suggests that Pammy's self is too fragmented to form a whole. When walking beneath a flophouse marquee that reads "TRANSIENTS," Pammy feels a vague familiarity: "What it conveyed could not itself be put into words.... Pammy stopped walking, turned her body completely and looked once more at the sign. Seconds passed before she grasped its meaning" (*Players* 207). Pammy's delay in understanding the meaning of the sign reflects the distance created between her and her identity. She is utterly immersed in technocultural superficiality. She depends on elevators, lobbies, and signs in order to develop a hermeneutical perception of who she is and where she is located.

Even if Pammy's profession is to council mourners, death itself "terrorizes the margins of her awareness" (Dewey 55). When faced with difficulties, Pammy retreats to her superficiality to avoid dealing with deep feelings. Being a transient in her own life, Pammy is "casually playing at life" in an uncomplicated context of public life.[61] For Cowart,[62] her approach to life

148   *The Phenomenology of Technocultural Space*

attests to her ultimate sterility of existence (49). When she is addressed, Pammy has the impression that people "were communicating *out* to her from some unbounded secret place" (*Players* 51; emphasis in original). Pammy's failure to experience an authentic engagement with others "compels [her] to create second selves, and to contrive plots designed to regain [her] lost spiritual and emotional property" (Osteen 145).

The second self, or persona, that Pammy creates to respond to the world is not a mere way of appearing; it is a way of being, or rather a way of *not* being. As Yehnert suggests, DeLillo's characters "may be shaped by [the environment], but they have created the milieu that will grant them relief from the burden of existence" (358).[63] Pammy's willingness to be guided by her physical environment seems to emanate from existential boredom:

> Pammy examined the uses of boredom. Of late she'd found herself professing to be bored fairly often. She knew it was a shield for deeper feelings. Not wishing to express conventional outrage she said again and again, "How boring, so boring, I'm bored." Pornography bored her. Talk of violence made her sigh. Things in the street, just things she saw and heard day to day, forced her into subtle evasions…. Flying made her yawn. She yawned on the elevators at the World Trade Center. Often she yawned in banks, waiting on line to reach the teller.
>
> (*Players* 51–52)

The sort of activities she adheres to, or has to accomplish, do not necessitate depth, so she usually finds herself "yawning." Pammy immerses herself in the static standing of the Twin Towers and in the repetitive movement of the elevators in order to avoid facing her finitude.[64] She chooses boredom as a "shield" against the awareness of her imminent mortality. As described by Baudelaire, "Boredom, fruit of dejected indifference, / takes the magnitude of immortality…." [my translation].[65] Pammy's boredom is reflected in technocultural space, a space that sustains her persona.

Pammy creates her own environment to avoid facing her vulnerability and uncertainty in the metropolis. However, a change of environment leads to a change in attitude. As will be shown, if the metropolis keeps Pammy controlled, the suburbs shake her principles.

The Suburban Unboxing of the Self

After completely drifting apart from Lyle, Pammy decides that it is time for "a separation from the world of legalities and claims" (*Players* 88). She accompanies her superior Ethan Segal and his partner Jack Laws to Maine. She believes that spending her holidays in the suburbs would allow her to gain a fresh view of life. However, Pammy is unable to channel with

The Phenomenology of Technocultural Space   149

the suburban atmosphere of Maine. She could not believe that "the sky was everywhere" (*Players* 136). The lack of enormous buildings produces a change in her sense of location. Everything is foreign to her around the house they have rented. "She'd always lived in apartments. This was a house in the woods.... she couldn't tell the difference between the sounds of wind and rain, or bats and squirrels, or rain and bats" (*Players* 113). The fact that Pammy is unable to distinguish between sounds attests to her unfamiliarity with a technocultural space that contains distinct variations of species. Even the sound of rain, which cannot be stopped in the world of skyscrapers, seems undefinable. Her confusion, therefore, is furthered by an inability to recognize the anatomy of the suburbs. Pammy is unable to find "a sense of renewal or purity in the landscape; instead, the landscape disorients [her] grasp of time and space and, consequently, [her] sense of self" (Martucci 39).

Pammy views nature and culture as independent spheres, a bifurcation triggered by her need to pause her mode of thinking as much as her mode of life. In the wilderness, Pammy is seeking to take a break not only from her work but also from the very responsibility of maintaining a self. Henri Lefebvre explores this disassociation of the self when exposed to different contexts such as work-life and leisure time.[66] He explains that city-dwellers conceive a utopic vision of leisure activities. The purpose of these activities is to respite the boundaries of repetition and social limits. However, because of the nature of their existence, city-dwellers are unable to break free from the fragmentation and the monotony of their dailiness (Lefebvre, *Critique of Everyday Life* 247). Pausing their routine by going on holidays becomes an exposure to the unfamiliar and unrecognizable.

In Pammy's case, the lack of skyscrapers brings her face to face with herself. "All this stuff is flashing your way. It's like a mirror, ultimately. You end up with yourself minus all the familiar outward forms, the trappings and surroundings. If it's too new, it's frightening. You get too much feedback that's not predetermined" (*Players* 139). Pammy seeks to remain numb to the self-exploration that the suburbs can suggest, but her bodily space threatens to bring her face to face with her nemesis: "Her life. She hated her life. It was a minor thing, though, a small bother. She tended to forget about it" (*Players* 32). Pammy thinks about her life as a "vague presence."[67] In the technoculturally advanced space of the metropolis, she finds enough distraction from this vague presence. The distraction is not available in the suburbs. Everything becomes real and proximate. Landscapes and sensations deromanticize the idea of perfect holidays. " 'Do you believe this water?' 'Cold, I know' " (*Players* 112). "Grass, it stings. It's not like movie grass" (*Players* 164). The properties of real suburbs assault Pammy's and Jack's expectation of movie-flat notion of pleasant pictorial space. Ethan believes that Pammy and Jack lack the "references" necessary

150 *The Phenomenology of Technocultural Space*

to gain familiarity with the suburbs. "What you don't know is a whole era of things. You've been gone right by. It must be solid void to live without the references" (*Players* 140).

The suburban "realness" contributes to dredging up Pammy's sense of alienation. Her body seems to respond to the dislocation: "she stepped out of the shower and felt pain, momentary pressure, at the side of her head. She would be dead within weeks" (*Players* 136). Even her language is altered by the primitiveness she senses around: " 'Fire come', she said. 'Make big for heat the body' " (*Players* 136). These "pseudo-primitive constructions"[68] are not totally deliberate. Pammy feels compelled to respond to her environment no matter how alien it proves to be.

Because of her gradual frustration at the lack of distractions, Pammy seeks to counter the disorientation through the only way she knows. Once again, she turns to the technocultural space within which she is "thrown." She starts to "explore the messages of her body and the physical world" (Osteen 150). As she is taking a walk with Jack, they reach a field labeled "PRIVATE" (*Players* 163). Similarly to the flophouse marquee that describes her transient attitude toward life, the sign stirs in Pammy a vague familiarity.

When Pammy enters the private property, she undresses and Jack complies. It seems that a private pastured square stimulates in her the desire for intimacy. "It was to be a serene event, easefully pleasant sex between friends" (*Players* 165). Playing on his earlier confession concerning his bisexuality, Pammy pushes Jack to act on his desire to experiment. In a way, she dubs the cloak of the adventurer described by Simone de Beauvoir.[69] Pammy brackets her allegiances in an attempt "to offset years of sensory and emotional deprivation" (*Players* 166). Indulging in adultery seems to be, for Pammy, a temporary freedom from the restrictions of the body and of moral codes. As LeClair states, "[Pammy's] clandestine relationships with Jack arise not from a simple desire for sexual satisfaction.... but from a complicated desire created by failed fulfillment, the absence of play, and denial of the body" (159). Setting aside remorse, Pammy discovers the power of ethical transgression. She seeks a minor but significant "dominance in a symbolic possession of the self and in power over the rival" (160). Similarly to de Beauvoir's adventurer,[70] Pammy's ultimate goal is to subdue the "rival." Pammy's "rival" is not Jack but an imposing technocultural space. She is symbolically testing her body against a world too powerful to be controlled and against an unstoppable decay of the flesh.

In the aforementioned scene, the narration highlights "body-centered spatial processing," which clarifies the implication of technocultural space in Pammy's actions and reactions. "Body-centered spatial processing" is a narrative method "where the source of information about space is the body itself and its immediate environment" (Farmasi 54). The narrator describes the intercourse with a degree of spatial awareness: "This crossing

The Phenomenology of Technocultural Space   151

over. The recomposition of random parts into something self-made. For a time it seemed the essential factors were placement, weight and balance. The meaning of left and right. The transpositions" (*Players* 168). Pammy is more aware of the position of bodies than the act itself. This recalls the importance Gary gives to the positioning of bodies. Similarly to Gary, Pammy considers the positioning of bodies as the only lasting and significant information.

The narration seems to temporarily focus on the bodily release that Pammy and Jack experience, a technique used by DeLillo to stress the characters' embodied experiences.[71] However, Pammy's "victory" over the tyranny of the earth is short-lived. "The earth had hurt. The goddamn ground" (*Players* 169). Pammy realizes that the transgression may have consequences, as she is slightly concerned about Jack. "Did it mean what they'd done had less effect on her than it did on Jack?" (*Players* 169). Pammy denies the seriousness of the question as she repeatedly invites Jack to pursue their affair, but the duration of this denial is brief. Confused by his bisexuality and his growing guilt, Jack commits a ritualistic suicide. He immolates himself a few days after the affair had started, an action that Pammy finds hard to understand.

Pammy as always tries to protect herself from acknowledging her responsibilities. She avoids looking at Jack's corpse by "situating" herself in a way that enacts larger objects as shields. "After that second look she was diligent in keeping a large object between herself and Jack's body. First the car and now the bulldozer" (*Players* 198). After a failed attempt at comforting Ethan, Pammy decides to take "an eleven-hour bus ride" (*Players* 203). John A. McClure argues that her choice of transport is a way to acknowledge the truth (81). He believes that the role of distance and time consists of bringing her face to face with her feelings. On the bus, her facial expression reflects her state-of-mind. "Pammy smiled, close to tears, her face developing cracks around the eyes and becoming lustrous, showing complex regret" (*Players* 203).

While McClure is right to suggest that Pammy attempts to face the truth, the ride home is too early a stage to mourn properly. She rather projects her sorrow onto the landscape that she watches unfold before her eyes:

The dead elms along the road brought a graver response. She'd never seen them in such numbers, silenced by blight, dark rangy things, their branches arched. It was startling, all this bareness, and the white frame houses, sometimes turreted or capped by a widow's walk, and the people who lived there, how different the dead elms made them seem, more resonant, deepened by experience, a sense about them of having lived through something, although she knew she was projecting this.

(*Players* 203–204)

152   *The Phenomenology of Technocultural Space*

Pammy uses the landscape as an anesthetic relief despite, or because of, its bareness. Either way, she finds, as Gary has found, a landscape capable of projecting her emotions. She is directing her grief outward. She declares that she longs for her apartment, "closed away again, spared the need to react tenderly to things" (*Players* 204). It seems that Pammy rides the bus in order to watch her own grief represented on the landscape. In this way, she is spared being alone with her guilt. The view unfolding in front of her "was startling" not because of its intrinsic depth, but because Pammy sees the "dead elms" as the personification of the "stump [that] was Jack" (*Players* 197).

Pammy's projection of grief is readjusted to the changed technocultural space of New York, that is, to a "truer necropolis, the outlying zone to which all bleak neon aspires" (*Players* 204). She finds herself "thrown" in "a ray system of desolation" (*Players* 204). When she reaches her apartment, Pammy is immediately reassured. "The apartment was serene. Objects sat in pale light, reborn. A wicker basket she'd forgotten they had…. Her memory in things" (*Players* 204). The "necropolis" atmosphere she has been feeling while walking the streets is dispersed with the "rebirth" of objects around her. Her restlessness, however, does not completely disappear. "The long ride was still unraveling in her body" (*Players* 204). Pammy turns on television and watches a black-and-white "inept and boring" movie (*Players* 204). Despite the cheapness of the movie, Pammy is transfused by its drama. "The cheapness was magnetic. She experienced a near obliteration of self-awareness" (*Players* 205). The tragic events of the movie, though artificial, stimulate Pammy's emotions. For McClure, the movie is attractive despite its cheapness because it makes ordinary fleeting life seem precious.[72] As the movie becomes more tragic, Pammy grows more upset; but is it because she is thinking about the meaning of life, death, and morality?

As Pammy herself declares, the cheapness of the movie leads her to experience "a near obliteration of self-awareness." The movie does highlight her sorrow, but she experiences it as a shallow state-of-mind:

> Pammy was awash with emotion. She tried to fight it off, knowing it was tainted by the artificiality of the movie, its plain awfulness. She felt it surge through her, this billowing woe. Her face acquired a sheen. She ran her right hand over the side of her head, fingers spread wide. Then it came, on-rushing, a choppy sobbing release. She sat there, hands curled at her temples, for fifteen minutes, crying, as the wife died, the boy recovered, the brother vowed to regain his self-respect, the hero in his pleated trousers watched his youngest child ride a pony.
>
> (*Players* 205)

Pammy forms a loop that helps her externalize her sorrow, using the mediation of technocultural space. Despite being a Grief Management

The Phenomenology of Technocultural Space   153

counselor, Pammy goes to great lengths to avoid her own grief. She channels the repressed emotions she has felt in the bus with the "artificiality of the movie, its plain awfulness." Being open to the possibilities of the screen allows Pammy to lose connection with reality. She immerses herself in the hyperreal. "The bus window had become a TV screen filled with serial grief" (*Players* 205). Pammy orbits around the simulacrum of her feelings. The memorized symbolic effect of the dead elms refers back to Jack's torched corpse, and the grief in the movie refers back to the dead elms she has "visualized" through the bus window. In a way, Pammy keeps the symbolic and physical representations of technocultural space between her and her grief.

The technocultural space builds a wall around the devastating knowledge of her implication in Jack's death. On the surface of this wall, screens are switched on for a visualization of a simulacrum of her grief. Similarly to the way Pammy has kept vehicles between her and Jack's corpse, she keeps the screen of television and the "boxed in" atmosphere of her bedroom between her and her guilt. The reason behind going through this detour is to remain within the context of outward perception of grief.

Akin to an elevator "being hollowed out"[73] by employees numbed by tiredness, Pammy feels empty and tired after the movie. She is famished after her sobbing release. "Her face looked recently finished; an outer surface of raw tissue" (*Players* 206). She goes to the kitchen with a new attitude. The temporary outburst is already being distanced. Pammy rationalizes her experience according to her training as a grief counselor: "Movies did that to people, awful or not.... She supposed she'd been building up to this. There were baffled pleasures everywhere, whole topographies rearranged to make people react to a mass-market stimulus" (*Players* 205–206). This practical explanation of her outburst reflects the efficiency of postmodern technology. As Katja F. Aas posits, "the new technologically mediated world tends to eschew moral considerations of acts and individuals and replaces them with partial, technical evaluations" (154).[74] For Cowart, the movie "hints at a significant collapse of the distinction between 'real life' and its simulacrum" (51). Pammy tries to convince herself that her outburst has been a necessary inconsequential moment of artificial grief. "No harm done succumbing to a few bogus sentiments" (*Players* 206). It seems that the serenity of the apartment is already helping her recover her composure. She gradually re-adopts her transient attitude. Not finding anything to eat but "envelopes of soup," she decides to treat herself with a roast beef sandwich.

When she steps outside the building, Pammy has already forgotten her grief. The streets seem "warm," and everyone seems to reflect her hunger. "Everyone was eating. Wherever she looked there were mouths moving, people handling food" (*Players* 206). It could be said that Pammy views

154 *The Phenomenology of Technocultural Space*

these people as transient sets of data. As Steve F. Anderson explains, "the surveilled body is little more than a transient conduit for data flows, the aggregation of which far surpasses the significance of any individual's action" (136).[75] To anticipate Chapter 5, perception itself adopts the visual representation of information. When Pammy "emerged with a small bag of groceries," the city reflects the synthetic beauty of her plastic bag. "The city was unreasonably insistent on its own fibrous beauty, the woven arrangements of decay and genius that raised to one's sensibility a challenge to extend itself" (*Players* 206–207). Pammy carries on the superficiality that restrain any perception of the previous week's real happenings. She finds herself in the familiar space of the lobby, protected and superficial.

End Zone as much as *Players* wander away from the deafening presence of latent history. While Gary Harkness seeks "de-multiplication" in barren lands, Pammy becomes a corrosive construct in the technocultural context within which she is "thrown." However, they both fail to escape the waves and radiations of information. As has been demonstrated, Gary automatically transitions to the environmental multiplicity of the desert, and Pammy is constantly in transit, similarly to fleeting data. Their perception responds to a new sort of technocultural context, a context that rebuilds the way one is positioned within the world. Chapter 5 explores the manner in which information is at the heart of this repositioning.

Notes

1 DeLillo, Don. *End Zone*. New York, New York, Penguin, 1986 [1972].
2 Williams, Raymond. *Problems in Materialism and Culture: Selected Essays*. London, Verso, 1980.
3 Shaw, Debra B. *Technoculture: The Key Concepts*. Oxford, Berg, 2008.
4 Tom LeClair points to the importance DeLillo gives to Gary's spatial environment. The critic suggests that, in *End Zone*, "DeLillo's interest moves beyond mass communications to include systems of geopolitics and ecology" (59).
5 Osteen, Mark. *American Magic and Dread Don DeLillo's Dialogue with Culture*. Philadelphia, University of Pennsylvania Press, 2000.
6 In *Understanding Don DeLillo* (2014), Henry Veggian suggests that the title of DeLillo's second novel is multilayered.

> DeLillo's title refers both to the literal space of the end zone on a football field.... and also a philosophical plane that Gary, the novel's narrator, ultimately reaches as he crosses the genres of the sports novel, the war novel, the campus novel, and so forth.
>
> (40)

> Veggian, Henry. *Understanding Don DeLillo*. Columbia, University of South Carolina, 2014.

7 Osteen, *American Magic and Dread Don DeLillo's Dialogue with Culture*, p. 33.

The Phenomenology of Technocultural Space   155

8 See also LeClair, Tom. *In the Loop: Don DeLillo and the Systems Novel.* Champaign, University of Illinois Press, 1987, p. 59; and Yehnert, Curtis A. "'Like Some Endless Sky Waking Inside': Subjectivity in Don DeLillo." *Critique: Studies in Contemporary Fiction*, vol. 42, no. 4, 2001, p. 363.

9 The cycle is symbolized through the repetitive soft noise of rocking chairs, for instance. Paying attention to basic technologies such as chairs distracts Gary from more advanced visual technologies. Basic technologies are enclosed and controlled within an organized and minimalistic space, but do they offer the emptiness that Gary seeks?

10 Osteen, *American Magic and Dread Don DeLillo's Dialogue with Culture*, p. 33.

11 Lefebvre, Henri. *The Production of Space.* Translated by Donald Nicholson-Smith, Cambridge, Blackwell, 1991.

12 Eliot, T. S. *Collected Poems: 1909–1962.* Orlando, Harcourt, 1991, p. 66.

13 Cronon, William, editor. *Uncommon Ground: Rethinking the Human Place in Nature.* New York, W.W. Norton, 1995.

14 Martucci, Elise. *The Environmental Unconscious in the Fiction of Don DeLillo.* New York, Routledge, 2007.

15 Martucci, *The Environmental Unconscious*, p. 20.

16 The desert as a space rich with history is a recurring theme in DeLillo's novels. It is notably found in *Point Omega* (2010). While driving, the protagonist notices "the history that runs past the window, mountains forming, seas receding, Elster's history, time and wind, a shark's tooth marked on desert stone" (121).

17 Eliot, *Collected Poems*, p. 67.

18 DeLillo, *End Zone*, p. 88.

19 Yehnert, "Like Some Endless Sky Waking Inside," p. 361.

20 Haraway, Donna Jeanne. *Simians, Cyborgs, and Women: The Reinvention of Nature.* London, Free Association, 1991, p. 149.

21 DeLillo, *End Zone*, p. 45.

22 Haraway, *Simians, Cyborgs, and Women*, p. 150.

23 DeLillo, Don. "An Interview with Don DeLillo." Interview by Thomas LeClair. *Conversations with Don DeLillo*, edited by Thomas DePietro, Jackson, University Press of Mississippi, 2005, p. 8.

24 Merleau-Ponty, Maurice. *Phenomenology of Perception.* Translated by Colin Smith, London, Routledge, 1962.

25 Nietzsche, Friedrich Wilhelm. *On the Genealogy of Morals and Ecce Homo.* Translated by Walter Kaufmann and R. J. Hollingdalb, New York, Vintage, 1989.

26 It is important to note that, in this context, "ascetic actor" does not refer to individuals who experience *inauthentic* spiritual elevation in the desert. Rather, it refers to the manner in which Gary experiences the desert regardless of the nature of the experience. Focus is given to how Gary interacts with his environment, not on his failure or success to develop an ascetic self.

27 McClure, John A. *Partial Faiths: Postsecular Fiction in the Age of Pynchon and Morrison.* Athens, University of Georgia, 2007.

156 *The Phenomenology of Technocultural Space*

28 Heidegger, Martin. *Being and Time.* Translated by John Macquarrie and Edward Robinson, Oxford, Blackwell, 1967.

29 In *Civilization and Its Discontents* (1930), Sigmund Freud argues that individuals are reigned by their desire to find pleasure or to avoid unpleasantness. Each person follows their own method of saving.

> It is a question of how much real satisfaction he can expect to get from the external world, how far he is led to make himself independent of it, and, finally how much strength he feels he has to altering the world to suit his wishes.
>
> (30)

Freud, Sigmund. *Civilization and Its Discontents.* Translated by James Strachey. New York, W.W. Norton, 1962.

30 Joyce, James. *A Portrait of the Artist as a Young Man.* Oxford, Oxford University Press, 2008.

31 DeLillo, Don. "The Art of Fiction CXXXV: Don DeLillo." Interview by Adam Begley. *Conversations with Don DeLillo*, edited by Thomas DePietro, Jackson, University Press of Mississippi, 2005, p. 101.

32 Lee, Benjamin. "Metalanguages and Subjectivities." *Reflexive Language: Reported Speech and Metapragmatics*, edited by John A. Lucy, Cambridge, Cambridge University Press, 1993, pp. 365–392.

33 Gourley, James. "Beckett's *Worstward Ho* and DeLillo's *The Body Artist*." *Literature and Sensation*, edited by Anthony Uhlmann, Paul Sheehan, Helen Groth, and Stephen McLaren, Newcastle, Cambridge Scholars, 2009, pp. 215–228.

34 Deleuze, Gilles. *Cinema 1: The Movement Image.* Translated by Hugh Tomlinson and Barbara Habberjam, Minneapolis, University of Minnesota, 1986.

35 Deleuze thinks of close-ups as processes that zoom into detailed and suggestive images. "There is thus an internal composition of the close-up, that is a genuinely affective framing, cutting [découpage] and montage" (Deleuze 103).

36 As suggested by Lilla Farmasi, DeLillo "foregrounds how language is intertwined with embodiment" (53).
Farmasi, Lilla. "'[P]ure, Dumb Canine Instinct': Narrative Space and Motion(lessness) in Don DeLillo's 'The Ivory Acrobat'." *Space, Gender, and the Gaze in Literature and Art*, edited by Ágnes Zsófia Kovács and László Sári, Newcastle, Cambridge Scholars, 2017, pp. 47–62.

37 In *The Spaces of Violence* (2006), James Giles suggests that DeLillo enacts the stylistics of both geographic space and extra-geographic space. "On the extra-geographic level the movement is from realistic and naturalistic to metaphoric and surreal visions of space(s)" (4).

38 Giles, James. *The Spaces of Violence.* Alabama, University of Alabama, 2006, p. 96.

39 John Johnston suggests that DeLillo constructs characters that seek simplicity either through suicide or through de-multiplication (6). His main statement is that the exposure of DeLillo's characters to a multiplicity of information produces a corrosive effect in their perception of culture and the self.

The Phenomenology of Technocultural Space 157

Johnston, John H. *Information Multiplicity: American Fiction in the Age of Media Saturation*. London, Johns Hopkins University Press, 1998.

40 As Osteen corroborates, "[Gary's] attraction to Myna is thus coupled with his fascination with nuclear holocaust" (42).

41 Jencks, Charles. *Critical Modernism: Where Is Post-modernism Going?* London, Wiley-Academy, 2007.

42 Mini-cities here refers to that which Slavoj Žižek calls "urban space." "[P]ostmodern buildings tend to function as their own urban spaces (like parks inside malls, self-contained capsule-worlds)" (Žižek 263).
Žižek, Slavoj. *Living in the End Times*. London, Verso, 2010.

43 Jameson, Fredric. *Postmodernism, or, the Cultural Logic of Late Capitalism*. Durham, Duke University Press, 2003.

44 Many critics seem to look at DeLillo's interest in the Towers as a prophetic event and not as a curiosity about the nature of skyscrapers. Emphasis has been put on the 9/11 attack, but the symbolic importance of the Twin Towers as technocultural constructs is overlooked. Therefore, in this section, the Towers do not represent the enactment of a tragedy but the implication of skyscrapers in dailiness. See www.theguardian.com/books/2001/dec/22/fiction.dondelillo

45 Žižek, *Living in the End Times*, p. 250.

46 DeLillo, Don. *Cosmopolis*, London, Picador, p. 103.

47 DeLillo, Don. "In the Ruins of the Future." *The Guardian*. Guardian News and Media, December 22, 2001. Web. November 5, 2018. www.theguardian.com/books/2001/dec/22/fiction.dondelillo. Accessed November 5, 2018.

48 Potentiality and actuality can be considered as a process going from theory to substance then to change. "The possession of a potentiality just is the possession of a potentiality to act, and such a potentiality is not unconditional but depends on the obtaining of propitious circumstances" (322). The ability of the Towers to come into actuality depends on the evolution of technology, which allows their construction. However, this evolution has not been accompanied by the appropriate response in human beings.
Aristotle. *Metaphysics*. Translated by Hugh Lawson-Tancred. London, Penguin, 1998.

49 This is a modified quote from Merleau-Ponty's *Phenomenology of Perception*. "To experience a structure is not to receive it into oneself passively: it is to live it, to take it up, assume it and discover its immanent significance" (301).

50 Žižek borrows the term "parallax" from the philosopher Kojin Karatani in *Living in the End Times* (2010).

51 DeLillo, Don. "In the Ruins of the Future."

52 Osteen, *American Magic and Dread Don DeLillo's Dialogue*, p. 143.

53 At some point in the novel, lobbies are compared or mistaken for rooms, which implies a degree of comfort and familiarity. "That's the lobby where we stayed. Or that's the room. I think that was someone's room" (*Players* 76).

54 Jameson, *Postmodernism, or, the Cultural Logic*, p. 42.

55 As suggested by Jameson,

> [w]e know in any case that recent architectural theory has begun to borrow from narrative analysis in other fields and to attempt to see our physical

158 *The Phenomenology of Technocultural Space*

trajectories through such buildings as virtual narratives or stories, as dynamic paths and narrative paradigms which we as visitors are asked to fulfill and to complete with our own bodies and movements.

(42)

56 In Martucci's words, "[t]he way in which his characters understand themselves is often revealed through their relationships to the particular places they come from or they reside" (23).

57 Osteen, *American Magic and Dread Don DeLillo's Dialogue with Culture*, p. 145.

58 DeLillo, Don. "An Interview with Don DeLillo," p. 6.

59 Pammy knows exactly where she must be and when. For instance, "[t]he class was on West Fourteenth Street, two evenings a week, eight-thirty to ten" (*Players* 78).

60 Dewey, Joseph. *Beyond Grief and Nothing: A Reading of Don DeLillo.* Columbia, University of South Carolina Press, 2006, p. 56.

61 In the Heideggerian philosophy, public life refers to the shallow existence that individuals drift in when they fail to construct their own understanding of life.

62 Cowart, David. *Don DeLillo: The Physics of Language.* Georgia, University of Georgia Press, 2003.

63 See also Martucci, *The Environmental Unconscious*, p. 21.

64 LeClair agrees that one of the principles upon which *Players* is built is the fear of "rotten flesh." The characters try to repress their "own physical complexity" in a desperate attempt to escape this fear (LeClair 147).

65 Baudelaire, Charles. *Les Fleurs du Mal.* Paris, Chêne, 2007, p. 289.

66 Lefebvre, Henri. *Critique of Everyday Life.* Translated by John Moore, vol. 1, London, Verso, 1991.

67 DeLillo, Don. *Players*, New York, Vintage, 1989, p. 32.

68 Cowart, *The Physics of Language*, p. 50.

69 Beauvoir, Simone de. *Pour une Morale de L'ambiguïté.* Paris, Gallimard, 1947, p. 78.

70 Beauvoir, *Pour une Morale de L'ambiguïte*, p. 79.

71 As corroborated by Farmasi, "The embodied experiences are so emphatic that narrative time and space move with the character's body" (59).

72 "The film seems to work, in the manner of a secular wisdom story, to drive home the grievous facts of mortality and to make ordinary life seem precious" (McClure 82).

73 DeLillo, *Players*, p. 177.

74 Aas, Katja F. *Sentencing in the Age of Information: From Faust to Macintosh.* London, GlassHouse, 2005.

75 Anderson, Steve F. *Technologies of Vision: The War between Data and Images.* Cambridge, MIT Press, 2017.

5   Perception in the Informational Era

The "Dominant Metaphor" of Postmodern Technoculture

Information in DeLillo's Novels

In *Theories of the Information Society* (1995), Frank Webster voices the individual's inquiries into the nature of contemporary society

> It seems to me that most people ask themselves, at one time or another, what sort of society is it in which we live? How can we make sense of what is going on with our world? And where is it all taking us?[1]

By asking these questions, Webster aims to shed light on the fast and radical transformation noticed in the post-industrial society. The British sociologist argues that locating these transformations begins with "information," as it represents "a distinguishing feature of the modern world" (2). Webster believes that information is lived and interpreted in various ways yet remains critically vague. Even if it is christened the "dominant metaphor"[2] of the postmodern technocultural age, information maintains an impermeable resistance to a full definition. As confirmed by Katherine Hayles, "even if information provides the basis for much of contemporary U.S. society, it has been constructed never to be present itself" (25).[3] Because of this elusiveness, the discussion on information starts on the basis that the term as such is never fully perceived.

DeLillo does not pretend giving an unproblematic answer as to the nature of information in the age of postmodern technoculture, but he does inscribe in his novels its modes of appearance. Joseph Conte ascribes DeLillo's interest or inclination toward information theory to the author's academic background:[4] "One presumes that [DeLillo's] program in the communication arts involved some component of information theory, which had been proposed by Claude Shannon only ten years earlier, since the conveyance of information would be the essential aim of communication"

DOI: 10.4324/9781003407768-6

160 *Perception in the Informational Era*

(113). Having a formal discernment on the theory has informed DeLillo's novels to an extent, but he does not limit his novels to its abstractness. Indeed, DeLillo does not seek to unveil the workings of information only as a dematerialized aspect of communication and, to a degree, as knowledge. He seeks to locate the subtle embodied manifestation of information in technocultural dailiness. In this way, DeLillo does not celebrate the complete disappearance of the body. Rather, as Hayles would put it, he establishes his characters' subjectivity "at the crossing of the materiality of informatics with the immateriality of information" (193). Information becomes the immaterial discourse to which embodied circumstances respond, preferably without entrapment.

Drawing on Ludwig Wittgenstein and Jean-François Lyotard, Gregory H. Davis explains that postmodern technoculture has reconfigured the role of language to become a game of information.[5] Language, as a system of communication and as a programming language, becomes a city of multiplicity. The multiplicity of language gives infinite fragmented possibilities. These possibilities represent the never-exhausted reservoir of information, and technocultural space is the field within which this reservoir is built. DeLillo seems interested in this discursive game of chance and possibilities that form a dialogue between abstract possibilities and embodied subjectivity. In DeLillo's novels, the endless flow of information in the characters' dailiness contributes to determining their beliefs, behaviors, and activities.

Since information appears by the mediation of different technologies and since it touches different aspects of life, it is necessary to begin this chapter by introducing the different facets of the term. The aim of the following paragraphs, therefore, is to examine these facets as conceived by DeLillo.

In general, "information" refers to "knowledge obtained from investigation, study, or instruction (2): intelligence, news (3): facts, data."[6] This definition is neither complete nor precise in an age when "information" is the idiom of everyday existence.[7] The polymorphic characteristic of "information" complicates the measurement of a straightforward definition of the term. Mark C. Taylor[8] argues that despite witnessing an "information revolution," the only thing that individuals know for sure is that the presence of information is overwhelming (100). The information revolution, which is supposed to clarify the cultural, technological, and spatial contexts of the postmodern world, is itself a controversial societal development.

Kevin Robins and Frank Webster[9] attempt to locate what makes information revolutionary in postmodern society. They suggest that the "Information Revolution" is not the product of technological advance as much as the product of power. For them, even if technological advance has contributed in establishing a wide range of data gathering systems,

Perception in the Informational Era   161

"Information Revolution" is about the collaboration of efficiency and knowledge to establish power (91). However, Robins and Webster remain trapped in the economic and political analysis of the mechanization of information. Despite their attempt to expand their analysis to cultural praxis, they approach the everyday life of individuals as consumers mainly. In DeLillo's novels, the technocultural approach to information is not limited to its socioeconomic aspect. DeLillo is particularly interested in the changes brought to ontological and psychological systems in a time when dailiness is rich with information sources.

When Constance Penley and Andrew Ross had popularized the term "technoculture," they were witnessing a radical transformation brought about by the information revolution. They suggest that the importance of this revolution lies in its capacity to provide counter-narratives to governmental accounts. The two editors gathered texts that stress the role of image and communication technologies in emancipating information from the tyranny of power. This emancipation allows the emergence of countercultures, as diversity ascends from a state of marginalization. Such emancipation is expressed, for instance, in the accounts of latent history. Instead of being filtrated and imposed, information has found in image technologies a medium of liberation. In this way, information is no longer imposed and accepted; it is contested and individualized.

The age of postmodern information is expressed through the technologies that have been developing since the seventies. The fast evolution and expansion of information technologies has led to an unprecedented societal reconstruction. DeLillo touches upon the evolution of information technologies in everyday technocultural space. In *Ratner's Star* (1976), for instance, he describes a "Space brain," an enormous computer that increasingly expands in space. In *White Noise* (1985), he focuses on television and the radio as necessary components of the living room. In *Cosmopolis* (2003), he focuses on "spycams," monitors, vehicles, and various advanced gadgets. These technologies do not leave society unchanged, as they extend the body and the nervous system. As indicated by Ian McNeil,[10] "[i]nformation technologies (which we will take to include communications) may be regarded as extensions of human sensory-motor capabilities: particularly, the senses of sight and hearing; and memory, speech and manipulative skills, such as writing" (686). DeLillo suggests that the profound sensory exposure to technology, which has grown with the passing of time, is bound to contribute to the reconstitution of ontological and psychological perception. Despite his indirect approach to information technologies, or because of it, DeLillo demonstrates the conversion of information by the means of technologies.

In DeLillo's novels, information appears primarily as noise filling technocultural space. For instance, supermarkets are described as a space

162 *Perception in the Informational Era*

"awash in noise" (*White Noise* 43). Supermarkets offer different recognizable products, products that are enlivened by shiny symbols, but it also stifles "a dull and unlocatable roar" (*White Noise* 43). When characters are unable to distinguish and untangle the incredible flow of information, they suffer from "information sickness." This sickness is described in DeLillo's novels as, for instance, the "innate disturbance of low frequency in the grain of the physical city, a ghostly roar" (*Players* 148), or "the panic data that fed into [one's] life" (*Mao II* 90).

If information overload, background noise, becomes a source of sickness or even terror, it is also the basis of perception. This view is compatible with Michel Serres' definition of "background noise."[11]

> Background noise is the ground of our perception, absolutely uninterrupted, it is our perennial sustenance, the element of the software of all our logic. It is the residue and the cesspool of our messages. No life without heat, no matter, neither; no warmth without air, no logos without noise, either. Noise is the basic element of the software of all our logic, or it is to the logos what matter used to be to form. Noise is the background of information, the material of that form.
>
> (7)[12]

The indiscernibility between noise and information pushes the characters to select actively the data that they translate into meaning. In this way, the initial encounter of the characters with information comes in the form of noise to be deciphered. As reminded by Murray, the supermarket is "full of psychic data.... Everything is concealed in symbolism, hidden by veils of mystery and layers of cultural material" (*White Noise* 44). In *Mao II*, Brita describes a similar sensation: "Everything feeds in, everything is coded, there is everything and its hidden meaning" (*Mao II* 90). These veils of mystery conceal meaningful data within technocultural space. The characters are usually challenged to distinguish relevant information from the noise of technocultural space.[13]

The manner in which information is obtained, or selected from a state of disorder, differs from character to character. In DeLillo's novels, information is processed through physical and mental extensions. As has been shown, Endor chooses to approach the world the way it is perceived by his senses, while other characters are continuously exposed to screens. Sense organs are the primary mediums of information as they filtrate data from noise. The father of cybernetics, Norbert Wiener, lays down the manner in which an individual processes information.[14]

> Information that he receives is co-ordinated through his brain and nervous system until, after the proper process of storage, collation, and

Perception in the Informational Era   163

selection, it emerges through effector organs, generally his muscles. These in turn act on the external world, and react on the central nervous system through receptor organs such as the end organs of kinaesthesia; and the information received by the kinaesthetic organs is combined with his already accumulated store of information to influence future action.

(17)

The way information is sent is not necessarily the way it is received, as information is constantly under the threat of being swamped up by noise. Wiener believes that individuals perpetually need to fight against entropy. Still, the environment, or technocultural space, does not only "degrade" information but it also opens it to new connections.

As shown, these usual or unusual connections are not only physical but also abstract. They are represented by facts but also by imaginative possibilities. Information, therefore, appears in many forms. It appears in the form of David's pixels, and Jack's attempt for protection. It appears in the form of historical events as the transmitted "waves and radiations" where information is brought to living rooms or is found in uncanny footages. Information is history rendered personal and viewed under "superreal" and "underreal" lenses. In short, the manner in which information is processed depends on the characters' technocultural space and on their embodiment.

Since individuals are receptors to the information found in technocultural space, they respond to information received both by human interaction and by the surrounding machines. This is relevant to the extent that embodied interaction with technocultural space allows feedback. The liberation of information, through forming a feedback reaction, has brought a radical change in communication. Instead of having various possible sets of information, one piece of information opens many possibilities through feedback. According to Wiener, when information creates a dynamic performance that changes the method and pattern of a system, it promotes learning (61). Since feedback is a process that allows learning, the characters' interaction with their respective technocultural space provides them with insight.

The characters gathered in this chapter are pushed to adopt certain beliefs according to the insights they gain from interacting with technocultural space. They are hence gnostic, as defined by Harold Bloom. For the critic, "Gnosticism was (and is) a kind of information theory."[15] He argues that the "American Religion manifests itself as an information anxiety," by encouraging questions such as: "Where were we?" and "Where are we journeying?"[16] With the advance of technology, these characters have gained the possibility to select the aspect information they deem credible so that they fabricate their own truth. They believe in a post-Kennedy America, a space where trauma and freedom of interpretation are not too

164   *Perception in the Informational Era*

far apart. Their theological rationale, if it could be called so, is based on information. As expressed by David F. Noble,[17] "modern technology and modern faith are neither complements nor opposites, nor do they represent succeeding stages of human development. They are merged, and always have been, the technological enterprise being, at the same time, an essentially religious endeavor" (4–5). Information, as a technoculturally veiled source of belief, invites the characters to regain some control over their dailiness, no matter how hopeless their quest might be.

Adapting belief to information becomes a way of fighting against the overwhelming presence of noise, entropy, and the disappearance of the self. This view could be loosely read in terms of Wiener's comparison between the "life" of the machine and the life of the human being.

> When I compare the living organism with such a machine, I do not for a moment mean that the specific physical, chemical, and spiritual processes of life as we ordinarily know it are the same as those of life-imitating machines. I mean simply that they both can exemplify locally anti-entropic processes, which perhaps may also be exemplified in many other ways which we should naturally term neither biological nor mechanical.
>
> (32)

Wiener believes that a "living phenomenon" such as the machine and the human being share a capacity to maintain anti-entropic processes. It will be argued that, in accordance with these processes, the characters' need for self-preservation is manifested in everyday techno-activities. This assertion is underlined by the miscellaneous forms of information, especially the spiritual, ontological, and psychological forms.

The Vitality of Information: a Reading of Cosmopolis

The Micro-Liveliness of Dailiness

Among DeLillo's novels, *Cosmopolis*[18] offers the starkest manifestation of information as a distinct feature of postmodern technoculture. DeLillo's thirteenth novel narrates the last day of Eric Packer. Eric is a billionaire who wakes up in his prestigious penthouse in 1st avenue, New York, and perishes in the derelicts of Hell's Kitchen. Published in 2003, the novel is DeLillo's post 9/11 attack.[19] However, it does not so much deal with terrorism and capitalism as much as with the anatomy of technology at the beginning of the twenty-first century.[20] The 28-year-old investor feels at ease in a highly advanced technocultural space. His ease emanates from the gift of profiting from information by manipulating financial markets.

Perception in the Informational Era 165

Cosmopolis is constituted of two parts. Each part is divided into two chapters separated by the counter-narrative of Eric's killer, Richard Sheets. The main concern of the novel is the dilemma created by the abstract understanding of information. A large part of the novel takes place in Eric's limousine, which is a vessel connecting screened flows of information and physical locations.

The novel investigates the spiritual, ontological, and psychological changes that have accompanied technological innovations reached at the beginning of the twenty-first century. The narrative focuses on Eric's use of technology with the aim of hosting new technocultural possibilities. His ambitious nature holds contempt for available technological extensions. Eric is "dedicated to knowing,"[21] and in order to acquire knowledge he accumulates data, using his limousine as vessel. He moves through the streets of New York to reach what Dewey calls Eric's "epiphanic journey beyond."[22] The aim of this "journey beyond" is to unlock the key to more advanced technologies. Their role is to build a new form a being, unrestricted by the limitations of the body.

Eric is disappointed in primitive information technologies and, at the same time, fascinated by advanced ones. As he gazes at the technology surrounding him, Eric realizes that it is becoming obsolete. ATMs and flat-screens seem to him outdated and inadequate. ATMs remain exposed to the "inference of fuddled human personnel and jerky moving parts" (*Cosmopolis* 54). The fact that humans are involved in the steps taken by the machine renders it "anti-futuristic, so cumbrous and mechanical" (*Cosmopolis* 54). ATMs contradict their automation legacy, so Eric questions their very existence. Flat screens, too, no longer seem to him flat enough. He is unhappy with their cumbersome size. As the narrator conveys, "[Eric] was tired of looking at screens. Plasma screens were not flat enough. They used to seem flat, now they did not" (*Cosmopolis* 140). Because of the fast progress of technology, machines become rapidly mundane. Eric is assailed by devices he wishes no longer existed. He spots technological deficiencies wherever he directs his attention. When Eric spots a police lieutenant, for instance, he comments on his walkie-talkie. The protagonist declares that he wanted to ask the lieutenant why he is still using this "contraption." The outdated device offends Eric because it belongs to the past. The lieutenant does not realize that he is "carrying the nitwit rhyme out of the age of industrial glut into smart spaces built on beams of light" (*Cosmopolis* 102).

Eric longs for a future when he is free of primitive tools and decaying bodies. As he is being examined by Dr. Ingram, Eric draws a distinction between two sorts of technologies. Ingram's stethoscope seems to belong to "lost tools of antiquity, quaint as bloodsucking worms" (*Cosmopolis* 43). Conversely, the echocardiogram that Dr. Ingram does afterward

166   *Perception in the Informational Era*

seems fascinating. Eric is not sure whether he is watching "a computerized mapping of his heart or a picture of the thing itself" (*Cosmopolis* 44). The images he observes on the monitor open a distant dimension from which emanates "raptures of a galaxy in formation" (*Cosmopolis* 44). Eric's curiosity about the advanced and complicated medical and communication technologies grows. However, when he is informed that his prostate is asymmetrical, Eric becomes overwhelmed by uneasiness. This fact frustrates his need for perfection. He often tries (and succeeds) in attaining "mastery over ideas and people. But there was something about the idea of asymmetry...." (*Cosmopolis* 52). Asymmetry slips out of his control because it exists in "the world outside the body" (*Cosmopolis* 52). The body, in this context, does not refer only to human anatomy but also to anything that touches and approximates Man, the biosphere. Eric is referring to the mystery of life itself, a mystery he would like to unravel down to the "subatomic, that made creation happen" (*Cosmopolis* 52).

Eric is convinced that if he succeeds in accumulating enough information about the body, he could learn to manipulate it. With this aim in mind, Eric is increasingly drawn to the microscopic workings of his environment. Laist remarks that, in *Cosmopolis*, "we are seeing familiar material treated to an unfamiliar degree of microscopic inspection" (153). The characters in the novel witness Eric's unusual obsession with the newest gadgets, gadgets that attest to his futurism. These gadgets, which are increasingly discreet, convey ductile information. His wife "of 22 days," Elise Shifrin, seems to realize this even if they have not spent a lot of time together. "I think you acquire information and turn it into something stupendous and awful" (*Cosmopolis* 19). Eric unconsciously proves Elise's statement by turning his attention to the "ear plug" of his bodyguard, Torval. As he watches Torval answering someone who "speaks in his ear," Eric reflects on the practicalities of such extension. He realizes that Elise is gone, but this does not concern him much. He is absorbed in calculating the worth of the earplug. "He knew these devices were already vestigial. They were degenerate structures. Maybe not the handgun just yet. But the word itself was lost in blowing mist" (*Cosmopolis* 19). Even if these technologies never seem advanced enough to accomplish catharsis, they offer Eric a glimpse of a life *beyond*. The microscopic inspections that they mediate amplify his desire to transcend the present.

Eric's microscopic inspection of the external world and the struggles within is quintessentially technocultural in nature. DeLillo chooses "Cosmopolis" as the title of the novel because of the interactional possibilities opened by technological advance and cultural imperatives. During his last day, Eric "reprograms" his perception to acquaint himself with both "technocrowds"[23] and the human figures that constitute these crowds. In an interview, DeLillo declares that with *Cosmopolis* he wanted to place

Perception in the Informational Era   167

a character in a "stretched" vehicle and simply go from there.[24] As Eric travels the streets of New York, he is frequently stopped for a reason or another. His advance is slowed down by the arrival of the president, because of whom "whole streets were wiped out from the map" (*Cosmopolis* 11). Eric's limousine stops because of the anger of protestors. He takes time to meet his newlywed wife several times throughout the day. He witnesses the moving funerals of his favorite rapper. He sees for the first time his driver, and ultimately, he meets his assassin.

Eric's rising ambivalence is one of the reasons that pushes him to travel the streets in his well-equipped limousine. "Technology as a cultural undertaking, as a way to being in the world…. is the manner in which *homo technologicus* becomes what he is," Laist declares (156; emphasis in original). Eric is tempted to abandon a spiritual quest to "live on disk…. An idea beyond the body."[25] However, is Eric *destined* to become data on disk? He faces a dichotomy that emerges from the complexity of information, information obtained on a daily basis. Because of the multilayered nature of information, Eric is torn between reading it as code for pursuing a spiritual journey or as a call to transcending everything that makes him human. The micro-information that magnifies to macro-conclusions constantly changes his perception. It will be shown that Eric embarks on a journey that is too technological to be spiritual and too transcendental to be a shallow materialistic trip.

Information has an unprecedented vitality in the digitalized technocultural era. This vitality is already observed at the beginning of the novel when the reader is introduced to an insomniac Eric. Since he cannot sleep, Eric decides to watch the world rouse from his 88 stories above ground window. The liveliness of information represents the manner in which Eric understands his environment. The landscape Eric observes through his window is not an isolated instance of his method of daily information processing. His perched penthouse gives him the advantage of optimal panorama.

He is caught marveling at sunrise, which is "beginning to roar" behind the George Washington bridge. For him, the bridge is "the noblest thing" not only because it connects different contexts, but also because it offers freedom from the restricts of a particular place.[26] Eric desires to cross realms. He does not fear the other world. He believes, or wishes, that the bridge may open a technologically transcendental realm. For Dewey, this morning gaze is one of the examples that reveal Eric's parable structure.[27] However, Eric does not linger over the beauty of the view. He soon shifts to a more pragmatic process of thought.

Eric notices that dawn brings a change of human categories. As "whores were all fled from the lamplit corners," other "kinds of archaic business" have just woken up (*Cosmopolis* 6). He reads the scene as information. The unfolding details of the scene or "screen" attest to the insertion of

168 *Perception in the Informational Era*

information in the most ordinary activities. The particularity of this instance is that Eric looks through the window in the way he looks at his limousine's screens. The screens' "bits of information," Crystal Alberts suggests, "have not only become inseparable from life (human and otherwise), but Eric implies they also have a vitality of their own" (17).[28] This vitality refers to the fast change in the landscape that layers the fast unfolding of data on his computer screens, as will be shown later.

While observing the coexistence of random and contradictory energies, such as the retreat of prostitutes and the filling of the streets with vehicles, Eric watches "a hundred gulls trail a wobbling scow downriver" (*Cosmopolis* 7). He attempts to know the birds as they "ripple in a furl of air" (*Cosmopolis* 7). When the last gull takes off, Eric finds himself "admiring the bird, thinking into it, trying to know the bird, feeling the sturdy earnest beat of its scavenger's heart" (*Cosmopolis* 7). This encounter between Eric and the gulls could be understood preliminarily in terms of Wiener's conception of information. "Information is a name for the content of what is exchanged with the outer world as we adjust to it, and make our adjustment felt upon it" (Wiener 17). In its simplest form, the adjustments made on the outer world, in general, and the gull, in particular, consist of such building as the skyscraper in which Eric resides. In a way, the gull adjusts to Eric in the sense that it has to adapt to a technocultural reconstruction of ground and sky. Eric's perspective is positioned on a higher level than the flying gulls, as he stands 900 feet above ground. In their turn, the flying gulls provide Eric with an epiphany. While watching the birds, Eric "didn't know what he wanted. Then he knew. He wanted to get a haircut" (*Cosmopolis* 7). Thus, his journey is mysteriously encouraged by an encounter with flying birds, that is, with the natural world.

Eric's interest in the gulls has a deeper facet that comes in the form of micro-information. While Eric's perception of the gulls takes place in the material world, his mode of understanding is virtual. He does not merely observe a natural phenomenon of birds flying. He processes them microscopically, by depicting their internal composites. Eric has already "mastered the teeming details of bird anatomy" (*Cosmopolis* 7). He is able to picture gulls' "large strong heart" and "hollow bones" (*Cosmopolis* 7). He has developed the capacity to break down a random scenery as he would break down the data he observes on his screens. Eric looks not only at the birds themselves, but also at a micro-information version of them. Microscopic inspection allows him to "encipher, arrange, store and process strings of binary symbols"[29] about gulls.

The digitalized version of information seeps in the natural world, and the natural world provides the material for depiction. The future of the postmodern technocultural era is digitalized information, as perceived by Eric. Still, the material world in which he has been "thrown" has a grip

Perception in the Informational Era 169

on him. He understands the physical world through digital information. Simultaneously, he gains epiphanies by observing the outer world through the windows of his penthouse and limousine.

The Limo-Stage of Data

The condensed nature of the novel is not the result of DeLillo's inability to produce another mammoth such as *Underworld* or a memorable plot such as *White Noise*'s. Even if critics describe *Cosmopolis* as his "black sheep,"[30] the novel is not a failure. It describes Eric's perception of information as he interacts with its techno-compartments. Eric's limousine does not testify to his wealth only. It is his technocultural vessel. Indeed, DeLillo employs the limousine as a vehicle moving through various aspects of life before reaching its destination. The limousine takes the role of a window to the external world, an office, a space for spiritual and philosophical reflections, and a protection against external violence. Eric has enough space in the limousine to meet his employees and his doctor. He understands his employees better as he welcomes them "on stage."

The fact that Eric is able to watch his employees emerge from their respective "wings" gives him a glimpse of their lives outside the office. He becomes familiar with their beliefs, behaviors, and activities. He uncovers their weaknesses as they are not protected by their office attire, and they are stripped of authority. Moreover, because of its flat theatrical structure, the limousine offers a horizontal understanding of the roles the employees play in developing Eric's own self-discovery. His own beliefs, behaviors, and activities are revealed as he dialogues with them. Even if he pays them to advise him, their role consists mainly of being the targets of his contempt and derision. They vote against borrowing more Yen to avoid bankruptcy. Instead of giving weight to their warnings, Eric prefers to trust his instinct and the data on screens.

In addition to the various individuals Eric meets in his limousine, he has space for various screens and cameras. Vija Kinsky, Eric's "chief of theory," is mesmerized by the radiance that emanates from the screens that adorn the walls of the limousine. For her, there is a sort of liveliness in the screens that is hard to ignore. "Oh and this car, which I love. The glow of the screens. I love the screens. The glow of cybercapital. So radiant and seductive" (*Cosmopolis* 78). In addition to the data and news screens, Eric is exposed to a "spycam" which records his every movement. He is able to see the reflection the camera gives of him thanks to a small screen attached to it. The role that this one particular screen plays in the novel is primordial. Contrarily to the others, it depicts his every gesture and offers him a different perception of himself. The spycamera creates a loop that brings Eric back to himself.

170 *Perception in the Informational Era*

Everything in *Cosmopolis* goes back to the protagonist as the narrative structure of the novel focuses on the radiance of Eric's last day. This radiance consists of the way he is seated in the limousine, the way he interacts with others, and the way he responds to the glow of his gadgets. The rear leather club chair, which lends authority, is the central element of Chapter 1, Chapter 2, and Chapter 3 of the novel. The Scribner Tie-In edition of the novel uses the theatrical release poster of the movie *Cosmopolis*, released in 2012. It shows Eric Packer, starred Robert Pattinson, seated in his club chair in order to assert its importance.[31] The technological and cultural interconnection, which Eric observes throughout the day, is symbolized by this leather club chair. He keeps returning to his chair as he moves toward Hell's Kitchen. The leather chair radiates both authority and protection. As seen in Chapter 3, the "Womb Chair" is a vessel that contain one's body and fears. Eric constantly returns to the leather chair because it offers safety and because it creates a loop generated by a complex technoculture.

The role of the chair does not end here. It highlights *Cosmopolis* as a theatrical performance. The theatrical aspect of the novel emanates from DeLillo's tendency to create characters "eavesdropped on" by the reader as they voice their struggles. Jon D. Rossini confirms this assertion when he argues that "DeLillo uses the theater itself and performance elements in his novels as sites for negotiating both the denial and the acceptance of death" (46).[32] As Eric moves toward his doom, he is aware that he stands between life and death. Getting a haircut at the other side of the city is not so much driven by the desire to get a restyle. Eric is intrigued by how the day would end.

Eric's ultimate desire is to surpass his current state, as has been stated. For this reason, he decides to acquire information in a different manner. Even if Eric's chief of security declares that the "ride crosstown does not happen unless we make a day of it,"[33] Eric decides to slowly move in the crowded streets of New York City. This slow movement brings out the interaction between screened data and the cultural movement happening outside his window. In order to impregnate himself with this interaction, most of the novel unfolds as back and forth movement to his leather club chair. Eric either observes the "wings" of the streets or the fleeting data on his screens.

The Grin without a Body: Uncertainty in Fleeting Data

When Eric gets in his limousine, he finds Shiner, his chief of technology, waiting for him. After ascertaining that the system is secure, Eric observes all the "medleys of data on every screen, all the flowing symbols and alpine charts, the polychrome numbers pulsing" (*Cosmopolis* 13). The vitality felt by Eric represents the translated symbols of micro-information, being

Perception in the Informational Era   171

binary. "Binary, digitized data have become the new informational 'given' of our contemporary culture."[34] While standing at the window of his penthouse, Eric has processed the gulls at the micro-information level. While sitting in the leather chair of his limousine, Eric describes information in terms of the natural world. He views the unfolding data as "medleys," he imagines strings of charts as "alpine" trees, and he paints the pulsing numbers in various colors. It could be said that Eric fuses the horizons of the digital and the natural worlds. He seeks to transcend the limited mode of understanding, which fails to concretize the exactness of binary and to extract nature from physicality. For him, information should be a collaboration between the natural world and the digitalized data. However, the fleeting nature of information restricts Eric's ability to control its mode of appearance.

Information *appears* rather than *presents itself* because it is "conceptually distinct from the markers that embody it" (Hayles 25). In this way, the information Eric receives is represented by pattern rather than presence. Even more, it is represented by "the absence of pattern," that is, by randomness.[35] The "medleys of data," "the alpine charts," and "the polychrome numbers" comprise not only clear-cut sets of data but absent significant data. Information could be perceived as a "convenient formula for describing what happens where it isn't" (qtd. in Hobert and Schiffman 225). "Like the Cheshire cat," Hobert and Schiffman explain, "both an atom and a datum fade before us as we seek their hard lumps, only to reappear again as we turn our backs and start applying rules of logic" (225).

The grin without a cat is to be understood as the inability of human perception to process fast combinations of a datum with other data. Information is obtained when a datum is set in motion, which must involve unambiguous steps in algorithms.[36] Through its complex steps, this motion gives the information age its "central power," and from its application emerges the 1s and 0s patterned strings.[37] Since the entirety of the steps is too quick to be measured, a degree of uncertainty arises about the exactitude of information. This could explain the uncertainty that provokes fissures on the ground of reality. When seen in terms of information, reality becomes a game of appearance and disappearance of meaning, which must be grasped before it fades away. The Cheshire metaphor could be understood as the lack of an undisputed perception of reality because of uncertainties. These uncertainties are the result of the speed, the internal ambiguity, and the multiplicity of information in the postmodern technocultural era.

The spread of uncertainty caused by the fleeting nature of information is felt intensely by Eric during his last day. He is overwhelmed by the presence of information when he starts asking questions whose answers he could not immediately summon. "Where do all these limos go at night?"

172 *Perception in the Informational Era*

he asks a confused Shiner. Even if their job is to process information, it still slips from their grasp; Eric and Shiner are unable to follow the course of "Cheshire's body." Shiner reluctantly admits that he does not fully grasp the depth of his job.

> All this optimism, all this booming and soaring. Things happen like bang. This and that simultaneous. I put out my hand and what do I feel? I know there's a thousand things you analyze every ten minutes. Patterns, ratios, indexes, whole maps of information. I love information. This is our sweetness and light. It's a fuckall wonder. And we have meaning in the world. People eat and sleep in the shadow of what we do. But at the same time, what?
>
> *(Cosmopolis* 14)

The structure of this passage attests to Shiner's confusion. The information overload, which he has to process, exceeds his capacities. His hopelessness is the result of his incompatibility with the speed of data. Even if Eric relies on his ease with the chaotic workings of data, a degree of doubt has crept into his understanding of its "sweetness and light." When Eric meets Didi Fancher, his mistress, she informs him that "an element of doubt began to enter [his] life" (*Cosmopolis* 31). The talent he has developed for reading data is slowly vanishing. Eric is uncomfortable with this remark, as it means that he is failing at what he does best, that is, predicting information. It also means that the reality that he has been building threatens to crumble down at any moment. In other words, Eric becomes the target of the Cheshire uncertainty.

Mark Osteen[38] borrows the Cheshire metaphor to demonstrate the growing uncertainty of reality. The critic uses his reading of "Moholean relativity" to give weight to his assertion. DeLillo develops the "Moholean relativity" in *Ratner's Star*. During Billy's stay in the scientific center, he is summoned by Orang Mohole. This last is a theoretician who develops the Moholean Relativity:

> A mohole traps electromagnetic information, among other things, and then either releases it or doesn't. It's as though the mohole were a surface that absorbs light and sound and then reflects either or both to another part of the universe. But it's not a surface and it doesn't absorb. It's a mohole. It's part of a theoretical dimension lacking spatial extent and devoid of time value. Value-dark in other words.
>
> *(Ratner's Star* 181)

Osteen argues that similarly to the cat's appearance and disappearance, the cosmos, as theorized by Mohole, might have a Wonderland-like structure

Perception in the Informational Era   173

where existence is about summoning and dismissing data (71). For Eric, the cosmos is supposed to be glimpsable set of data that, sometime in the future, can be caught, collected in tangible masses, and manipulated to fit his goals. However, in Eric's world, one that still uses, to a large degree, "degenerate" technology, glimpsable data mainly amplifies uncertainty.

Although transcending his state is Eric's main objective, critics differ in the main methods used for reaching that goal. Using Osteen's assertion about the Cheshire metaphor, Marc Schuster argues that Eric's reality is shaped and satisfied by the economic system.[39] Eric's environment constantly changes as he pleases, thanks to his wealth. He spirals "ever more deeply into self-absorption and alienation from the world at large" (183). Eric's self-absorption, Schuster argues, is a result of his influence on world economies and his desire to improve his financial prospects by manipulating information.[40] Conversely, for Laist, "it is clear that Eric's (and presumably DeLillo's) interest in money is secondary to his infatuation with the latest technologies" (155). According to what has been said so far, the weight of technological advance is heavier than the weight of economic gain for Eric.

The Zero-Oneness of Being

Eric processes his way to fusing completely with technology through the possibilities of "zero-oneness." Reading nature in particular and the world in general in terms of "zero-oneness" has incited the reaction of several critics. The manner in which it is depicted moves toward two distinct directions. There are those who believe that zero-oneness turns the world into a shallow construct of zeroes and ones, and those who believe that it does not. Aaron Chandler, among others, believes that the "zero-oneness" allows Eric to reduce all the cultures he encounters into easily read data. Drawing on Levinas, Chandler argues that instead of beholding the Other as a legitimate and different entity, Eric views this Other as a "reproduction of the same" (247).

Difference in itself does not scare Eric. In fact, he encourages the diversity of the Cosmopolis. However, he needs to be able to convert this diversity into his own possessions. He needs to be able to use the information he accumulates on the Other to his own capitalist ends. To do so, he turns the world into a coherent set of data. As reinforced by Per S. Petersen,[41] Eric forms an understanding of the zero-oneness in terms of the "abstract and rigid digital discourse of hyper/cybercapitalism" (73). Nevertheless, Petersen acknowledges the growing posthuman inclination.[42]

Alberts interprets Eric's use of "zero-oneness" as an innovative scientific method for reading the human being. Eric hopes that being able to understand the new definition of the world as a set of data may allow

174　*Perception in the Informational Era*

him to "read the signs hidden within [that] could, potentially, unlock its secrets" (17). Alberts investigates this unlocking from a nearly utopic scientific perspective. In accordance with Alberts' interpretation, Laist defines Eric's description of data and technology not as mere stream of consciousness but as a databased form of intuition (158). The more inserted is information in dailiness, the less distinct it becomes from Eric's view of the ontology of the human being. The human being, or as Haraway would say, the "cyborg," has become a semi-technological construct.[43] This poses questions concerning the extent of Eric's integrity or absorption in an advanced technocultural world. Is Eric using technology as an extension of his body and nervous system, or is he becoming an extension of technology?

This question will be answered next as it concerns the posthuman. In light of what has been said so far, "zero-oneness" could be understood as a mode of data processing that Eric adopts to redefine and act upon the world. He interprets the external world as the other, either to be understood or dominated. The billionaire strives to reach futuristic interrelatedness between data and understanding, information and modes of being. His observations, in general, are not the result of passing thoughts. He attempts to uncover that which lies outside the range of being human. He impregnates himself with the method of information processing. As a result, the distinction between reality and fantasy is blurred.

Eric is not an isolated case in this regard. As will be shown, other characters also seek to transcend their human capacities through various sorts of information technologies. They no longer limit their humanity to the properties of the human per se. They rather embrace the possibilities of technological expansion, even evolution.

DeLillo's Posthumans

With its momentous expansion, information generates irrevocable uncertainties, but it also opens unprecedented possibilities to the human being. As Hayles insists, the new form of information processing allows human agency to reach beyond the capabilities found in a particular time. This is how the posthuman is born, Hayles suggests. Indeed, the "posthuman" does not refer to the eradication of the human body, as the "human being is first of all embodied being" (283). "Posthuman" designates rather the possibilities opened through the interaction between various technologies and the embodied being. "Located within the dialectic of pattern/randomness and grounded in embodied actuality rather than disembodied information, the posthuman offers resources for rethinking the articulation of humans with intelligent machines" (287). True to technocultural discourse, Hayles looks beyond the polarities built between humans and

Perception in the Informational Era 175

machines. She explores the dynamic dialogue woven between information and consciousness, which always pushes the limits of what it means to be human.

This underlies a technocultural avant-gardism that continuously reconfigures culture to accept new forms of technology as a complementary necessity. As seen in the previous section, the way Eric views technology, as either primitive tools to be discarded or as potential allies, is the basis of technological selection that promises the betterment of one's extensions. The increasing insertion of technology in dailiness changes the way human beings make use of technology. It could be said that, with the advance of technology, human beings always seek new technological hosts for their beliefs, behaviors, and activities. This readiness to adopt new forms of technologies, to expand one's consciousness, gives "posthuman" its full meaning in the postmodern world.

In some of his novels, DeLillo pays particular attention to the posthuman manifestation of his characters. *Underworld* (1997), *Cosmopolis* (2003), *Point Omega* (2010), and *Zero K* (2016) attest to a continuously crafted wave of technological implication. Such implication blurs the boundaries between reality and virtuality, between embodiment and disembodiment. As the field of pattern and randomness, virtuality redefines the meaning of reality insofar as it offers the characters an alternative to the physical world.

DeLillo declares in an interview that this semi-transition, this in-betweenness, gives birth to a new belief. "Technology has suggested a new language and a new belief. What was unthinkable fifteen years ago has become realizable today. This advance has displaced the core of belief" [my translation] (39).[44] Using the Internet as an example, DeLillo propounds the idea that new technologies inevitably foster new expectancies. They also conceal new pitfalls. DeLillo seems to believe that technology nests an inescapable paradox. Technology has the potential to extend one's physical and mental capacities. However, the attractiveness toward that which lies *beyond* becomes problematic when the characters start to forget that they are embodied beings.

This section brings forth characters that strive to achieve posthuman forms. In this context "posthuman," as derived from Hayles, means that which breaches the limits of what it means to be human in a particular time. In DeLillo's latest novels, reaching beyond the limits of the available technologies is grounded in the characters' dailiness. Information is used in various ways. It is notably used as an important if not decisive element of the posthuman. This last is investigated from the lens of transhumanism and virtuality. Each character develops their own conception of the posthuman. Eric desires to be resurrected as a set of data in cyberspace. Artis seeks a transhuman vessel for the body, and Sister Edgar struggles to renew her faith through using virtual reconstruction. Because these

176   *Perception in the Informational Era*

possibilities are formed in the realm of pattern/randomness, the question concerning the embodiment of the characters is posed. Do the characters lose their humanity the longer they are exposed to information technologies? Or do they attest to new forms of what it means to be human?

Seeking the Beyond: the Other Side of the Screen

A return to the last day of Eric would help in setting the premises of the posthuman. Even if Eric's experience is abortive, it touches upon the irresistible need to push the limits of the body and mind. Eric's ultimate goal revolves around freeing his mind from the shackles of corporal deficiencies. This goal is described by Laist as an endeavor to achieve "mental reality" (157). Inspired by Hayles's notion of the posthuman, Laist describes "mental reality" as a new form of consciousness. Its peculiarity consists of freeing the mind from "psycho-sexual" tension[45] and physical malformation. By inference, this means for Laist that Eric is adapting his mind to the logic of time and space. Eric's understanding of himself depends more on the physics of space than on his fellow humans, as has been shown. He is "programmed" by the technology with which he identifies as extensively as it is programed by him. This identification pushes him to construct a fantasy that matches his aspirations. Consequently, Eric seems to make no difference between the object aspect of tools and the subject aspect of humans. Eric is thus posthuman, for he does not resist the possibilities offered by his advanced technocultural space. These possibilities appear to Eric as a set of zeros and ones to be translated and adapted to his needs.

It is assumed so far that Eric's process of becoming posthuman consists of favoring a technological extension of the biological body. Laist bases this insertion on the way Eric uses time and space in order to reach a reality unrestrained by asymmetry. Seen from a different lens, Eric channels his psychological state to his surroundings with the aim of finding answers to his growing anxiety. "His psychology is not that of a human subject contrasted against a world of inert objects, but rather incorporates those objects and the spatio-temporal permutations they represent" (158). Eric is convinced that "Freud is finished, Einstein's next" (*Cosmopolis* 6). His anxiety cannot be tamed through a Freudian process that goes back to his roots. The novel barely refers to his life before his last day. Eric's psychological state can be read more accurately in terms of time and space. However, it would be shortsighted to limit Eric's seemingly grand enterprise to the satisfaction of being impregnated by the suggestions of his (techno)surroundings.

Near the end of Eric's last day, he is faced with two choices. He must decide whether he can reinsert himself in contemporary technocultural space or take a leap of faith. The former would imply being exposed to

Perception in the Informational Era 177

primitive technology, as the available gadgets are not advanced enough to contain him. The second choice necessitates a leap of faith toward an uncertain digital reprogramming.

Eric believes that returning to the neighborhood of his childhood, Hell's Kitchen, would provide him with an answer. This answer is channeled not to the place itself as much as to the prospect of danger. A serious threat to his life has been signaled earlier, but he has insisted on pursuing his journey. As he walks toward the shop of his childhood barber, Anthony Adubato, Eric tries to summon a feeling of belonging. However, "this had never been his home or street" (*Cosmopolis* 159). The semi-spiritual pilgrimage toward Hell's Kitchen seems to symbolize a return to a primitive reality. Anthony is the only connection that Eric has maintained. Once installed on a half-broken barber chair, Eric's eyes wander all over Anthony's small shop. The elderly proceeds to cutting Eric's hair while recounting for the millionth time how Eric's father had died. "This is what he wanted from Anthony. The same words. The oil company calendar on the wall. The mirror that needed silvering" (*Cosmopolis* 161). Eric realizes that the elderly and his shop represent the ruins of time.

The old flawed technocultural space puts Eric face to face with the real world. "Paint was coming off the walls, exposing splotches of pinkish white plaster, and the ceiling was cracked in places" (*Cosmopolis* 160). It seems that the old shop and the luxurious limousine are no longer considered different. At the end of the day, the limousine is described as "a striking sight under the streetlamp, with a bruised cartoonish quality" (*Cosmopolis* 157). Both the shop and the limousine have expiration dates, and so does Eric. As he gazes upon the "old stubbed head and pale eyes,"[46] Eric sees his own aging body. Anthony attests to the mercilessness of time and the unstoppable marks of the years.

Eric becomes afflicted with Icarian impatience. The unbearable slow evolution of technology pushes him to seek a quick death. Half through the haircut, Eric interrupts the hairdresser and leaves. The need for symmetry no longer a requirement, Eric makes his way toward his antagonist, who also seems to be the source of his salvation.[47] Eric believes that the assassination would not mark his end. "When he died he would not end. The world would end" (*Cosmopolis* 6). Half prediction half hope, Eric seems to think that if technology advances enough in the future, his surviving particles would merge with cybernetic mechanisms. He chooses to take a leap of faith toward an uncertain posthuman state. He orchestrates the ending for his bodily restrains with the hope that he would transition to the other side of his screens.

When Eric finds himself face to face with his killer, Richard Sheets, who uses the pseudonym Benno Levin, they enter a long dialogue. Its purpose is to attempt an understanding of each other's reasoning. Eric does

178 *Perception in the Informational Era*

not remember that Levin has worked for him, but he remembers seeing him earlier in front of a cash machine. Eric believes that Levin's about-to-be crime is not authentic because it is an imitation that he has "caught" from the others (or rather from the Internet).[48] The fact that Levin has not taken a real action makes his crime "stale fantasy" (*Cosmopolis* 193). "It's another syndrome, a thing you caught from others. It has no history," Eric protests (*Cosmopolis* 193). Levin insists that the crime is necessary because of everything for which Eric stands; Eric's very existence, as a man owning a vessel that displaces "the air that people need to breathe in Bangladesh" (*Cosmopolis* 202), is reason enough to murder him.

Eric's failure to predict the Yen, which has led to bankruptcy, represents the last straw in Eric's trial. Levin explains that this failure is the result of Eric's insistence on finding the perfect balance. Balance is not always the answer to "misshapes," such as the rise of the Yen. Levin declares that there are "cross-harmonies between nature and data" (*Cosmopolis* 200). The link between nature and information is not to be discarded. This link is chaotic and not always balanced. Eric, however, has forgotten that he is part of a chaotic system (Alberts 21). Levin states that Eric has forgotten how "market cycles can be interchangeable with the time cycles of grasshopper breeding, wheat harvesting" (200).[49] In his obsession for perfection, Eric does not process the "cycles of grasshopper breeding" that may converge with the "market cycles." The point is that Eric fails to consider the world as a "randomly" layered technoculture. Such structure beholds the movement of random connections formed between the environment, human beings, technology, and information. Eric remains rigid in his interpretation of the hints that have been conveyed to him through nature and electronic data. His aim for precision and clarity clouds his judgment. This results in the birth of doubt, the loss of his legacy, and ultimately his upcoming death.

Immediately before his death, Eric looks at his watch. He notices that it shows his own image instead of time. Thinking about violence as something that needs "a burden, a purpose" makes Eric shoot the middle of his hand. He thinks about all the people he has wronged and killed. This action is the most direct self-harm he has come to inflict upon himself but it is not the first. As the novel unfolds, this disquiet is felt through, first of all, borrowing more Yen, through asking one of his bodyguards Kendra Hays to electrify him with her Taser, and through allowing the protestors to destroy his limousine. The reason for his self-destruction is never clearly stated but it is implied by the doubt that has crept up on Eric's life. It could be interpreted as the burden of being. Pain is Eric's way to "to attain release from the demands of being human" (Wright 174).[50] Because of the burden, he wants to "fail more, lose more, die more than others, stink more than others," as Levin words it (*Cosmopolis* 193).

The shot hand makes Eric realize that he has accidentally activated the "electron camera." He is fascinated with the camera. The "hand device,"

Perception in the Informational Era 179

as he calls it, does not seem to belong to the present. "It is so microscopically refined it was almost pure information. It was almost metaphysics" (*Cosmopolis* 204). This epiphanic moment is reinforced with the camera's ability to zoom in onto a beetle nearby and expose all its details. Eric feels that, at that moment, "something changed around him.... the image on the screen was a body now, facedown on the floor" (*Cosmopolis* 205). The system that he has been manipulating is now manipulating him. He sees himself as standing in "midbeing."[51] He is still breathing in the natural world, but he feels already projected into the afterlife. He is fascinated by the ability of the watch not only to divulge the hidden information of the beetle but also to predict the future.

The image remains blocked on the dead body even if Eric points the hand device toward six different directions. The watch stops responding to Eric even when he directs the camera to the beetle. Afterward, it shows him in an ambulance then in the morgue with a tag for Male Z, a term for "the bodies of unidentified men in hospital morgues" (*Cosmopolis* 206). Eric is not saddened that he will remain unidentified. He projects his elevated self as "quantum dust, transcending his body mass" (*Cosmopolis* 206). The supernatural (or illusory) atmosphere that this scene provokes is not out of context. Eric has been feeling the "imminence" and "semi-mythical" power of technology throughout the day. For him, this is "the natural next step.... an evolutionary advance that needed only practical mapping of the nervous system onto digital memory" (*Cosmopolis* 207). His advance toward the future is not being stopped, as "the perpetuity Packer seeks, even in death, is a continuation of his obsession with the future" (Chandler 253).[52]

The fact that the obsession is amplified minutes before his death reassures him as he may now "live outside the given limits, in a chip, on a disk, as data, in whirl, in radiant spin, a consciousness saved from void" (*Cosmopolis* 206). Eric understands the possibilities opened by information. Instead of being limited to the body, Eric would like to become an entity living on "disk." His goal consists of displacing the body and making technology its equal, or even its better alternative. This could be read in analogy with Artificial Life (AL). One of the prominent researchers of AL, Christopher Langton, suggests that when the body is transcended, consciousness is not completely obliterated:

> The principle [*sic*] assumption made in Artificial Life is that the "logical form" of an organism can be separated from its material basis of construction, and that "aliveness" will be found to be a property of the former, not of the latter.
>
> (qtd. in Hayles 231)

If Eric has understood this, he dies with the conviction that future innovations in technology could restore his life. This works in accordance

180 *Perception in the Informational Era*

with the appearance and disappearance of data. The "zero-oneness" that characterizes this perception becomes a dynamic "memory" thrown in nature. Even if it is invisible to the eye, the atoms and data that have once constituted Eric could find a host in cybernetic mechanisms similar to his watch, or so he seems to believe.

Eric unusual death stands true to his nature, as it mirrors his desire "to be one civilization ahead of this one" (*Cosmopolis* 152). Be it fantasy or prediction, the images appearing in his watch point out the relevancy of the posthuman to postmodern technoculture. The civilization Eric longs for breaks the boundaries between the body and the machine. It is believed that technology holds the key not only to a longer life but also to immortality. While downloading consciousness in a computer is one way to achieve perpetuity, cryonics is another.

Transhumanism: the Emancipation of Consciousness in Point Omega *and* Zero K

Thirteen years later, DeLillo considers a new form of consciousness, imagined thanks to a slightly more advanced technology. *Zero K* describes a secret world where transcending what it means to be human is possible. As seen in Chapter 1, Jeffrey Lockhart is invited to the Convergence to witness the cryopreservation process of his mother-in-law, Artis Martineau. Jeffrey is described as "the judgmental observer in the book, oscillating between the new religion of technology promising transcendence and the gross, unspiritual life of contemporary America" (Glavanakova 96).[53]

Jeffrey is skeptical about the promise of technological advance. He questions particularly the way consciousness would function once the body is obsolete:

> When does the person become the body? There were levels of surrender, I thought. The body withdraws from one function and then possibly another, or possibly not—heart, nervous system, brain, different parts of the brain down into the mechanism of individual cells.
>
> (*Zero K* 139)

It is believed, in the Convergence that, as the body can dissolve into "individual cells," it can also be reconstructed anew. "We are here to reconsider everything about life's end. And we will emerge in cyberhuman form into a universe that will speak to us in a very different way" (*Zero K* 67). This new method seems to favor information as a key element to maintaining negative entropy. Simply put, entropy is the state of disorder and negentropy is the struggle for a state of order.[54] These definitions are applied in biology primarily but they are also used in information theory. Negentropy, an already formed set of data, represents the path through

Perception in the Informational Era 181

which more information can be formed, or through which the universe may "speak to us in a very different way." Even if information is perpetually disordered, it also constructs itself anew. It forms new associations leading to increasingly "accurate" conclusions.

The idea that one's environment and technological means hold the key to the improvement of the human condition is shared by transhumanism. The transhumanist goal consists of projecting today's ambition of betterment, even immortality, toward a more advanced technoculture. The Swedish philosopher, Nick Bostrom, explores this idea with the aim of defending the transhumanist goal:[55] "[Transhumanism] holds that current human nature is improvable through the use of applied science and other rational methods.... Transhumanists promote the view that human enhancement technologies should be made widely available" (203–204). Transhumanism as an idea works toward the objective of using the amalgamation of technologies and possibilities to reach the omega point. As suggested by M. Castillo, "[w]hen transhumanists speak about the Omega Point, they refer to the point when our use of science and technology will improve our human state."[56] However, technologies themselves are not enough to sustain the transhumanist goal. Believing in the idea and centering one's activities and behaviors around it is also necessary, as seen in Chapter 1.

The Convergence holds the idea that if enough information is gathered, it could form a path toward the omega point. The notion of "Omega Point" was coined by the French Jesuit Pierre Teilhard de Chardin. Teilhard de Chardin suggests that we are advancing toward a more and more accurate and transcending consciousness. This consciousness would involve all human beings in a collective thought.[57] DeLillo borrows and edits the notion to write his novella, *Point Omega* (2010).[58] In the latter, Richard Elster, a 73-year-old scholar and war specialist, imagines a future where everything that escapes entropy moves toward a centripetal force.

> Consciousness accumulates. It begins to reflect upon itself. Something about this feels almost mathematical to me. There's almost some law of mathematics or physics that we haven't quite hit upon, where the mind transcends all direction inward. The omega point.... Whatever the intended meaning of this term, if it has a meaning, if it's not a case of language that's struggling toward some idea outside our experience.... Paroxysm. Either a sublime transformation of mind and soul or some worldly convulsion. We want it to happen.
>
> (*Point Omega* 91)

Either as fantasy or as erudition, Elster suggests that the human being strives toward an illusory or real "sublime transformation." DeLillo's interest in the notion of the omega point is felt in *Zero K*. He uses the omega point to

182 *Perception in the Informational Era*

represent the transition toward a new form of life. As posited by Pavlina Radia,[59] "DeLillo suggests.... that death is not only the end, but also the very beginning: the omega point of existence" (41). In this way, the omega point is the objective, and transhumanism is the *belief* that this objective is attainable.

Julian Huxley suggests that the physical world has been mapped, so it is time to explore the realm of the human possibility:[60]

> The human species can, if it wishes, transcend itself—not just sporadically, an individual here in one way, an individual there in another way, but in its entirety, as humanity. We need a name for this new belief. Perhaps transhumanism will serve: man remaining man, but transcending himself, by realizing new possibilities of and for his human nature.
>
> (17)

For Huxley, transhumanism is initially a belief, as it holds the promise of a better destiny. *Zero K* is grounded on the assumption that transhumanism itself is about technocultural belief.[61]

The certainty of the founders of the Convergence is juxtaposed with Jeffrey's demurral. The founders seem to believe that cyberhuman represents the accumulation of relevant data for the survival of consciousness. If, as Langton suggests, consciousness is not eradicated after the death of the body, the possibility of attaining an omega point is not total fantasy. However, if as Antonio R. Damasio argues, the mind cannot survive without the body,[62] the idea of immortality remains fiction. Jeffrey would like to believe in the possibility of Artis's revival, but he cannot help asking questions about the consequences of body alteration.

> Do you think about the future? What will it be like to come back? The same body, yes, or an enhanced body, but what about the mind? Is consciousness unaltered? Are you the same person? You die as someone with a certain name and with all the history and memory and mystery gathered in that person and that name. But do you wake up with all of that intact? Is it simply a long night's sleep?
>
> (*Zero K* 48)

Jeffrey learns later that brains, and sometimes entire heads, are removed and stored. When technology is advanced enough, the heads are meant to be "grafted to a healthy nanobody" (*Zero K* 147). Jeffrey wonders once again: "would all the revivified lives be identical, trimmed tight by the process itself? Die a human, be reborn an isometric drone" (*Zero K* 147). Jeffrey is reluctant to conceive a technocultural time when the "dehumanization"

Perception in the Informational Era   183

of individuals becomes the norm. This view is shared by DeLillo. When he is asked whether he would like to live eternally, if it were possible, DeLillo answers with a question found in the novel: "what's the point of living if we don't die at the end of it?"[63] For DeLillo, the body is not meant to live forever. He believes that the mind must thrive, in the current technocultural regime, not despite the body but in accordance with it.

The question of self and identity is thus raised. How would the supposedly revived brain identify itself as regards the "nanobody"? Damasio argues that the mind and the body are each other's sensors. The well-functioning of the mind depends partly on the adjustments brought to the body and vice versa. "All of these adjustments depend on signals going from brain to body and on related signals going from body to brain" (224). The neural basis of the self, Damasio insists, resides in the continuously reactivated representations of one's history (identity) and of one's body (238). Identity depends on "sensory maps" related to one's unique personal history. During a conference held in the Convergence, a nameless speaker ponders the question concerning identity.

> Will new technologies allow the brain to function at the level of identity? This is what you may have to confront. The conscious mind. Solitude in extremis. Alone. Think of the word itself. Middle English. *All one.* You cast off the person. The person is the mask, the created character in the medley of dramas that constitute your life. The mask drops away and the person becomes you in its truest meaning. All one. The self. What is the self? Everything you are, without others, without friends or strangers or lovers or children or streets to walk or food to eat or mirrors in which to see yourself. But are you anyone without others?
> (*Zero K* 67; emphasis in original)

The self-refuting question asked in this passage indicates the importance of the physical world in forming one's identity. Identity is not the set of data concocted in isolation. It is "a sense of unity and coherence that can be felt, lived, and attributed"[64] in a whole technocultural context. Conversely, being stripped from all the "medley of dramas" uncovers the self in its "truest meaning," the realization of the omega point. However, is the omega point the alteration of what it means to be human or a better version of it?

For Bostrom, transhumanism seeks to extrapolate the limits of human beings because they are encoded in a way that allows their amelioration. "Human nature in this broader sense is dynamic, partially human-made, and improvable" (213). Sustaining consciousness without a body does not seem as dehumanization, in this case, but as a movement toward the next version of the posthuman. The question that comes to mind is: What kind

184 *Perception in the Informational Era*

of identity can emerge from reaching the state of omega point sought by transhumanism?

In a section interjecting Part One and Part Two of *Zero K*, the protagonist attempts to answer this question. The section, entitled "Artis Martineau," seems to represent the omega point of Artis's consciousness after the cryopreservation. Jeffrey imagines Artis, or what remains of Artis, existing with "minimal consciousness" (*Zero K* 272). To form this perception, he borrows the information gathered during his stay in the Convergence. On the one hand, Jeffrey provides the reader with a possibility where Artis is not dead, "against [his] firm belief" (*Zero K* 272). On the other hand, Jeffrey reduces Artis to basic "sentences" or data expressions. "I think of her in a state of virgin solitude. No stimulus, no human activity to incite response.... Then I try to imagine an inner monologue, hers, self-generated, possibly nonstop" (*Zero K* 272). The basis of this monologue is a set of minimal data scripts. It starts with Artis's attempt to develop a self. "But am I who I was" (*Zero K* 157). Without a question mark, this sequence of words seems incomplete. "I think I am someone. There is someone here and I feel it in me or with me" (*Zero K* 157, 161, 162). These "zeros" and "ones" are repeated throughout the section with variations. Artis struggles to become a full-fledged self, but she always digresses into a state of "minimal" existence.

If reaching the omega point implies that everything outside the self has burnt out, is "minimal consciousness" the truest representation of the self? In the mentioned section, the narrator remarks that "*she* [Artis] *is the residue, all that is left of an identity*" (*Zero K* 160; emphasis in original). Artis's identity, in contemporary technoculture, is described at the beginning of the novel. She is "the Second Wife," "the Stepmother," "the Archaeologist" (*Zero K* 13). Her beautiful face is "attenuated by illness," and she is the sort of person who gives "a certain kind of life to the drop of water" (*Zero K* 13, 18). Artis has a quiet soothing voice and an elevated understanding of art. When everything that constitutes Artis dissolves, she becomes a barely functional virtual construct. Unable to remember her body and her personal history, she remains trapped in a temporally stretched set of sentences. "How much time am I here.... I try to know who I am. But all I am is what I am saying and this is nearly nothing" (*Zero K* 161). However, the very possibility that she develops "a minimal consciousness," no matter how "meagre" it seems, might indicate that she has transcended herself, that she has reached the *beyond*.

When asked if transhumanism holds a degree of humanism, DeLillo answers that "it is about expanding the limits of what it means to be human" [my translation].[65] Eric and Artis represent DeLillo's attempt to consider the possibility of a future that defies death. For DeLillo, death is no longer envisaged in terms of religion alone but in terms of technology

Perception in the Informational Era 185

as well. Eric reveals a shift in the human perception that has become more apparent by the end of the first decade of the twenty-first century. One's process of thought is no longer exclusive to human properties. If Eric shows that the time of the posthuman is still young, Artis shows that the possibilities opened through the interaction between information and technologies are still not to be underestimated.

This is also true for contemporary technoculture. Indeed, DeLillo does not investigate the possible future of technological innovations only. He also goes back in time to locate an important shift in the representation of the posthuman, which is virtuality. The virtual world, more specifically the Internet, may not give eternal life, as cryonics promises, but it still represents man's attraction toward the _beyond_, as will be shown.

Toward a Virtual Reality

In an interview,[66] DeLillo proclaims that he tries not to take for granted the force of postmodern technology. The aim of his constant retrospection toward the hidden workings of technology is to detect the extent of its implication in one's self-realization. "I wonder if there is a secret drive in technology that tends toward a kind of totalitarian perception.... Or whether there's something in us that's brought to realization by technology itself."[67] DeLillo broaches this hypothesis in _Underworld_ and _Cosmopolis_. He calls upon the growing intersection of the virtual world with one's mode of understanding. This intersection has already been shown in the way Eric looks at the natural world as if it were a screen. A landscape becomes for him a field full of data, and data becomes a landscape to be read. This interrelatedness of data and image is significant for investigating the manner in which information is part of technocultural dailiness. As the privileged child of postmodern technoculture, how does information inform beliefs, behaviors, and activities? And how does its manifestation through virtuality invoke the posthuman?

As the virtual world has become more normalized, the way it is implicated in the individual's dailiness is overlooked. Reflectively and cautiously, DeLillo treads on the premises of the virtual world in dailiness. He realizes that the virtual world does not merely suggest a different view. It also plants the seed of change in his characters' minds. Their beliefs, behaviors, and activities are reoriented toward abstract conceptions. Seen from the lens of the posthuman, it could be said that the virtual world offers an alternative to the epiphanies that have been suggested mainly in the physical world. This technocultural expansion indicates the subtle but strong insertion of information technologies in dailiness.

As it is usual with technological terminologies, "virtuality" is widely used while upholding a degree of vagueness. For a long time, virtuality has

186　*Perception in the Informational Era*

referred to the "refracted or reflected image of an object" (Woolley 219).[68] This unequivocal definition is no longer sufficient in the postmodern technocultural world. By moving from being a technical term in optics and physics to defining the essence of cybernetics, "virtuality" is no longer unambiguous. Richard Norton opens his article "What is Virtuality?"[69] with the presupposition that virtuality is not a "nonactual" reality. "Virtual reality is not the same as being nonactual.... it is not the 'off' position and actual reality the 'on' position (because nonactual is the 'off' position)" (500). Deleuze reinforces this assertion in terms of the image of thought.[70] As he puts it, "the virtual is not opposed to the real; it possesses a full reality by itself" (Deleuze *Difference and Repetition* 211). What is relevant to this context is that virtual reality is not an illusion even if it does not take place in actuality. Nevertheless, virtuality remains a simulation mediated by image technologies. The interaction between screens and the virtual produces "an abstract entity or process that has found physical expression, that has been 'realized'. It is a simulation, only not necessarily a simulation of anything actual" (Woolley 224). Virtuality is, therefore, understood as a reality perceived through screens. It does not actualize itself in the physical world but it remains *real* insofar as it constitutes the experience of the self, especially the virtual self.

The fact that the virtual experience is a real experience provokes a degree of confusion in the minds of DeLillo's characters. Virtual technoculture refers to the blurring of boundaries between the real and the mirrored image in the context of dailiness. The brightness and "waves and radiations" implanted in technocultural space bring modifications in the characters' behaviors and activities. As described by Steve F. Anderson,[71] virtuality represents one of the most significant visual modifications in postmodern technoculture: "Machine vision and human vision have achieved a precarious balance that is currently playing out across various technologies of vision. The relationship of these two regimes is as irreducible to metaphors of human cognitive processes as to algorithmic ones" (230). In DeLillo's novels, virtual technoculture is implicated in the way the characters behave both around the other and around technology. This technoculture is expressed through the manner in which the actions of the characters are translated into zero-oneness. As corroborated by Lelia Green, "Virtual reality (VR) technocultures immerse users in a computergenerated environment that responds to their moves or actions" (196).[72] Virtual technoculture has grown in proportion, and the extent of its impact on the human psyche remains for the most part unrecorded. Its expansion is mainly expressed through cyberspace. This last is represented in DeLillo's novels as a door toward a new mode of being.

In *Neuromancer* (1984),[73] William Gibson describes cyberspace as a "graphic representation of data abstracted from the banks of every

Perception in the Informational Era 187

computer in the human system. Unthinkable complexity. Lines of light ranged in the nonspace of the mind" (51). The brightness of cyberspace is compared to the brightness of physical technocultural space, with its "clusters and constellations of data. Like city lights" (51). Such brightness opens a dimension that marginalizes the physical world and absorbs one's attention inward. Cyberspace becomes thus a technocultural personification of the mind, as posited by Green:

> Cyberspace can be constructed as the conceptual domain within which Internet interactions take place. If the Internet is the equivalent of the physiological brain—with technological hardware equivalent to neurons, synapses, cells, neurotransmitters and the like—cyberspace is the technocultural equivalent of the mind.
>
> (198)

A reading of how the mind processes and selects data could be extracted through the exploration of the workings of cyberspace. Cyberspace favors the sense of vision, but it can also submerge the being with a synesthetic experience. Through the limitless possibilities of cyberspace, the mind weaves together previously unrelated images. This leads to the provocation of new forms of self-realization.

The growth of cyberspace has provoked a mutation in the individual's perception processings. Slavoj Žižek had suggested in 1997 that cybernetics is contributing to a movement toward the "postmodern epoch of dissemination."[74] It is a movement "from *the modernist culture of calculation to the postmodernist culture of simulation*" (167; emphasis in original). Žižek argues that the postmodern world has moved toward a "transparency" that conceals the working of physical machines. Such transparency connects the nervous system directly to the images of the screen, discarding most of physical involvement. In the same year, *Underworld*[75] was published. In its epilogue, DeLillo explores the transition of one's hermeneutical experience of virtuality as described by Žižek. On the verge of losing her faith, or transitioning her faith, a nun in her sixties finds herself submerged by the promise of technology. Sister Edgar sees her physical world crumbling down after a breakdown caused by her failure to save a homeless child. The 12-year-old Esmeralda Lopez is raped and murdered a few hours after Sister Edgar and Sister Grace had tried to rescue her from homelessness. For Edgar, the murder attests to the closeness of danger. "All terror is local now. Some noise on the pavement very near, the stammer of casual rounds from a passing car.... Ancient fears revived" (*Underworld* 816). Edgar loses faith in the "serenity of immense design" (*Underworld* 817). She retreats to a safer technocultural space to be oblivious to the weakness of the body and new forms of terror. The way she adapts to her

188 *Perception in the Informational Era*

new environment provides a reading of the early appealing manifestations of virtual technoculture.

Edgar has always feared the unknown, which is symbolized by her use of latex gloves. The gloves are a hindrance to her asceticism, as she gives herself the luxury of physical distance from any "organic menace." Read as her way to be wired to consumer technoculture, the gloves represent her purchased "purity." Laist suggests that it is because of Edgar's latex gloves rather than because of faith that she is connected to the world. The gloves "bespeak a sense in which she is wired to a consumer technoculture of synthetic commodities" (148). Edgar refuses to be "infected" by bodily viruses, which indicates her mistrust of Providence.

> Edgar force-fitted the gloves onto her hands and felt the ambivalence, the conflict. Safe, yes, scientifically shielded from organic menace. But also sinfully complicit with some process she only half understood, the force in the world, the array of systems that displaces religious faith with paranoia. It was in the milky-slick feel of these synthetic gloves, fear and distrust and unreason.
>
> (*Underworld* 241)

In this context, Edgar is still connected to a physical world. Though belonging to synthetic production, the protection that the gloves provide does not separate Edgar from actuality. If anything, the gloves push her to question her faith and locate her deeply rooted hypocrisy. Edgar fears to be contaminated by the people she serves. Her paranoia is accurately read by Casey McCormick in terms of the overwhelming presence of information in the postmodern world:[76] "Sister Edgar's crisis of faith is inextricably tied to her pervasive paranoia, a theme that DeLillo uses throughout his fiction to describe one possible response to an information-saturated postmodern world" (98). Because Edgar is continuously *informed* about new pervasive dangers, she develops the habit of protecting herself from everything.[77]

Edgar claims that she "feels" the concealed diseases of the human body. Her piety responds to her need for protection from known and unknown dangers. This protection shatters after the murder of Esmeralda. Edgar realizes that nothing, not even her latex gloves, can protect her from local and unexpected tragedies. This pushes her, not without struggle, to seek new reference points, technologically advanced but still theist. "It is not a question of disbelief. There is another kind of belief, a second force, insecure, untrusting, a faith that is spring-fed by the things we fear in the night, and she thinks she is succumbing" (*Underworld* 817). Edgar succumbs to dread and superstition. When word reaches her that Esmeralda appears in a billboard near a traffic island, she decides to visit the "shrine." Despite Sister Grace's warning, Edgar is attracted to the promise of miracles. For

Perception in the Informational Era 189

Grace, the rumor exploits Esmeralda's death to create "tabloid superstition," and to broadcast "local news.... with all the grotesque items neatly spaced to keep you watching the whole half hour" (*Underworld* 819). Jack Gladney and Matt Shay are examples of the consumers that Sister Grace condemns as immoral. Their objective is to feed on local news, regardless of the truthfulness of televisual events. Edgar's objective is different. She is oblivious to Grace's assessment because she needs to *believe*.

Edgar reaches the site and picks her way through a multi-religious crowd, a contact she has always avoided. After anxiously waiting for 20 minutes, the headlights of a passing train hit the billboard. Edgar believes that she has seen in that half-second Esmeralda's face. This new perceptual lens offers Edgar a sudden but decisive reconstruction of her hermeneutical experience. Edgar's understanding becomes attuned to the crowd's pantheist suggestion. Risen to a "single consciousness,"[78] the crowd has witnessed "either a genuine irruption of the spiritual world or a group hallucination" (Osteen 257). Even if Edgar has never seen Esmeralda up close, she joins the crowd in their belief. Grace, who is more familiar with Esmeralda, believes that the image is a trick of the light. Grace's attempt at disillusionment is interrupted by the passing of another train. Edgar has the impression that she has seen the face more clearly. She feels an "Angelus of clearest joy" (*Underworld* 822). For her, the reappearance ascertains the authenticity of the image.

This moment marks Edgar's transition of faith. Viewed from Žižek's perspective, Edgar has reached the third and last stage of a complete emersion in virtuality.

> [F]irst, within "objective reality" itself the difference between "living" and "artificial" entities is undermined; then the distinction between "objective reality" and its appearance gets blurred; finally, the identity of the self which perceives something (be it appearance or "objective reality") explodes.
>
> (*The Plague of Fantasies* 171–172)

Edgar takes off her latex gloves and embraces whoever happens to be next to her. "Everything feels near at hand.... she is nameless for a moment, lost to the details of personal history, a disembodied fact in liquid form, pouring into the crowd" (*Underworld* 823). Edgar seems to be convinced that the image, which springs out of virtual space, marks the beginning of a new sort of belief. Expunged from hypochondria and enochlophobia, Edgar immerses herself in cybernetics. She no longer makes a difference between the physical world and virtuality. The way the image has been planted in her psyche blurs the distinction between the real and the virtual to the extent of indiscernibility.

190   *Perception in the Informational Era*

The way Edgar responds to Esmeralda's image could be read in parallel with the way Benno Levin develops his obsession with the image. Before expressing the need to kill Eric, Levin has lived *through* Eric; or rather, he has lived through the *image* of Eric. After being fired, Levin spends his days watching live video feeds from Eric's website. "I watched for hours and realistically days.... It was important to know where he was.... It put my world in order" (*Cosmopolis* 151). During that period, Levin expresses the need to monitor Eric. This need could be interpreted as the result of Levin's inability to develop an identity of his own. Instead, Levin develops what Gerard Raulet calls "floating identity:"[79]

> Of course, identity has always been a fiction constituted at the inter-section of individual and social games. But the new communication technologies challenge this very mechanism. The network creates a phe-nomenon of commutation which destroys the local and allows it only through ephemeral moments, floating identities, multiple and isolated language games or arbitrary associations.
>
> (51)

Levin does not live as an embodied being but as an arbitrary facsimile of Eric's image. All that interests him is the formed "floating identity" which is connected to Eric. "I wanted to pinpoint him in my mind. It was important to know where he was, even for a moment. It put my world in order" (*Cosmopolis* 151). Levin confesses that it is hard for him to talk to people, that he has to build lies to survive in the social context. "To speak directly to a person was unbearable" (*Cosmopolis* 151). He does not feel equipped to live like a normal person, so he *watches* how it is like to live and to speak. Levin's "floating identity" becomes so intertwined with Eric's daily activities that he can no longer distinguish the two. "My life was not mine anymore. But I didn't want it to be. I watched him knot his tie and knew who he was" (*Cosmopolis* 153).

When the live streaming stops because of "security issues," Levin's whole life crumbles down. The goal behind keeping a degree of anonymity of Eric's whereabouts is supposed to protect him from danger. Ironically, it leads to his death. Levin addresses Eric in his confession saying, "[w]hen you shut down the site I was I don't know, dead, for a long time after" (*Cosmopolis* 198). When Levin's online persona is no longer fed with a possibility to be, an imbalance is created which makes him feel dead in the physical world. In her attempt to explore the fate of the body in cyberspace, Alessandra Lemma suggests that when one's online life is producing a posi-tive impact, it can be felt or integrated with the "offline" life.[80] However, "where this kind of integration is not possible, the potential for patho-logical splitting is considerable" (79). This splitting is already triggered by Levin's virtual identification after his wife left him. "I'm susceptible to

Perception in the Informational Era 191

global strains of illness. I have occasions of *susto*, which is soul loss, more or less, from the Caribbean, which I contracted originally on the Internet" (*Cosmopolis* 152). In this satirical passage, DeLillo shows how cyberspace "implants" ideas in the minds of his characters. Levin is convinced that his life cannot have meaning unless he is either watching Eric live or provoking his death. Conversely, Edgar is convinced that she should join Esmeralda in the technological afterlife. While Levin kills Eric in order to find peace, Edgar transitions to cybernetic faith and dies peacefully.

After Edgar fulfills her true vocation, which consists of having faith in the image, she dies with the conviction that the afterlife is cybernetic in nature. It seems that moments before her death Edgar visualizes herself as a "floating identity," activated by the keystroke "enter." This is pointed out by a final section called "keystroke 2," which seems to symbolize Edgar's transition to the virtual world. A keystroke "links signifier to signified in direct correspondence."[81] It could be said that Edgar's body (signifier) is linked to its cybernetic equivalent (signified). After her physical death, that is, after the keystroke for "delete" is pushed, Edgar's mind/soul becomes the language, the zero-oneness, inscribed in the hyperlinked nature of the Internet. "Edgar's soul takes the form of electronic data, her afterlife becomes the World Wide Web" (Laist 149). Half satirical half predictive, DeLillo identifies the growing attraction toward the posthuman. The technological afterlife could be read as the individual's need for an experience *beyond* time and space. Such experience transcends the restrictiveness of the body.

In Edgar's case, DeLillo remains elusive about the truthfulness of her cybernetic transition. Has she truly integrated a "techno-afterlife,"[82] or is the reader part of a group hallucination if they think so? If Edgar's experience of the techno-afterlife is the last thing she is visualizing in her mind, is it her postsecular representation of faith? The last few pages of *Underworld* describe Edgar's experience in the techno-afterlife. Similarly to the miracle in the billboard, Edgar's afterlife, or techno-afterlife, is represented as a possibility glimpsed in half a second.

> When you decide on a whim to visit the H-bomb home page, she begins to understand. Everything in your computer, the plastic, silicon and mylar, every logical operation and processing function, the memory, the hardware, the software, the ones and zeroes, the triads inside the pixels that form the on-screen image—it all culminates here.
>
> (*Underworld* 825)

Everything culminates in the images of the screen, or in the "opaque transparency" of postmodern technology. By being wired directly to the content of the screen, the physical aspect of the computer is forgotten. The narrator is inviting the reader, "you," to re-question his or her familiarity

192 *Perception in the Informational Era*

with the Internet. *Underworld* is written in a time when the "image-and data-saturated culture"[83] is radiating a postsecular manifestation of faith. This faith is based on the connectivity read, previously, through latent history, and currently, through the Internet.

The unusual connections found in the net are different from the ones formed in the physical world. Edgar's previous reluctance to breathe the same air as the infected other is not translated in her digital self. McCormick agrees that in cyberspace Edgar is no longer afraid of being connected to the other: "the proliferation of connections is no longer menacing, inducing paranoia, or suggesting conspiracy, but instead emerges as freeflowing, liberating, and at once comprehensible in its perpetual connectedness" (104). Freed from her weakening embodiment, Edgar becomes open to the information suggested in the Internet.

> In her veil and habit she was basically a face, or a face and scrubbed hands. Here in cyberspace she has shed all that steam-ironed fabric. She is not naked exactly but she is open—exposed to every connection you can make on the world wide web.
>
> (*Underworld* 824)

Edgar's "naked body" becomes a set of coded data that write her posthuman "version."

Once the dichotomy between subject and object breaks down, Edgar experiences the full force of virtual reality. She becomes a set of data perpetually linked to more data. This implies that her personal history and her embodiment have elapsed. "There is no space or time out here, or in here, or wherever she is" (*Underworld* 825). Once Edgar has become no one, she is free to "float" as an empty numerical sequence that can represent anything. As posited by Lemma, once connected to cyberspace, the individual becomes amnesiac as regards the physical environment: "the link to the anchor of the past is eroded, especially as it is recorded in the body. Multiple identities, like the Windows program, can be opened and closed at will" (78). Having multiple identities, or floating identities, leads to the abolishment of a reality based on difference and uniqueness. As a result, Edgar becomes no one but can be anyone. At some point, Edgar is hyperlinked to J. Edgar Hoover. "The bulldog fed, J. Edgar Hoover, the Law's debased saint, hyperlinked at last to Sister Edgar—a single fluctuating impulse now, a piece of coded information. Everything is connected in the end" (*Underworld* 826). Unfazed by the "closeness," Edgar welcomes the connection as pure information, which attests to her shift in perspective.

Instead of thinking about the connection as a violation of personal space, and as a possibility of catching a disease, Edgar processes the

Perception in the Informational Era 193

Internet as the merging of different sets of data. As explained by Green, the "Internet offers a variety of degrees of interactivity within technocultural contexts from simple access (consumption) to full content creation (production) as part of the communication exchange" (197). In cyberspace, the focus is given to the information itself, directly connected to the nervous system. The medium of the body is marginalized if not eradicated. All that remains are endless hyperlinked differences. "Sister and Brother. A fantasy in cyberspace and a way of seeing the other side and a settling of differences that have less to do with gender than with difference itself, all argument, all conflict programmed out" (*Underworld* 826). Edgar seems however incapable of completely giving up her embodied expressionism, "veil and habit,"[84] as the human being is, first of all, an embodied being. The narrator once more stresses the ambivalence of her transition. It is remarked that Sister Edgar "*sees* the flash, the thermal pulse. She *hears* the rumble building, the great gathering force rolling off the 16-bit soundboard. She *stands* in the flash and feels the power" (*Underworld* 825; emphasis added).

If her expressions attest to a sort of "bodily memory," not yet translated in cyberspace, they still do not rule out Edgar's belief in the "intersecting systems"[85] of cyberspace. As the connections intensify, the distinction between the physical world and the virtual world is gradually blurred. This leads the narrator to ask, either curiously or alarmingly: "Is cyberspace a thing within the world or is it the other way around? Which contains the other, and how can you tell for sure?"[86]

Notes

1 Webster, Frank. *Theories of the Information Society*. 4th ed. London, Routledge, 2014.
2 Hobart, Michael E., and Zachary S. Schiffman. *Information Ages: Literacy, Numeracy, and the Computer Revolution*. Baltimore, Johns Hopkins University Press, 2000, p. 3.
3 Hayles, N. Katherine. *How We Became Posthuman: Virtual Bodies in Cybernetics, Literature, and Informatics*. Chicago, University of Chicago Press, 1999.
4 Conte, Joseph M. *Design and Debris: A Chaotics of Postmodern American Fiction*. London, University of Alabama Press, 2002.
5 Davis, Gregory H. *Means without End: A Critical Survey of the Ideological Genealogy of Technology without Limits, from Apollonian Techne to Postmodern Technoculture*. Lanham, University Press of America, 2006, p. 164.
6 www.merriam-webster.com/dictionary/information
7 As Michael E. Hobart and Zachary S. Schiffman suggest in *Information Ages: Literacy, Numeracy, and the Computer Revolution* (1998), "we really do not know much about this idiom. Dictionaries assume it, rather than explain it" (3).

194 Perception in the Informational Era

8 Taylor, Mark C. *The Moment of Complexity: Emerging Network Culture*. London, University of Chicago Press, 2001.

9 Robins, Kevin, and Frank Webster. *Times of the Technoculture: From the Information Society to the Virtual Life*. London, Routledge, 2005.

10 McNeil, Ian, editor. *An Encyclopaedia of the History of Technology*. London, Routledge, 1990.

11 Serres, Michel. *Genesis*. Translated by Genevieve James and James Nielson, Ann Arbor, University of Michigan, 1995.

12 See also Taylor, *The Moment of Complexity*, p. 100.

13 Separating noise from information is not only a challenge on a daily basis. The theoretical framework of information has been concerned about the manner in which information is to be extracted from noise. In fact, one of the main challenges of the founder of information theory, Claude Shannon, has been to distinguish a meaningful message from turbulent noise, to separate "order from disorder" (qtd. in Conte 117).

14 Wiener, Norbert. *The Human Use of Human Beings: Cybernetics and Society*. Boston, Da Capo Press, 1954.

15 Bloom, Harold. *The American Religion*. E-book, Chu Hartley, 2013.

16 Bloom, *The American Religion*, E-book.

17 Noble, David F. *The Religion of Technology: The Divinity of Man and the Spirit of Invention*. New York, Alfred A. Knopf, 1998.

18 DeLillo, Don. *Cosmopolis*. London, Picador, 2011 [2003].

19 DeLillo declares in an interview that *Cosmopolis* was "almost done" before the events, and that he did not feel the need to change anything in it. http://perival.com/delillo/interview_henning_2003.html

20 As Randy Laist suggests, "DeLillo's thirteenth novel is arguably his most focused meditation on the theme of technology and subjectivity" (153).

21 DeLillo, *Cosmopolis*, p. 19.

22 Dewey, Joseph. *Beyond Grief and Nothing: A Reading of Don DeLillo*. Columbia, University of South Carolina Press, 2006, p. 142.

23 Laist redefines the term "Cosmopolis" to include what he calls technocrowds. For him, Cosmopolis "itself is a microcosm of the increasingly all-inclusive technocrowd of global citizenry in which history, identity, memory, and other footholds of humanist subjectivity are effaced in favor of a collective narcosis" (174).

24 "Don DeLillo New Millenium." *YouTube*, uploaded by Eugenio Sánchez Bravo, March 30, 2014, www.youtube.com/watch?v=aQlYnbWR3pI. Accessed July 13, 2018.

25 DeLillo, *Cosmopolis*, p. 105.

26 Similarly to Eric, Brian Glassic a waste manager in *Underworld* (1997) experiences a strong sensation when he approaches or crosses a bridge, as "[t]he longer and higher the span, the greater his sense of breathless abyss" (167). Crossing the George Washington bridge gives him the sensation of undertaking a "mobius gyration" to another realm. However, whereas the bridge provokes in Brian a feeling of foreboding, Eric is freed by its supernatural aura. Eric's perception of the bridge may be further explained in the light of Ivo Andrić's *The Bridge over the Drina*. For Andrić, the Drina bridge is not

Perception in the Informational Era   195

only a stony structure. Rather, it involves "tales and legends associated with the existence and building of the bridge, in which reality and imagination, waking and dream, were wonderfully and inextricably mingled" (15).

27

His every action reveals the typical makeup of a parable character: a yearning for transcendence constantly undercut by an inordinate need to control and by a stubborn delight/addiction in the stimulations of the horizontal plane of experience, its pleasures and its pains.

(Dewey 140)

28 Alberts, Crystal. "'Freud Is Finished, Einstein's Next': Don DeLillo's *Cosmopolis*, Chaos Theory, and Quantum Entanglement." *Orbit: A Journal of American Literature*, vol. 4, no. 2, 2016, https://doi.org/10.16995/orbit.196. Accessed May 20, 2018.

29 Hobart and Schiffman, *Information Ages*, p. 224.

30 "In terms of critical reception," argues Laist, "*Cosmopolis* is the black sheep of DeLillo's recent novels.... it is as if he has exhausted bigness with *Underworld* and has become newly entranced with the possibilities of the minute, the inward, and the evanescent" (152).

31 http://perival.com/delillo/cosmopolis_editions.html

32 Rossini, Jon D. "DeLillo, Performance, and the Denial of Death." *Death in American Texts and Performances: Corpses, Ghosts, and the Reanimated Dead*, edited by Lisa K. Perdigao and Mark Pizzato, London, Routledge, 2016, pp. 45–62.

33 DeLillo, *Cosmopolis*, p. 19.

34 Hobart and Schiffman, *Information Ages*, p. 224.

35 For more details, see Hayles, *How We Became Posthuman*, p. 25 and Hobert and Schiffman, *Information Ages*, p. 224.

36 Hobert and Schiffman, *Information Ages*, p. 225.

37 Ibid.

38 Osteen, Mark. *American Magic and Dread Don DeLillo's Dialogue with Culture*. Philadelphia, University of Pennsylvania Press, 2000.

39 Schuster, Marc. *Don DeLillo, Jean Baudrillard and the Consumer Conundrum*. New York, Cambria Press, 2008.

40 Schuster, *Don DeLillo, Jean Baudrillard and the Consumer Conundrum*, p. 181.

41 Petersen, Per S. "Don DeLillo's *Cosmopolis* and the Dialectics of Complexity and Simplicity in Postmodern American Philosophy and Culture." *American Studies in Scandinavia*, vol. 37, no. 2, 2005, pp. 70–84. https://rauli.cbs.dk/index.php/assc/article/view/4508. Accessed May 27, 2018.

42 "Like Hayles, Packer is now convinced that human identity and self-consciousness cannot be separated from its material substrate, its organic embodiment, and converted to digital data" (Petersen 78).

43 Haraway, Donna Jeanne. *Simians, Cyborgs, and Women: The Reinvention of Nature*. London, Free Association, 1991.

196 *Perception in the Informational Era*

44 "La technologie a proposé un nouveau langage. Et une croyance. Ce qui était impensable il y a seulement quinze ans devient aujourd'hui faisable. Cela déplace le cœur de la croyance" (39).
   DeLillo, Don. "Le Grand Entretien: Don DeLillo." Interview by François Busnel. *America: L'Amérique Comme Vous Ne L'avez Jamais Lue*, August 2017, pp. 25–43.
45 Laist, Randy. *Technology and Postmodern Subjectivity in Don DeLillo's Novels*. Frankfurt, Peter Lang, 2010, p. 157.
46 DeLillo, *Cosmopolis*, p. 162.
47 As Dewey posits, "it is Sheet's clumsy assassination plot that will provide Packer the moment necessary for spiritual confirmation" (144).
48 This point is elaborated in the "Toward a virtual reality" section.
49 Alberts interprets Levin's suggestion in terms of the butterfly effect. To do so, she borrows James Gleick's definition of the concept. Gleick explains that "a butterfly stirring in the air today in Peking can transform storm systems next month in New York" (qtd. in Alberts 14).
50 Wright, Nicholas. "Tendering the Impossible: The Work of Irony in the Late Novels of Don DeLillo: A Thesis Submitted in Fulfilment of the Requirements for the Degree of Doctor of Philosophy in the University of Canterbury." *University of Canterbury*, 2006, https://ir.canterbury.ac.nz/handle/10092/932. Accessed February 15, 2017.
51 DeLillo, *Cosmopolis*, p. 205.
52 Chandler, Aaron. " 'An Unsettling, Alternative Self' ": Benno Levin, Emmanuel Levinas, and Don DeLillo's *Cosmopolis*." *Critique: Studies in Contemporary Fiction*, vol. 50, no. 3, 2009, pp. 241–260, https://doi.org/10.3200/CRIT.50.3.241-260. Accessed May 8, 2018.
53 Glavanakova, Alexandra K. "The Age of Humans Meets Posthumanism: Reflections on Don DeLillo's *Zero K*." *Studies in the Literary Imagination*, vol. 50, no. 1, 2017, pp. 91–109. *Project MUSE*, https://doi.org/10.1353/sli.2017.0007
54 The physicist Erwin Schrodinger suggests that "a living organism continually increases its entropy—or, as you may say, produces positive entropy, which is death. It can only keep aloof from it, i.e., alive, by continually drawing from its environment negative entropy" (qtd. in Avery 88).
   Avery, John. *Information Theory and Evolution*. Singapore, World Scientific Publishing, 2003.
55 Bostrom, Nick. "In Defense of Posthuman Dignity." *Bioethics*, vol. 19, no. 3, 2005, pp. 202–214.
56 Castillo, M. "The Omega Point and Beyond: The Singularity Event." *American Journal of Neuroradiology*, March 1, 2012, www.ajnr.org/content/33/3/393
57 Teilhard de Chardin, Pierre. *The Phenomenon of Man*. Translated by Bernard Wall, New York, Harper Perennial Modern Thought, 2002.
58 DeLillo, Don. *Point Omega*. London, Picador, 2011.
59 Radia, Pavlina. *Ecstatic Consumption: The Spectacle of Global Dystopia in Contemporary American Literature*. Newcastle, Cambridge Scholars Publishing, 2016.
60 Huxley, Julian. *New Bottles for New Wine*. London, Chatto & Windus, 1957.

Perception in the Informational Era 197

61 "We share a feeling here, a perception. We think of ourselves as transrational. The location itself, the structure itself, the science that bends all previous belief. The testing of human viability" (*Zero K* 128).

62 Damasio, Antonio. *Descartes' Error: Emotion, Reason and the Human Brain.* New York, Avon Books, 1995.

63 DeLillo, "Le Grand Entretien: Don DeLillo," p. 39. See also DeLillo, Don. *Zero K.* New York, Scribner, 2016, p. 40.

64 Slack, Jennifer Daryl, and J. Macgregor Wise. *Culture and Technology: A Primer.* New York, Peter Lang, 2015, p. 198.

65 DeLillo, "Le Grand Entretien: Don DeLillo," p. 38.

66 DeLillo, Don. "Unmistakably DeLillo." Interview by Mark Feeney. *Conversations with Don DeLillo*, edited by Thomas DePietro, Jackson, University Press of Mississippi, 2005, pp. 169–172.

67 DeLillo, "Unmistakably DeLillo," p. 171.

68 Woolley, Benjamin. "Virtuality." *The New Media and Technocultures Reader*, edited by Seth Giddings and Martin Lister, London, Routledge, 2011, pp. 217–225.

69 Norton, Richard. "What Is Virtuality?" *The Journal of Aesthetics and Art Criticism*, vol. 30, no. 4, 1972, pp. 499–505. *JSTOR*, www.jstor.org/stable/429465

70 Deleuze, Gilles. *Difference and Repetition.* Translated by Paul Patton, New York, Columbia University Press, 1994.

71 Anderson, Steve F. *Technologies of Vision: The War between Data and Images.* Cambridge: MIT Press, 2017.

72 Green, Lelia. *Technoculture: From Alphabet to Cybersex.* Crows Nest, Allen & Unwin, 2002.

73 Gibson, William. *Neuromancer.* New York, The Berkley Publishing Group, 1984.

74 Žižek, Slavoj. *The Plague of Fantasies.* 2nd ed., London, Verso, 2008.

75 DeLillo, Don, *Underworld.* London, Picador, 2011 [1997].

76 McCormick, Casey J. "Toward a Postsecular 'Fellowship of Deep Belief': Sister Edgar's Techno-spiritual Quest in Don DeLillo's *Underworld.*" *Critique: Studies in Contemporary Fiction*, vol. 54, no. 1, 2013, pp. 96–107, https://doi.org/10.1080/00111619.2010.540593. Accessed June 17, 2019.

77 As Žižek points out, "[w]e have only to recall the all-pervasiveness of the logic of victimization, from sexual harassment to the dangers of food and tobacco, so that the subject itself is increasingly reduced to 'that which can be hurt' " (*The Plague of Fantasies* 175).

78 DeLillo, Don. *Underworld.* London, Picador, 2011, p. 821.

79 Raulet, Gérard. "The New Utopia: Communication Technologies." *Telos.* Translated by Hassan Meley, vol. 1991, no. 87, 1991, pp. 39–58, https://doi.org/10.3817/0391087039

80 Lemma, Alessandra. "An Order of Pure Decision: Growing up in a Virtual World and the Adolescent's Experience of the Body." *Psychoanalysis in the Technoculture Era*, edited by Alessandra Lemma and Luigi Caparrotta, London, Routledge, Taylor & Francis, 2014, pp. 75–96.

81 Hayles, *How We Became Posthuman*, p. 26.

82 McCormick, "Toward a Postsecular 'Fellowship of Deep Belief'," p. 97.

198 *Perception in the Informational Era*

83 In his reading of *Underworld*, Sven Birkerts suggests that the novel depicts a transitional phase in the American technoculture. "Our image- and data-saturated culture is pushing us toward some sort of critical mass. We are at the moment in the paradigm shift when the old has clearly given way but the new has not yet announced itself" (256–257).
Birkerts, Sven. *Readings*. Saint Paul, Graywolf Press, 1999.

84 DeLillo, *Underworld*, p. 824.

85 Ibid., p. 826.

86 Ibid.

Conclusion

Most of Don DeLillo's novels are born out of striking images he tries to understand,[1] and understanding them requires breaching the limits of ostensible interpretations. It could be said that one of the things DeLillo has understood is that beyond the "neutrality" of tools, there is a thread that weaves technology to culture. More than ever, culture and technology are indiscernible, which gives technoculture its full meaning. DeLillo seems to believe that technology is the expression of culture no matter how advanced the former can be. Indeed, the advance of technology does not necessarily stifle culture. On the contrary, culture as a set of beliefs, behaviors, and activities is able to acclimatize itself with technological progress. Particularly important is the manner in which the author reveals usual and unusual connections built between dated and advanced technologies and ordinary settings. The same set of technologies may have diverse spiritual and behavioral outcomes, and similar beliefs and behaviors may emerge from different technologies. Through these dynamics, DeLillo's fiction anatomizes subtle and overt transitions in the nature of the American dailiness. Such transitions disclose the historical, spatial, and informational changes that characterize the postmodern world.

One of DeLillo's focal points is the injection of new technologies in familiar contexts. Technological innovation, the integration of the new in dailiness, does not eliminate old practices. DeLillo describes this process as an increasingly moving set of intersecting rings.[2] These intersecting rings do not obliterate authentic past beliefs, behaviors, and activities; they paint these cultural imperatives in new colors, which are elaborated through the historical, spatial, informational changes. Other aspects of technocultural manifestation, such as language, memory, and aesthetics have not been integrated in this study. Despite the connections that DeLillo has constructed between them and technologies, these aspects are either already investigated[3] or uphold a weak connection with the particular technologies examined in this project.

DOI: 10.4324/9781003407768-7

200   *Conclusion*

DeLillo supports the idea that spiritual beliefs, non-manufactured behaviors, and long-established activities are not dead in postmodern technoculture. On the contrary, they form new rings that highlight "radiance in dailiness." From Chapter 1 to Chapter 5, unusual connections are continuously engendering new rings that fuse the familiar with the innovative, the ordinary with the transcendental. The correlations built between the characters generally show that beliefs no longer have a closed context and that technological innovations do not necessarily oppose one's simpler background, as the postmodern world breathes multiplicity. This does not mean that DeLillo's intersecting rings never become blurry. It is noticed that at times transparency decreases between cultural imperatives and technology. This is provoked, for instance, by the opacity of guns and skyscrapers, as seen in the first and fourth chapters. DeLillo is not indifferent to the dangers of technological opacity nor is he unaware of the omnipresence of technology.[4] Nevertheless, he does not promote a rejection of technological advance. By acknowledging technological omnipresence, the author seeks to draw attention to a thread connecting culture to technology. Without this thread, expressed through "radiance in dailiness," technoculture in DeLillo's novels would dissolve.

It is undeniable that technology's expressions have never been as conspicuous as today's possibilities, but DeLillo keeps reminding the reader that technology has been implied in the reorientation of one's culture from the beginning of time. Characters such as Katheryn Axton and Henrik Endor attest to the necessity of technological extensions no matter how primitive they are. These extensions are not useful only on the material level but also on the spiritual level. The spiritual uplift felt by Katheryn while digging into the Athenian ruins in search of jars is as strong as Jack Gladney's search for bright products in the supermarket. The "brightness" of craft and the daily exposure to "waves and radiations" have always been part of *Homo Faber*. The stance adopted in the chapters seeks to highlight DeLillo's technocultural views while avoiding technological determinism. To do so, DeLillo's approach to technological opacity is rarely equated to the death of beliefs, the rise of robotic behaviors, or the control of activities. With the exception of Keith Neudecker and, to an extent, Pammy Wynant, all the characters try to respond actively to technological suggestions rather than subdue to them. Nevertheless, if the opacity of technology is not the cause of the individual's disquiet, it does announce the rise of uncertainty.

Uncertainty is provoked by the restlessness of minds that is reflected through technology, as seen in Chapter 2. However, uncertainty needs not be always linked to an augmentation of hopelessness. It can also be an indicator of multiplicity. This is illustrated through the possibilities opened by image technologies. Historical events such as the Kennedy assassination, the establishment of filmed murders, and the 9/11 attack indicate the rise of randomness and fear. However, other broadcast events, such as natural

Conclusion 201

catastrophes, accounts on dictators, the revolt of the masses, are sought in order to mitigate a deadening routine. It is noticed that televisual images do not always stimulate a feeling of being a "zero in the system." In some instances, uncertainty is woven with televisual images in order to seek protection, as seen in the first and third chapters. This could explain why even traumatic events are not unsolicited. In the case of Jack Gladney or Matt Shay, it is better to be informed about calamities than to be kept in the dark. At times, this leads to the loss of ethical values, as the characters are not concerned with the struggles of the other. They rather feel entertained or relieved that they are far away from harm. Therefore, the possibilities of the screen reconceptualize reality in a way that personal experience becomes connected to outer space.

Outer and inner space are implicated in the characters' dailiness as much as image technologies. As seen in Chapter 4, architecture does not leave the characters indifferent. Pammy's actions are woven with space, as her hermeneutical processes respond to the grandeur of skyscrapers as well as to the suburbs. This study has not elaborated on the ecological aspect of technological implication, as it has been covered extensively by critics such as Elise Martucci. It is suggested rather that the behaviors and activities of the characters adapt to the technocultural space within which they are thrown because space itself is a source of information.

This point is elaborated in Chapter 5 where different spaces are woven with cultural imperatives. Unusual connections and sensations are not experienced in supermarkets and living rooms solely; limousines, secret organizations, and virtual spaces incite in the characters unusual responses as well. Information is thus not a mere set of neutral zeros and ones, as it implants belief in the otherwise cynical posthuman. The characters that choose to adhere to a technologically loaded culture, such as Eric Packer, Artis Martineau, and Sister Edgar maintain a high degree of belief. Their capacity to experience spiritual enhancement is not "unplugged" once they pursue their avant-gardist journeys. On the contrary, their journeys are fueled by an embedded capacity to believe in the transcendental.

The characters' capacity to believe, which has been adapting to image and information technologies, divulges a mutating ontology. The characters rely on technologies to develop an understanding of the world and the self. To complete this process in a complex technocultural space, their ontology becomes binary in nature. The characters' environment either adjusts to their field of vision or becomes a phenomenological source of reference. Accordingly, their embodiment responds to their interaction with the visual/virtual realm. The characters at times disassociate from their physical environment. To counter the uncertainty that ensues, some of them have recourse to a remolded version of beliefs. These remolded beliefs are born, for instance, to interpret unfamiliar physical or virtual events. The neglected correlations between visual/virtual experiences and

202 *Conclusion*

physical space were central to this project. The correlations show that the technocultural experience has many folds as it functions on different levels.

DeLillo thus writes about phenomena he seeks to understand, and the phenomena he seeks to understand usually have a technocultural undertone. When it comes to daily exposure, there are technologies that DeLillo has not covered such as the progress of the telephone. Additionally, DeLillo has not elaborated on the new "smart" televisions, cars, and screens. Perhaps DeLillo is not interested in understanding these technologies, or perhaps he has not found yet cultural connotations or expressions allowing him to write about them. Nonetheless, it is undeniable that Don DeLillo has built his fiction in a way that it offers his readers an infallible aptitude to understand how technology and culture have always been woven in overt and concealed layers, and understanding these layers is needed today more than ever before.

Notes

1 "Most my novels are born out of striking images" [my translation] (34). Later in the interview DeLillo declares that he writes simply to understand (43).
   "La plupart de mes romans sont nés d'images marquantes" (34).
   DeLillo, Don. "Le Grand Entretien: Don DeLillo." Interview by François Busnel. *America: L'Amérique Comme Vous Ne L'avez Jamais Lue*, August 2017, pp. 25–43.
2 DeLillo, Don. "'An Outside in this Society': An Interview with Don DeLillo." Interview by Anthony DeCurtis. *Conversations with Don DeLillo*, edited by Thomas DePietro, Jackson, University Press of Mississippi, 2005, p. 69.
3 See the writings of Cowart, Wolf, and Coyle.
4 "It is impossible to resist technology. It is omnipresent. It dominates our lives" [my translation] (39).
   "Il est impossible de résister à la technologie. Elle est omniprésente. Elle domine nos vie" (39).
   DeLillo, "Le Grand Entretien: Don DeLillo."

Works Cited

Aas, Katja F. *Sentencing in the Age of Information: From Faust to Macintosh.* London, GlassHouse, 2005.

Alberts, Crystal. "'Freud Is Finished, Einstein's Next': Don DeLillo's *Cosmopolis*, Chaos Theory, and Quantum Entanglement." *Orbit: A Journal of American Literature*, vol. 4, no. 2, https://doi.org/10.16995/orbit.196. Accessed May 20, 2018.

Anderson, Steve F. *Technologies of Vision: The War between Data and Images.* Cambridge, MIT Press, 2017.

Andrić, Ivo. *The Bridge over the Drina.* Translated by Lovett F. Edwards. London, The Harvill Press, 1995.

Aristotle. *Metaphysics.* Translated by Hugh Lawson-Tancred. London, Penguin, 1998.

Arnold, John. *History.* New York, Sterling, 2009.

Avery, John. *Information Theory and Evolution.* Singapore, World Scientific Publishing, 2003.

Barglow, Raymond. *The Crisis of the Self in the Age of Information, Computers, Dolphins and Dreams.* London, Routledge, 1994.

Barthes, Roland. *Mythologies.* Translated by Annette Lavers, New York, Hill and Wang, 1972.

Baudelaire, Charles. *Les Fleurs du Mal.* Paris, Chêne, 2007.

Baudrillard, Jean. "Fatal Strategies." *Jean Baudrillard: Selected Writings*, edited by Mark Poster, Cambridge City, Polity Press, 2001.

———. *L'illusion de la Fin: Ou la Grève des Evénements.* Paris, Galilée, 1992.

———. *Simulacra and Simulation.* Translated by Sheila Glaser, Ann Arbor, University of Michigan, 1994.

———. "The Vanishing Point of Communication." *The New Media and Technocultures Reader*, edited by Seth Giddings and Martin Lister, London, Routledge, 2011, pp. 110–117.

Bawer, Bruce. "Don DeLillo's America." *The New Criterion*, April 1985, www.newcriterion.com/issues/1985/4/don-delilloas-america. Accessed May 23, 2016.

Beauvoir, Simone de. *Pour une Morale de L'ambiguïté.* Paris, Gallimard, 1947.

Birkerts, Sven. *Readings.* Saint Paul, Graywolf Press, 1999.

Bloom, Harold. *The American Religion.* E-book, Chu Hartley, 2013.

204　*Works Cited*

Boorstin, Daniel Joseph. *The Image: A Guide to Pseudo-events in America.* New York, Vintage, 1992.

Borgmann, Albert. *Technology and the Character of Contemporary Life: A Philosophical Inquiry.* London, University of Chicago, 1984.

Bostrom, Nick. "In Defense of Posthuman Dignity." *Bioethics*, vol. 19, no. 3, 2005, pp. 202–214.

Boxall, Peter. *Don DeLillo: The Possibility of Fiction.* London, Routledge, 2006.

Bugliosi, Vincent. *Reclaiming History: The Assassination of President John F. Kennedy.* Kindle ed. New York, W.W. Norton, 2007.

Burger, Henry G. " 'Technoculture'." *Technology and Culture*, vol. 2, no. 3, 1961, pp. 260–261. *JSTOR*, www.jstor.org/stable/3101029

Cantor, Paul A. "Adolf, We Hardly Knew You." *Don DeLillo's White Noise*, edited by Harold Bloom, Philadelphia, Chelsea House Publishers, 2003, pp. 51–72.

Carmichael, Thomas. "Lee Harvey Oswald and the Postmodern Subject: History and Intertextuality in Don DeLillo's 'Libra', 'The Names', and 'Mao II'." *Contemporary Literature*, vol. 34, no. 2, 1993, pp. 204–218. *JSTOR*, www.jstor.org/stable/1208548

Carr, Edward H. "What Is History?" *Reading Architectural History*, edited by Dana Arnold, London, Routledge, 2004, pp. 14–23.

Castillo, M. "The Omega Point and Beyond: The Singularity Event." *American Journal of Neuroradiology*, March 1, 2012, www.ajnr.org/content/33/3/393. Accessed July 5, 2019.

Cecchetto, David, et al. *Ludic Dreaming: How to Listen Away from Contemporary Technoculture.* New York, Bloomsbury Academic, 2017.

Chandler, Aaron. " 'An Unsettling, Alternative Self' ": Benno Levin, Emmanuel Levinas, and Don DeLillo's *Cosmopolis*." *Critique: Studies in Contemporary Fiction*, vol. 50, no. 3, 2009, pp. 241–260, https://doi.org/10.3200/CRIT.50.3.241-260. Accessed May 8, 2018.

Charles, Ron. "Don DeLillo's 'The Silence' is an absurdist look at our technology dependence." *The Washington Post*, 2020, www.washingtonpost.com/entertainment/books/don-delillos-the-silence-is-an-absurdist-look-at-our-technology-dependence/2020/10/12/01b656ea-0beb-11eb-b1e8-16b59b92b36d_story.html

Coale, Samuel. *Quirks of the Quantum: Postmodernism and Contemporary American Fiction.* London, University of Virginia Press, 2012.

Coker, Christopher. *War in an Age of Risk.* E-book ed. Cambridge, Polity Press, 2009.

Conte, Joseph M. *Design and Debris: A Chaotics of Postmodern American Fiction.* London, University of Alabama Press, 2002.

Cooper, Simon. *Technoculture and Critical Theory: In the Service of the Machine?* London, Routledge, 2014.

Cowart, David. *Don DeLillo: The Physics of Language.* Georgia, University of Georgia Press, 2003.

Coyle, John F. "Don DeLillo, Aesthetic Transcendence and the Kitsch of Death." *European Journal of American Culture*, vol. 26, no. 1, Intellect, May 2007, pp. 27–39. https://doi.org/10.1386/ejac.26.1.27_1

Cronon, William, editor. *Uncommon Ground: Rethinking the Human Place in Nature.* New York, W.W. Norton, 1995.

Cytowic, Richard E. *Synesthesia: A Union of the Senses.* 2nd ed. London, MIT Press, 2002.

Works Cited 205

Damasio, Antonio. *Descartes' Error: Emotion, Reason and the Human Brain.* New York, Avon Books, 1995.

Davis, Erik. *TechGnosis: Myth, Magic & Mysticism in the Age of Information.* Berkeley, CA, North Atlantic Books, 2015.

Davis, Gregory H. *Means without End: A Critical Survey of the Ideological Genealogy of Technology without Limits, from Apollonian Techne to Postmodern Technoculture.* Lanham, University Press of America, 2006.

Deleuze, Gilles. *Cinema 1: The Movement Image.* Translated by Hugh Tomlinson and Barbara Habberjam, Minneapolis, University of Minnesota, 1986.

———. *Difference and Repetition.* Translated by Paul Patton, New York, Columbia University Press, 1994.

DeLillo, Don. *Americana.* New York, Penguin Books, 1989 [1971].

———. "American Blood: A Journey through the Labyrinth of Dallas and JFK." *Articles by Don DeLillo,* 1983, www.perival.com/delillo/ddarticles.html. Accessed June 5, 2018.

———. "The American Strangeness: An Interview with Don DeLillo." Interview by Gerald Howard. *Conversations with Don DeLillo,* edited by Thomas DePietro, Jackson, University Press of Mississippi, 2005, pp. 119–130.

———. "The Art of Fiction CXXXV: Don DeLillo." Interview by Adam Begley. *Conversations with Don DeLillo,* edited by Thomas DePietro, Jackson, University Press of Mississippi, 2005, pp. 86–108.

———. *The Body Artist.* London, Picador, 2011 [2001].

———. *Cosmopolis.* London, Picador, 2011 [2003].

———. "Dangerous Don DeLillo." Interview by Vince Passaro. *Conversations with Don DeLillo,* edited by Thomas DePietro, Jackson, University Press of Mississippi, 2005, pp. 75–85.

———. "DeLillo Interview by Peter Henning." Translated by Julia Apitzsch, *Perival,* 2003, www.perival.com/delillo/interview_henning_2003.html. Accessed December 19, 2018.

———. *End Zone.* New York, Penguin, 1986 [1972].

———. *Falling Man.* London, Picador, 2011 [2007].

———. *Great Jones Street.* London, Picador, 2011 [1973].

———. Interview by Kevin Connolly. *Conversations with Don DeLillo,* edited by Thomas DePietro, Jackson, University Press of Mississippi, 2005, pp. 25–39.

———. Interview by William Goldstein. *Conversations with Don DeLillo,* edited by Thomas DePietro, Jackson, University Press of Mississippi, 2005, pp. 47–51.

———. "In the Ruins of the Future." *The Guardian,* Guardian News and Media, December 22, 2001, www.theguardian.com/books/2001/dec/22/fiction.dondelillo. Accessed November 5, 2018.

———. "An Interview with Don DeLillo." Interview by Maria Nadotti. *Conversations with Don DeLillo,* edited by Thomas DePietro, Jackson, University Press of Mississippi, 2005, pp. 109–119.

———. "An Interview with Don DeLillo." Interview by Thomas LeClair. *Conversations with Don DeLillo,* edited by Thomas DePietro, Jackson, University Press of Mississippi, 2005, pp. 03–15.

———. "Le Grand Entretien: Don DeLillo." Interview by François Busnel. *America: L'Amérique Comme Vous Ne L'avez Jamais Lue,* August 2017, pp. 25–43.

———. *Libra.* New York, Penguin, 2006 [1988].

206 Works Cited

———. *Mao II*. London, Vintage, 1992 [1991].

———. *The Names*. London, Picador, 2011 [1982].

———. "'An Outside in this Society': An Interview with Don DeLillo." Interview by Anthony DeCurtis. *Conversations with Don DeLillo*, edited by Thomas DePietro, Jackson, University Press of Mississippi, 2005, pp. 52–74.

———. *Players*. New York, Vintage, 1989 [1977].

———. *Point Omega*. London, Picador, 2011.

———. "The Power of History." *The New York Times*. The New York Times, September 7, 1997, https://archive.nytimes.com/www.nytimes.com/library/books/090797article3.html. Accessed May 7, 2018.

———. *Ratner's Star*. New York, Vintage, 1980 [1976].

———. *Running Dog*. London, Picador, 2011 [1978].

———. "Seven Seconds." Interview by Ann Arensberg. *Conversations with Don DeLillo*, edited by Thomas DePietro, Jackson, University Press of Mississippi, 2005, pp. 40–46.

———. *The Silence*. Kindle ed. London, Picador, 2020.

———. *Underworld*. London, Picador, 2011 [1997].

———. "Unmistakably DeLillo." Interview by Mark Feeney. *Conversations with Don DeLillo*, edited by Thomas DePietro, Jackson, University Press of Mississippi, 2005, pp. 169–172.

———. *White Noise*. London, Picador, 2012 [1985].

———. "'Writing as a Deeper Form of Concentration': An Interview with Don DeLillo." Interview by Maria Moss. *Conversations with Don DeLillo*, edited by Thomas DePietro, Jackson, University Press of Mississippi, 2005, pp. 155–168.

———. *Zero K*. New York, Scribner, 2016.

Dewey, Joseph. *Beyond Grief and Nothing: A Reading of Don DeLillo*. Columbia, University of South Carolina Press, 2006.

"Don DeLillo New Millenium." *YouTube*, uploaded by Eugenio Sánchez Bravo, March 30, 2014, www.youtube.com/watch?v=aQlYnbWR3pI. Accessed July 13, 2018.

Duvall, John N. *The Cambridge Companion to Don DeLillo*. Cambridge, Cambridge University Press, 2008.

———. *Don DeLillo's Underworld: A Reader's Guide*. New York, Continuum, 2002.

———. "The (Super)Marketplace of Images: Television as Unmediated Mediation in DeLillo's *White Noise*." *Arizona Quarterly: A Journal of American Literature, Culture, and Theory*, vol. 50, no. 3, 1994, pp. 127–153. Project MUSE, https://doi.org/10.1353/arq.1994.0002

Eco, Umberto. "Cogito Interruptus." *Faith in Fakes: Travels in Hyperreality*. Translated by William Weaver, London, Vintage, 1998, pp. 221–238.

Eliot, T. S. *Collected Poems: 1909–1962*. Orlando, Harcourt, 1991.

Farmasi, Lilla. "'[P]ure, Dumb Canine Instinct': Narrative Space and Motion(lessness) in Don DeLillo's 'The Ivory Acrobat'." *Space, Gender, and the Gaze in Literature and Art*, edited by Ágnes Zsófia Kovács and László Sári, Newcastle, Cambridge Scholars, 2017, pp. 47–62.

Ferguson, Niall, editor. *Virtual History: Alternatives and Counterfactuals*. Cambridge, Basic Books, 1997.

Works Cited   207

Foster, Dennis A. "Alphabetic Pleasures: The Names." *Introducing Don DeLillo*, edited by Frank Lentricchia, Durham, Duke University Press, 1991, pp. 157–173.

Freud, Sigmund. *Civilization and Its Discontents*. Translated by James Strachey, New York, W.W. Norton, 1962.

Frisch, Max. *Homo Faber*. Translated by Michael Bullock, San Diego, A Harvest Book, 1987.

Frow, John. "The Last Things before the Last: Notes on *White Noise*." *Don DeLillo's White Noise*, edited by Harold Bloom, Philadelphia, Chelsea House Publishers, 2003, pp. 35–72.

Gajjala, Radhika, Sue E. Mccomas, Franklin Yartey, Anca Birzescu, Heather Sloane, and Yahui Zhang. "Layered Literacies and Nuanced Identities: Placing Praxis from Moo Space to Second Life." *Feminist Cyberspaces: Pedagogies in Transition*, edited by Sharon L. Collingwood, Alvina E. Quintana, and Caroline J. Smith, Newcastle upon Tyne, Cambridge Scholars, 2012, pp. 297–320.

Genosko, Gary. *When Technocultures Collide: Innovation from below and the Struggle for Autonomy*. Waterloo, Canada, Wilfrid Laurier University Press, 2014.

George, Sam. "Emerging Youth Cultures in the Era of Globalization: Technoculture and Terrorculture." *One World or Many?: The Impact of Globalisation on Mission*, edited by Richard Tiplady, Pasadena, William Carey Library, 2003, pp. 33–54.

Geyh, Paula, et al., editors. *Postmodern American Fiction: A Norton Anthology*. New York, W. W. Norton, 2006.

Giaimo, Paul. *Appreciating Don DeLillo: The Moral Force of a Writer's Work*. Oxford, Praeger, 2011.

Gibson, William. *Neuromancer*. New York, The Berkley Publishing Group, 1984.

Giles, James. *The Spaces of Violence*. Alabama, University of Alabama, 2006.

Glavanakova, Alexandra K. "The Age of Humans Meets Posthumanism: Reflections on Don DeLillo's *Zero K*." *Studies in the Literary Imagination*, vol. 50, no. 1, 2017, pp. 91–109. *Project MUSE*, https://doi.org/10.1353/sli.2017.0007

Gourley, James. "Beckett's *Worstward Ho* and DeLillo's *The Body Artist*." *Literature and Sensation*, edited by Anthony Uhlmann, Paul Sheehan, Helen Groth, and Stephen McLaren, Newcastle, Cambridge Scholars, 2009, pp. 215–228.

Green, Lelia. *Technoculture: From Alphabet to Cybersex*. Crows Nest, Allen & Unwin, 2002.

Hall, Edward Twitchell. *Beyond Culture*. New York, Anchor Books, 1989.

Halldorson, Stephanie S. *The Hero in Contemporary American Fiction: The Works of Saul Bellow and Don DeLillo*. New York, Palgrave Macmillan, 2007.

Haraway, Donna Jeanne. *Simians, Cyborgs, and Women: The Reinvention of Nature*. London, Free Association, 1991.

Hassan, Ihab. "Toward a Concept of Postmodernism." *Postmodern American Fiction: A Norton Anthology*, edited by Paula Geyh, et al., New York, W. W. Norton, 2006, pp. 586–595.

Haviland, William A., et al. *Cultural Anthropology: The Human Challenge*. 14th ed. Belmont, Wadsworth/Cengage Learning, 2013.

Hayles, N. Katherine. *How We Became Posthuman: Virtual Bodies in Cybernetics, Literature, and Informatics*. Chicago, University of Chicago Press, 1999.

208 Works Cited

Hazard, Patrick D. *AV Communication Review*, vol. 13, no. 1, 1965, pp. 71–75. *JSTOR*, www.jstor.org/stable/30217185

Hegel, Georg Wilhelm Friedrich. *Philosophy of History*. Translated by John Sibree, New York, Prometheus Books, 1991.

Heidegger, Martin. *Being and Time*. Translated by John Macquarrie and Edward Robinson, Oxford, Blackwell, 1967.

———. *The Question Concerning Technology and Other Essays*. Translated by William Lovitt, New York, Garland Publishing, 1977.

Hesiod. *Theogony and Works and Days*. Translated by Catherine Schlegel and Henry Weinfield, Athens, University of Michigan Press, 2006.

Hobart, Michael E., and Zachary S. Schiffman. *Information Ages: Literacy, Numeracy, and the Computer Revolution*. Baltimore, Johns Hopkins University Press, 2000.

Hoffmann, Gerhard. *From Modernism to Postmodernism: Concepts and Strategies of Postmodern American Fiction*. New York, Rodopi, 2005.

Howells, Richard, and Joaquim Negreiros. *Visual Culture*. 2nd ed. Cambridge, Polity Press, 2015.

Huxley, Julian. *New Bottles for New Wine*. London, Chatto & Windus, 1957.

Ihde, Don. *Postphenomenology: Essays in the Postmodern Context*. Evanston, Northwestern University Press, 1993.

Jameson, Fredric. *Postmodernism, Or, The Cultural Logic of Late Capitalism*. Durham, Duke University Press, 2003.

Jencks, Charles. *Critical Modernism: Where Is Post-modernism Going?* London, Wiley-Academy, 2007.

Jenkins, Keith. *Rethinking History*. London, Routledge, 2004.

Jennings, Humphrey. *Pandaemonium, 1660–1886: The Coming of the Machine as Seen by Contemporary Observers*. Kindle ed. London, Icon, 2012.

Johnston, John H. *Information Multiplicity: American Fiction in the Age of Media Saturation*. London, Johns Hopkins University Press, 1998.

Joyce, James. *A Portrait of the Artist as a Young Man*. Oxford, Oxford University Press, 2008.

Jung, Carl G. *Synchronicity: An Acausal Connecting Principle*. Translated by R. F. C. Hull, New York, Bolingen Foundation, 2010.

Kauffman, Linda S. "Bodies in Rest and Motion in *Falling Man*." *Don DeLillo: Mao II, Underworld, Falling Man*, edited by Stacey Michele, New York, Continuum, 2011, pp. 135–151.

Kavadlo, Jesse. *Don DeLillo: Balance at the Edge of Belief*. Frankfurt, Peter Lang, 2004.

Kellner, Douglas. *Media Spectacle*. London, Routledge, 2003.

Kelman, David. *Counterfeit Politics: Secret Plots and Conspiracy Narratives in the Americas*. Lewisburg, Bucknell University Press, 2012.

Knight, Peter. *Conspiracy Culture from Kennedy to The X Files*. London, Routledge, 2000.

Kosinski, Jersy. *Being There*. New York, Grove Press, 2007.

Kovach, Bill, and Tom Rosenstiel. *The Elements of Journalism: What Newspeople Should Know and the Public Should Expect*. Ebook ed. New York, Three Rivers Press, 2014.

Kranzberg, Melvin, and Carroll W. Pursell, editors. *Technology in Western Civilization*, vol. 1. New York, Oxford University Press, 1967.

Kretz, Donald R. "Experimentally Evaluating Bias-Reducing Visual Analytics Techniques in Intelligence Analysis." *Cognitive Biases in Visualizations*, edited by Geoffrey Ellis, Cham, Springer, 2018, pp. 111–136.

Lacan, Jacques. *The Four Fundamental Concepts of Psychoanalysis, the Seminar of Jacques Lacan Book XI*, edited by Jacques-Alain Miller. Translated by Alan Sheridan, London, W. W. Norton, 1998.

Laist, Randy. *Technology and Postmodern Subjectivity in Don DeLillo's Novels*. Frankfurt, Peter Lang, 2010.

LeClair, Tom. *In the Loop: Don DeLillo and the Systems Novel*. Champaign, University of Illinois Press, 1987.

Lee, Benjamin. "Metalanguages and Subjectivities." *Reflexive Language: Reported Speech and Metapragmatics*, edited by John A. Lucy, Cambridge, Cambridge University Press, 1993, pp. 365–392.

Lefebvre, Henri. *Critique of Everyday Life*. Translated by John Moore, vol. 1, London, Verso, 1991.

———. *The Production of Space*. Translated by Donald Nicholson-Smith, Cambridge, Blackwell, 1991.

Lemma, Alessandra. "An Order of Pure Decision: Growing up in a Virtual World and the Adolescent's Experience of the Body." *Psychoanalysis in the Technoculture Era*, edited by Alessandra Lemma and Luigi Caparrotta, London, Routledge, Taylor & Francis Group, 2014, pp. 75–96.

Lentricchia, Frank. *Introducing Don DeLillo*. Durham, Duke University Press, 1991.

Levinas, Emmanuel. *Totalité et Infini: Essai sur L'extériorité*. Paris, Kluwer Academic, 2017.

Lysloff, René T. A. "Musical Life in Softcity: An Internet Ethnography." *Music and Technoculture*, edited by René T. A. Lysloff and Leslie C. Gay, Middletown, Wesleyan University Press, 2003, pp. 23–63.

Maltby, Paul. *The Visionary Moment: A Postmodern Critique*. New York, State University of New York Press, 2002.

Martucci, Elise. *The Environmental Unconscious in the Fiction of Don DeLillo*. New York, Routledge, 2007.

Marvin, Carolyn. "Dazzling the Multitude: Original Media Spectacles." *The New Media and Technocultures Reader*, edited by Seth Giddings and Martin Lister, London, Routledge, 2011, pp. 38–47.

McClure, John A. *Partial Faiths: Postsecular Fiction in the Age of Pynchon and Morrison*. Athens, University of Georgia, 2007.

McCormick, Casey J. "Toward a Postsecular 'Fellowship of Deep Belief'': Sister Edgar's Techno-spiritual Quest in Don DeLillo's *Underworld*." *Critique: Studies in Contemporary Fiction*, vol. 54, no. 1, 2013, pp. 96–107, https://doi.org/10.1080/00111619.2010.540593. Accessed June 17, 2019.

McCrum, Robert. "Don DeLillo: 'I'm Not Trying to Manipulate Reality–This Is What I See and Hear'." *The Observer*. Guardian News and Media, August 7, 2010. Accessed May 16, 2017.

McLuhan, Marshall. *Understanding Media: The Extensions of Man*. London, Routledge, 2001.

210   Works Cited

McNeil, Ian, editor. *An Encyclopaedia of the History of Technology*. London, Routledge, 1990.

Merleau-Ponty, Maurice. *Phenomenology of Perception*. Translated by Colin Smith, London, Routledge, 1962.

Mitgang, Herbert. "Reanimating Oswald, Ruby Et Al. in a Novel on the Assassination." *The New York Times*. The New York Times, July 19, 1988. Accessed June 16, 2018.

Naughton, Jim. "Don Delillo, Caught in History's Trap." *The Washington Post*, WP Company, August 24, 1988, www.washingtonpost.com/archive/lifestyle/1988/08/24/don-delillo-caught-in-historys-trap/48a5b0b1-8bd9-412f-8426-843a405896fe/?utm_term=.509cbae73bd9

Nel, Philip. "DeLillo and Modernism." *The Cambridge Companion to Don DeLillo*, edited by John Noel Duvall, Cambridge, Cambridge University Press, 2008, pp. 13–26.

Nietzsche, Friedrich Wilhelm. *On the Genealogy of Morals and Ecce Homo*. Translated by Walter Kaufmann and R. J. Hollingdalb, New York, Vintage, 1989.

Noble, David F. *The Religion of Technology: The Divinity of Man and the Spirit of Invention*. New York, Alfred A. Knopf, 1998.

Norton, Richard. "What Is Virtuality?" *The Journal of Aesthetics and Art Criticism*, vol. 30, no. 4, 1972, pp. 499–505. JSTOR, www.jstor.org/stable/429465

O'Donnell, Patrick. "Obvious Paranoia: The Politics of Don DeLillo's 'Running Dog'." *The Centennial Review*, vol. 34, no. 1, 1990, pp. 56–72. JSTOR, JSTOR, www.jstor.org/stable/23738950

Osteen, Mark. *American Magic and Dread Don DeLillo's Dialogue with Culture*. Philadelphia, University of Pennsylvania Press, 2000.

Parrish, Timothy. *From the Civil War to the Apocalypse: Postmodern History and American Fiction*. Amherst, University of Massachusetts Press, 2008.

Partridge, Eric. *Origins A Short Etymological Dictionary of Modern English*. London, Routledge, 2009.

Penley, Constance, and Andrew Ross, editors. *Technoculture*. London, University of Minnesota Press, 1991.

Petersen, Per S. "Don DeLillo's *Cosmopolis* and the Dialectics of Complexity and Simplicity in Postmodern American Philosophy and Culture." *American Studies in Scandinavia*, vol. 37, no. 2, 2005, pp. 70–84. https://rauli.cbs.dk/index.php/assc/article/view/4508. Accessed May 27, 2018.

Plant, Sadie. *Zeros + Ones: Digital Women + the New Technoculture*. London, Fourth Estate, 1997.

Plato. "Republic Excerpts." *The Norton Anthology of Theory and Criticism*. Edited by Vincent B. Leitch, William E. Cain, Laurie Finke, John McGowan, T. Denean Sharpley-Whiting, and Jeffrey Williams, New York, W.W. Norton, 2018, pp. 49–80.

Radia, Pavlina. *Ecstatic Consumption: The Spectacle of Global Dystopia in Contemporary American Literature*. Newcastle, Cambridge Scholars Publishing, 2016.

Raulet, Gérard. "The New Utopia: Communication Technologies." *Telos*. Translated by Hassan Meley, vol. 1991, no. 87, 1991, pp. 39–58, https://doi.org/10.3817/0391087039

Works Cited 211

Robins, Kevin, and Frank Webster. *Times of the Technoculture: From the Information Society to the Virtual Life*. London, Routledge, 2005.

Roderick, Ian. *Critical Discourse Studies and Technology: A Multimodal Approach to Analysing Technoculture*. London, Bloomsbury Academic, 2016.

Rossi, Marianne Ingheim. "Constructing the Meanings of History, Identity, and Reality in Don DeLillo's *Libra* and *Mao II*." MA thesis, Oslo, The University of Oslo, 2008.

Rossini, Jon D. "DeLillo, Performance, and the Denial of Death." *Death in American Texts and Performances: Corpses, Ghosts, and the Reanimated Dead*, edited by Lisa K. Perdigao and Mark Pizzato, London, Routledge, 2016, pp. 45–62.

Rowe, John C. "Global Horizons in *Falling Man*." *Don DeLillo: Mao II, Underworld, Falling Man*, edited by Stacey Michele, New York, Continuum, 2011, pp. 122–134.

Rupprecht, Caroline. *Womb Fantasies: Subjective Architectures in Postmodern Literature, Cinema and Art*. Evanston, Northwestern University Press, 2013.

Russo, John Paul. *The Future without a Past the Humanities in a Technological Society*. London, University of Missouri Press, 2005.

Sample, Mark L. "Unseen and Unremarked On: Don DeLillo and the Failure of the Digital Humanities." *Debates in the Digital Humanities*, edited by Matthew K. Gold and Lauren F. Klein, Minneapolis, University of Minnesota, 2016.

Sartre, Jean-Paul. *Being and Nothingness: A Phenomenological Essay on Ontology*. Translated by Hazel E Barnes, New York, Washington Square Press, 1992.

Schuster, Marc. *Don DeLillo, Jean Baudrillard and the Consumer Conundrum*. New York, Cambria Press, 2008.

Serres, Michel. *Genesis*. Translated by Genevieve James and James Nielson, Ann Arbor, University of Michigan, 1995.

Shaw, Debra B. *Technoculture: The Key Concepts*. Oxford, Berg, 2008.

Shilling, Chris. *The Body in Culture, Technology and Society*. London, SAGE, 2005.

Slack, Jennifer Daryl, and J. Macgregor Wise. *Culture and Technology: A Primer*. New York, Peter Lang, 2015.

Smith, M. W. *Reading Simulacra: Fatal Theories for Postmodernity*. Albany, State University of New York, 2001.

Stephenson, Wen. "Oswald: Myth, Mystery, and Meaning." *PBS*. Public Broadcasting Service, November 20, 2003, www.pbs.org/wgbh/pages/frontline/shows/oswald/forum/. Accessed March 18, 2018.

Symons, Arthur. *The Symbolist Movement in Literature*. London, W. Heinemann, 1980.

Tabbi, Joseph. *Postmodern Sublime: Technology and American Writing from Mailer to Cyberpunk*. Ithaca, Cornell University Press, 1996.

Taylor, Mark C. *The Moment of Complexity: Emerging Network Culture*. London, University of Chicago Press, 2001.

Teilhard de Chardin, Pierre. *The Phenomenon of Man*. Translated by Bernard Wall, New York, Harper Perennial Modern Thought, 2002.

Underwood, Jr Robert Milton. *Musings of a Modern Man: Essays and Research Papers*. LULU COM, 2014.

Veggian, Henry. *Understanding Don DeLillo*. Columbia, University of South Carolina, 2014.

212 Works Cited

Virilio, Paul, and Philippe Petit. *Cybermonde la Politique du Pire*. Paris, Les éditions Textuel, 1996.

Webster, Frank. *Theories of the Information Society*. 4th ed. London, Routledge, 2014.

Wiener, Norbert. *The Human Use of Human Beings: Cybernetics and Society*. Boston, Da Capo Press, 1954.

Wilcox, Leonard. "Don DeLillo's *Libra*: History as Text, History as Trauma." *Rethinking History: The Journal of Theory and Practice*, vol. 9, no. 2–3, 2005, pp. 337–353.

———. "Don DeLillo's 'Underworld' and the Return of the Real." *Contemporary Literature*, vol. 43, no. 1, 2002, pp. 120–137. JSTOR, www.jstor.org/stable/1209018.

Williams, Raymond. "Culture Is Ordinary." *Raymond Williams on Culture and Society: Essential Writings*, edited by Jim McGuigan, London, Sage Publications, 2014, pp. 1–18.

———. *Problems in Materialism and Culture: Selected Essays*. London, Verso, 1980.

———. *Television: Technology and Cultural Form*. 2nd ed. London, Routledge, 2003.

Wisnicki, Adrian S. *Conspiracy, Revolution, and Terrorism from Victorian Fiction to the Modern Novel*. London, Routledge, 2008.

Wolf, Philipp. *Modernization and the Crisis of Memory: John Donne to Don DeLillo*. Amsterdam, Rodopi, 2002.

Woolley, Benjamin. "Virtuality." *The New Media and Technocultures Reader*, edited by Seth Giddings and Martin Lister, London, Routledge, 2011, pp. 217–225.

Wright, Nicholas. "Tendering the Impossible: The Work of Irony in the Late Novels of Don DeLillo: A Thesis Submitted in Fulfilment of the Requirements for the Degree of Doctor of Philosophy in the University of Canterbury." *University of Canterbury*, 2006, https://ir.canterbury.ac.nz/handle/10092/932. Accessed February 15, 2017.

Yehnert, Curtis A. " 'Like Some Endless Sky Waking Inside': Subjectivity in Don DeLillo." *Critique: Studies in Contemporary Fiction*, vol. 42, no. 4, 2001, pp. 357–366.

Žižek, Slavoj. *Living in the End Times*. London, Verso, 2010.

———. *The Plague of Fantasies*. 2nd ed. London, Verso, 2008.

Index

Note: Endnotes are indicated by the page number followed by "n" and the note number e.g., 157n44 refers to note 44 on page 157.

9/11 attack 7, 99–100, 157n44, 164, 200

actual possibilities *see* history
afterlife 22, 179; techno-afterlife 191
alienation 34, 54, 107, 110, 150, 173; self-alienation 141, 146
American consciousness 7, 12, 61, 66, 68, 70, 81, 91, 100
Americana 3, 5, 36, 37–46, 146
Andric, Ivo 194n26
Aristotle 157n48
Artificial Life 179
ascetic, ascetism 106, 109–110, 118, 120, 127–128, 133–135, 139, 155n26, 188

Barglow, Raymond 17, 78, 81
Barthes, Roland 40, 51n81
Baudelaire, Charles 14, 45, 148
Baudrillard, Jean 6, 60, 68, 72, 80, 95; "Fatal Strategies" 60, 83n23; hyperreal, hyperreality 6, 94–95, 98–99, 101–103, 153; *L'illusion de la Fin* 95; *Simulacra and Simulation* 80, 95–96
Beauvoir, Simone de 150
Bergmann, Albert 3, 23
Body Artist, The 3, 89, 105, 117
Bostrom, Nick 181, 183
brain fade 42
Burger, Henry 2, 5, 47n8

Carr, Edward H. 62
causality 28–29, 54, 68, 70, 75–76, 78, 83n20
Chaplin, Charlie 57, 107
Cheshire 171–173
Coale, Samuel 4, 29, 60, 73, 77, 87n92
consciousness 3, 16, 22–24, 34, 41, 45, 47, 110–111, 131, 136–140, 175–176, 179–184, 189; stream of 3, 136–138, 140, 174
consumerism 32, 37–38
Coover, Robert 53
Cosmopolis 3, 4, 161, 164–172, 175–180, 185, 190–191
Cowart, David 4, 14, 58, 61, 79, 147, 153, 202n3
cryonic, cryonics 16–17, 22, 180, 185
cryopreservation 17, 21, 180, 184
culture 1–6, 8, 12–13, 15, 22, 27–28, 46, 56, 78, 89, 92, 127, 129–132, 149, 156n39, 175, 199–202; cultural determinism 3, 29; cultural imperatives 1–2, 7, 40, 166, 199–200; culture/history 130; culture/image 73; electric stuff of 30–31, 33; media culture 79, 103; "spectacular culture" 54; "TerrorCulture" 100, 122n32
cybernetics, cybernetic 162, 177, 180, 186–187, 189; cybernetic faith 191
cyberspace 8, 117, 175, 186–187, 190–193

214 *Index*

cyborg 4, 13, 22, 24, 174; *see also* Haraway

dailiness *see* "radiance in dailiness"
Damasio, Antonio 182–183
Davis, Erik 13, 30, 34
Davis, Gregory H. 160
death 13, 16–17, 21–22, 26, 29–32, 36–37, 43, 46, 68, 70, 94, 98, 117, 126, 128, 147, 152–153, 170, 177–179, 180, 182, 184, 189–191
Deleuze, Gilles 6, 11, 72, 77, 138–139, 186; *Difference and Repetition* 77, 186
deprogramming 106–110, 112, 118, 120
Dewey, Joseph 12, 19, 59, 63, 67, 75, 135, 144, 147, 165, 167
Dick, Philip K. 1
disembodiment 109, 175
Doctorow, E. L. 53
dull and unlocatable roar 36, 46, 162

electricity 33–34, 38–39, 114
Eliot, T. S.: "The Wasteland" 130
embodiment 16, 22, 101, 107, 139, 163, 175–176, 192, 201
End Zone 3, 8, 55, 125, 126–140, 154
entropy 163–164, 180–181, 196n54
Epicurean 59
Epimetheus 35

Falling Man 3, 5, 55, 89, 90, 94, 100–105, 114, 122n36
Freud, Sigmund 156n29, 176
Frisch, Max 1

gaze 7, 105, 109, 111–113, 115, 119, 167; collective gaze 79; mediated gaze 111, 117; transfixed gaze 106–107; virtual gaze 118; *see also* Lacan
Genosko, Gary 47n8
Giaimo, Paul 4, 45
Gibson, William 1, 186
Gleick, James: butterfly effect 196n49
Gnosticism 22, 163
grand narratives 54
Great Jones Street 3, 53, 55–61, 62, 64, 90
Green, Lelia 186, 193

Hall, Edward T. 120
Haraway, Donna 4, 6, 22, 46, 131–132, 174
Hassan, Ihab 10n15
Hayles, Katherine 6, 159–160, 171, 174–175; *see also* posthuman
Hegel, Georg Wilhelm Friedrich 56, 143; Truth 56, 59, 61–64, 69, 97
Heidegger, Martin 6, 134, 158n61; thrown, thrownness 134, 144, 150, 152, 154, 168, 180, 201; state-of-mind 133–134, 136–137, 140, 151–152
Hesiod 35
history 3, 5, 7, 13, 47, 53–56, 58–62, 64, 67, 69, 71, 73–75, 78–79, 81, 94–95, 99, 104, 120, 127, 130, 155n16, 163; actual possibilities 56, 60–61, 65–66, 82; American history 67, 69; historiography 56, 65, imaginative possibilities 7, 54–57, 60–62, 65–66, 76–77, 80, 82, 96, 98, 104, 128, 135, 147, 163; latent history 7, 54–57, 60–61, 65–68, 72, 76–78, 80, 82, 89–91, 94, 96, 100, 125, 128–130, 133, 135, 140, 154, 161, 192; personal history 127–128, 144, 183–184, 189, 192; postmodern history 53, 62; third line of history 68, 70, 75–77, 80; traditional history 68, 80
Hitler, Adolf 31, 57, 75; Hitler Studies 31, 75
Huxley, Julian 182
hyperreal, hyperreality *see* Baudrillard

identity 4, 19, 20–22, 24, 78–79, 93, 108, 118, 133, 141–142, 147, 183–184; technocultural identity 62, 80, 82
"illusory correlation" *see* Kretz
imaginative possibilities *see* history
immortality 17, 23, 36–37, 180–182
information 5, 8, 13, 32, 38–42, 44, 55–56, 58, 60, 64, 82, 99, 100, 104, 120, 130, 132, 140, 154, 159–164, 171–175, 178–179, 181, 185, 188, 192, 201; information technologies 2, 5, 10n15, 32, 69, 161, 165, 174, 176, 185, 201; information theory

Index 215

6, 180, 194n13; micro-information 167, 168, 170–171
Internet 3, 175, 178, 185, 187, 191–193; *see also* virtuality

Jameson, Fredric 69, 141, 145
Jencks, Charles 141
Jenkins, Keith 53, 56, 58, 60, 62
Jennings, Humphrey: *Pandaemonium* 63, 84n35
Joyce, James 14, 64, 135–136
Jung, Carl 76

Kavadlo, Jesse 4, 14, 30, 36, 58, 71, 79, 93
Kellner, Douglas: *Media Spectacle* 100; media spectacle 104
Kennedy assassination 7, 50n55, 58–61, 66–67, 82, 91, 142, 200
Kosinski, Jersy: *Being There* 38
Kretz, Donald: "illusory correlation" 104

Lacan, Jacques 109, 111, 123n45
Laist, Randy 4, 12, 14, 32, 38, 40, 57, 166, 173, 176, 188, 191
Langton, Christopher 179
LeClair, Tom 127, 137, 150, 154n4
Lefebvre, Henri 129, 130, 133, 149
Lemma, Alessandra 190, 192
Levinas, Emmanuel 108, 110, 112, 173; Other 108–109
Libra 3, 5, 53–60, 62–64, 66–82, 86n72, 91

Mao II 3, 55, 89, 105–116, 118–119, 140–143, 147, 162
Martucci, Elise 4, 14, 32, 129, 146, 201
Marvin, Carolyn 73
McClure, John A. 31, 134, 151
McCoy, Horace 25
McLuhan, Marshall 6, 14, 38, 40, 43–45, 70, 74, 78, 80; autoamputation 13, 23; extension 13–14, 16, 20, 21, 43
Merleau-Ponty, Maurice 6, 132, 135, 144–145, 157n49
metafiction 53
metanarratives 56
multilayered narrative 136

multiplicity 4, 15, 22, 72, 74, 76–77, 79–80, 116, 140–141, 146, 154, 156n39, 160, 171, 200

Names, The 3, 31–35, 42, 66–67, 85n48
nature 41, 98, 127, 129, 130–132, 134, 149, 171, 173, 178, 180
Nietzsche, Friedrich 133

omega point 181–184; *see also* Teilhard de Chardin
ontology, ontological 5, 8, 14, 24, 35, 125, 130–131, 133–134, 138, 146–147, 161, 164–165, 174, 201
Osteen, Mark 4, 19, 33, 36, 38, 41, 75, 127, 146, 172, 189
Oswald, Lee H. 7, 58, 66, 68–78, 86n72, 88n100, 90–91; as a technocultural construct 78–82
Other *see* Levinas

parallax *see* Žižek
paranoia 70, 91–92, 114, 188, 192
perception (technocultural) 5, 8, 57, 59, 61, 72, 78, 81, 90–92, 96, 99, 101, 105, 108–113, 125–132, 135, 137, 140, 145, 147, 153, 161–162, 166–169, 171, 180, 185, 187; *see also* phenomenology
phenomenology 6, 8, 125, 131, 141; "phenomenology of surfaces" 36
placelessness 130
Plant, Sadie 2, 6, 11, 22
Plato 97
Players 3, 8, 97, 113, 125, 140, 141, 144–154, 162
Point Omega 3, 155n16, 175, 180–181
posthuman, posthumanism 3, 5, 8, 21–22, 173–177, 180, 183, 185, 191–192, 201
Prometheus 35
Pynchon, Thomas 1

"radiance in dailiness" 4, 11–14, 17, 20, 22, 24, 30, 39, 46, 59, 70, 200; brightness 3, 11, 14, 30–37, 46, 53, 132, 187, 200; "waves and radiations" 11, 14, 31–23, 37–39, 41–42, 44, 46, 71, 132, 154, 163, 186, 200

216   *Index*

randomness 27–29, 63, 90–93, 128, 175, 200
Ratner's Star 3, 13–21, 65, 161, 172
Raulet, Gerard: "floating identity" 190–191
reality 3, 5, 7, 15, 17, 31, 39, 42, 46, 54, 65, 70, 89, 94, 96–97, 99–102, 105, 113–114, 116, 120, 129, 153, 171–173, 175, 185–186, 201; superreal 94, 96, 99, 101–102, 104–107, 114–115, 117, 129, 163; third reality 105, 108–113, 115, 120; underreal 94–96, 99, 101–102, 104–107, 110, 114, 117, 129, 163; virtual reality 117, 135, 185, 186, 192
Roderick, Ian 17
Running Dog 3, 53, 55, 57, 64
Rupprecht, Caroline 109, 111

Sartre, Jean-Paul 112–113
Schrodinger, Erwin 196n54
Shannon, Claude 159, 194n13
Shaw, Debra B. 54, 127
Shilling, Chris 20, 49n24
Silence, The 3, 5, 89, 105, 114–116
supermarket 4, 7, 32, 36–37, 93–95, 128, 133, 141, 161–162, 200
synesthesia 3, 7, 43, 45–46, 71

Tabbi, Joseph 4, 89, 98
Taylor, Mark C. 160
technoculture 2–6, 11–14, 27, 29, 32, 35, 39, 46, 70, 78, 80–82, 89, 95, 100–104, 110, 131–132, 159–161, 164, 170, 178, 184–186, 188, 199–200; advanced technoculture 70, 181; as extension 6, 24, 41, 111, 166, 174; music technoculture 104; postmodern technoculture 5, 14, 16, 82, 100, 105, 159–160, 164, 180, 185; technocultural assemblage 38; technocultural space 89, 101, 102, 109, 110–111, 113, 116, 119–120, 125–128, 131–132, 134–137, 140–141, 143–144, 148, 150, 152–153, 160–163, 176, 177, 186–187, 201; technocultural weaving 22
technology 1, 11–31, 46, 54, 60, 69, 79, 90, 98, 104, 131–132, 138,

143, 153, 161, 165, 173–175, 180, 185, 199; advanced technology 4, 8, 16, 19, 20–22, 134–135, 142, 180; image technologies 2, 4, 5, 7, 47, 54, 55, 57–58, 61–66, 70, 77–79, 81–82, 89–90, 92, 120, 125, 132, 135, 161, 186, 200, 201; information technologies 2, 5, 32, 69, 161, 165, 174, 176, 185, 201; nanotechnology 2, 24; technological determinism 2–4, 6, 25, 29, 46, 114, 200; technological extension 17, 23, 176
Teilhard de Chardin, Pierre 181
television 3, 12, 30–32, 37–47, 57–58, 66, 68, 71, 73–77, 79, 80–81, 90, 92–94, 96–98, 101, 103, 111–115, 118, 153, 161, 202
tele-visual, tele-visuality 3, 7, 125, 135–136, 138, 140
Texas Highway Killer (THK) 90, 91, 99
transcendence, transcendental (*beyond*) 3, 6, 19, 22, 24, 30–32, 34, 38, 43–46, 108, 165–167, 175–176, 180, 184–185, 191, 200
transference 110
transhumanism, transhumanist 36, 175, 180–184
Truth *see* Hegel
Twin Towers 141–146, 148, 157n44

uncertainty 5, 29, 50n55, 53, 56, 58–59, 61–63, 66–70, 78, 82, 128, 142, 148, 170–173, 200
Underworld 3, 4, 25–28, 53, 55, 89, 90–99, 127, 169, 175, 185, 187–189, 191–193
unusual connections 5, 27, 29, 64, 72, 89, 163, 192, 199, 201

virtuality, virtual 5, 16, 112–113, 116–120, 123n46, 139, 168, 175, 184–193, 201

Warren Commission Report 64, 68
weaving 2, 17, 22, 30, 44, 137
White Noise 3, 31–43, 81, 127, 161, 162

Wiener, Norbert 162–164, 168
Williams, Raymond 33, 38, 46, 127
Wittgenstein, Ludwig 160
Wolf, Philipp 4, 202n3
Womb Chair 111, 114, 170
Woolf, Virginia 137
World Trade Center 142, 144, 145

Zapruder film 61, 68–70, 82, 91, 99
Zero K 3, 15, 18–25, 83n9, 175, 180–184
zero-oneness 173–174, 180, 186, 191
Žižek, Slavoj 6, 123n44, 143, 146, 157n42, 187, 189; Parallax 141, 143–144, 146, 157n50